THE ECONOMIC DEVELOPMENT OF
THE THIRD WORLD SINCE 1900

P9-AQU-228

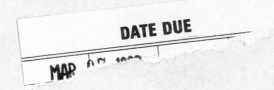

DATE DUE

MAR

The Economic Development of The Third World Since 1900

Paul Bairoch
translated by Cynthia Postan

UNIVERSITY OF CALIFORNIA PRESS
BERKELEY AND LOS ANGELES

University of California Press
Berkeley and Los Angeles, California

©1975 Paul Bairoch

California Paperback Edition 1977

ISBN: 0 520 03554 2
Library of Congress Catalog Card Number: 74 16706

Typeset in IBM Journal Roman by
Preface Limited, Salisbury, Wilts
and printed in Great Britain

NOTE TO THE USA EDITION

Throughout this book the word
billion has been used in
the sense of 1,000,000,000

Contents

viii   *Contents*

List of Statistical Tables

Note to the English Edition

The present edition, though based on the fourth French edition, differs from it in a number of respects, such as the addition of two Chapters (Urbanization and The Labour Force & Employment), the updating of practically all the figures, the numbering of the tables and notes, the presentation of certain tables and the contents of the bibliography, which has been specially adapted to the literature of the subject in the English language.

Unless otherwise stated the metric system of weights and measures has been used throughout.

Introduction

The subject of this book is the nature of under-developed economies and their behaviour over the long term. A study of economic evolution cannot ignore structural factors since the two are partly interdependent, for just as such factors are essential to the explanation of economic circumstances so changes in these circumstances will modify the structural factors themselves. I have discussed structural issues more specifically in my study *Révolution industrielle et sous-développement*,[1] and the research I undertook then made me aware that there is a notable gap in the large and often distinguished literature on the Third World -- the lack of comparative studies of its economic development. While there are several case studies on the development of individual countries, or small groups of countries, and also some studies of broader scope dealing with certain aspects of this development, there are none (as far as I know) which might help to single out the various characteristics of economic development in the Third World over a long enough period (i.e. the last seventy years) or for a large enough number of countries to make the analysis applicable to all the less-developed countries, or at any rate all the larger ones.

In writing this book I have attempted to fill this gap and to produce a study the aims of which are accordingly:

1. To extend the diagnosis over a sufficiently long period, which I have defined as from 1900 to 1970. In every case where the nature of the data makes this necessary annual averages have been calculated. For agricultural data averages have been calculated on a five-year basis, while for sectors less subject to fluctuations three-year averages have been used.

2. To include a large number of cases. Whenever index numbers or series relating to the entire Third World, or to large groups of less-developed countries, are available or can be calculated, these have been given precedence. In the case of individual countries, since it is obviously impossible to deal with every country or territory now in existence (the balkanization of former colonial empires has produced nearly 170 economic or political entities), I have thought it best to base the study mainly, but not wholly, upon a sample of twenty-four countries, chosen in the following manner:

(a) I have included a few countries from each of the larger geographical regions. Africa (both Black Africa and North Africa); Latin America; Asia; and the Middle East.

(b) A few countries from different economic and political regimes.

(c) A few countries with a large population.

The countries selected, whose population represents 80 per cent of that of the whole Third World, are:

AFRICA	AMERICA	ASIA	MIDDLE EAST
Ghana	Argentina	China	Egypt
Kenya	Brazil	Sri Lanka (Ceylon)	Iraq
Madagascar	Chile	India	Turkey
Morocco	Cuba	Pakistan	
Nigeria	Mexico	Indonesia	
Tunisia	Peru	Philippines	
Zaïre (until 1972 Dem. Rep. Congo)	Venezuela	Thailand	

The demographic significance of the country and the methodological importance of the 'Chinese way of development' demanded the inclusion of mainland China in this list, even though this entailed research on a massive scale out of all proportion to the addition of a single country.

This list of twenty-four countries is not treated as exclusive and will often be added to, or equally, in the absence of statistics, reduced. Finally, the Appendix contains two synoptic tables giving the principal economic and social data available for the 94 under-developed territories each possessing more than 400,000 inhabitants in 1965 and representing, from the economic and social point of view, more than 99 per cent of the Third World.

3. To differentiate various aspects of economic growth in the under-developed countries. The chapter titles of this study indicate its range of interest: 1. Population; 2. Agriculture; 3. Extractive industry; 4. Manufacturing industry; 5. Foreign trade; 6. The terms of trade; 7. The level of education; 8. Urbanization; 9. The labour force and employment; 10. Macro-economic data.

These chapters are not of equal importance. In the chapter on population, for instance, it is enough to give a brief summary of the quantitative material, while the chapter on the development of agriculture shows that the subject is of greater importance than almost any other. I have also attempted to fill in certain gaps in international documentation, in particular by calculating an index of agricultural productivity,[2] and an index of the production of the extractive industries.

Given the number of countries included and the importance of the factors under consideration, an in-depth examination of the conditions and situation peculiar to each country could not be expected of the present study. It has only been possible to make a diagnosis of the economic development of the Third World in its entirety. Needless to say, the exceptions to this diagnosis will be dealt with as they affect the different countries. I have tried to keep the argument as concise as possible by excluding any material which is superfluous or of doubtful usefulness.

To increase the value of the diagnosis, systematic comparisons have been drawn with the economic progress of the developed countries during the 'take off' period of their history always distinguishing as far as possible between those countries which industrialized early and those which entered the race at a later date.

The following remarks may clarify the methodology used.

1. *Terminology*. The terminology referrring to under-developed countries has been the subject of some controversy and there is no intention here of entering the lists. In this study I have used the terms 'less-developed', 'developing', 'under-developed', 'non-industrialized' and 'Third World' synonymously, and have used the word 'developed' solely in its economic sense.

2. *Geographical definition*. It has not been thought necessary to reclassify the territories considered to be under-developed. The classification used is based on that of the statistical services of the United Nations which, though not perfect (could any be?), has the advantage of being widely employed and understood. The U.N. statistical services distinguish three geographic regions: (a) developed countries; (b) developing countries; (c) communist countries (or centrally-planned economies).

Among the non-communist countries the following are considered to be under-developed: all those in Asia with the exception of Japan; all those in Africa with the exception of South Africa; all Latin-American countries; and all those in Oceania with the exception of Australia and New Zealand. This group will be referred to here as the 'non-communist under-developed countries'.[3]

In addition to the countries mentioned above, the under-developed world will, for the purposes of this study, include the communist states of Asia (China, Korea, North Vietnam and Mongolia). Readers are reminded, though, that till recently the statistical services of the United Nations included Cuba amongst the non-communist group of under-developed countries.

3. *How up to date is this study?* While very recent figures would not normally have been given special treatment in a long-term study of this kind, I have made every effort to include as much recent material as possible. This English edition (based on the revised fourth French one) incorporates all facts that are available up to the middle of 1973. Even so, it must be remembered that the 'statistical time lag' varies greatly from topic to topic and country to country.

4. *The provisional nature of recent statistics and the margin of error.* Methods used in compiling statistics, especially those based on estimates or sampling techniques (national accounting, agricultural and industrial production and population) mean that statistical institutions have to revise their figures periodically. Thus, as a general rule, it is wise to treat statistics relating to the last few years as provisional. This is in any case a necessary precaution with all published statistics.

It may be assumed, therefore, that an important part of the statistics used here contains margins of error. Wherever these are significant the reader's attention will be drawn to the fact. But to omit all statistics containing a margin of error would amount to renouncing any attempt at economic analysis.

I   *Population*

INTRODUCTION

Both the causes and consequences of demographic expansion afflicting the under-developed countries are so well known that it will suffice in the present chapter to deal briefly with a few quantitative facts.

The chapter is divided into two parts. The first is devoted to the long-term changes of population between 1900 and 1970, continent by continent and for the whole of the Third World. Details relating to separate countries will be found in the synoptic table which appears in the Appendix (p. 244) and which includes population in 1970 and the rates of demographic growth from 1960 to 1970 for most of the under-developed territories. The second part of the chapter will deal mainly with recent changes in birth rates and, very briefly, with population projections.

A. Changes in population of the under-developed countries from 1900 to 1970

Table 1 has been constructed on the basis of information published by the statistical office of the United Nations. With the exception of data prior to 1950, the table is based on the latest issue (for 1972) of the demographic year book (New York, 1973). It should be noted (a) that figures prior to 1950 contain a margin of error which gets progressively larger the earlier the period to which they refer and (b) that the data from 1900 to 1940 has been adjusted in order to take account of recent corrections made in the 1950 figures.

Data relating to the communist countries must be considered as approximate only, since so little is known about the population of China which, in fact, dominates the total. The figures reproduced here are taken from the demographic year books of the United Nations and assume a rate of population growth of 1.8 per cent per annum for the period 1950 to 1970. However, it appears after examination of the literature relating to Chinese demographic problems[1] that actual rates of growth were higher. From 1950 to 1957, a period during which figures were published by the Chinese authorities, demographic growth was of the order of 2.1 per cent. From 1957 to 1970 the indications are fragmentary and very crude. It appears that after the 'census' of 1953 new censuses or counts

Table 1   *Changes in the population of the less-developed countries and of the world*

Dates	Non-communist, less-developed countries				Asian communist countries[2]	Total less developed countries	World
	Africa	*Asia*	*America*	*Total inc. Oceania*			
Population (in millions)							
1900[1]	130	440	65	635	445	1,080	1,645
1920[1]	135	480	90	710	480	1,190	1,850
1930[1]	155	540	110	805	500	1,305	2,055
1940[1]	180	625	130	935	525	1,460	2,275
1950	205	716	162	1,086	556	1,642	2,486
1960	254	888	213	1,358	664	2,022	2,982
1970	324	1,152	283	1,763	801	2,564	3,632
Annual rate of growth (%)							
1900–20	*	*	*	0.5	*	0.5	0.6
1920–30	1.2	1.2	1.6	1.3	0.4	1.0	1.1
1930–40	1.5	1.4	1.9	1.5	0.5	1.1	1.0
1940–50	1.4	1.4	2.3	1.5	0.6	1.2	0.9
1950–60	2.2	2.2	2.8	2.3	1.8	2.1	1.8
1960–70	2.5	2.6	2.9	2.6	1.9	2.4	2.0

*The margin of error is too great for these figures to be worth including.
[1] Round figures.
[2] See text for comments on usefulness of these figures.
Sources: Various editions of *Demographic Yearbook* of the United Nations; *World Population Prospects* as assessed in 1963 (United Nations, New York, 1966); J. Durand, 'World population estimates, 1750–2000', *World Population Conference 1965* (U.N., 1967).

were undertaken in 1958 and in 1964; but, up till now, no results for 1964 have been made public. Since the cultural revolution the data is obviously even more uncertain. The only 'official' figure recently divulged was, first of all, 750 million, then 700 million, without in either case indicating the year to which the figure relates.[2] This naturally leaves us to imagine that it refers to the 1964 'census'. Klatt is probably right when he writes that 'nobody inside or outside China is likely to know the true size of the country's population'; he himself keeps the figure of 750 million for 1970/71. But in Field's view the figure should lie somewhere between the lower and the higher hypothesis resulting from the calculations in Aird's well-documented study, that is to say, between 788 and 814 million in 1970.[3] In my opinion the figure of 750 million is probably too low, since if the censuses or counts of 1953 (582.6 million) and 1958 (646.5 million) are taken as a basis, we obtain an annual rate of growth between those two dates of 2.1 per cent, and, between 1958 and 1970 of only 1.2 per cent, which is obviously too low. For this reason a figure for 1970 slightly below the average of Aird's two hypotheses, i.e. 800 million (in mid-year), is preferred here. In my view, therefore, instead of the figure of 801 million inhabitants for the total population of the communist less-developed countries in 1970, as accepted by the United Nations, a figure of the order of 840 million would be nearer reality.

In the absense of any more valid information, the statistical office of the United Nations, until the Monthly Statistical Bulletin for August 1971, were content to add 10 million each year to the figure of China's population in the preceding year. These 10 million represent an annual growth for 1958 of the order of 1.6 per cent which is rather low, but for 1970 they represent no more than 1.3 per cent, which is most certainly too low. Since August 1971, however, the data has been revised upwards and the statistical office now postulates an annual rate of growth of 1.8 per cent, which is probably nearer the truth.

Always allowing for margins of error, there are three phases of population change in the Third World that can be distinguished between 1900 and 1970. The first, which begins well before 1900 and lasts until about 1920, is characterized by what one might call the demographic evolution of a traditional or *ancien régime* economy, i.e. by a population movement marked by short-term variations of a positive or negative kind related to harvests or epidemics, and whose average rate of growth over longer periods was very low (well below 1 per cent per annum). During this period the factors of demographic change were birth and death rates which were equally high, i.e. crude rates of the order of 40 per thousand. It should be noted, however, that in a large number of regions population change was being, or had already been, influenced by the introduction of western medical techniques.

From 1910–20 until about 1950, a second phase can be distinguished which marked a break with traditional demographic trends. During these decades appeared the first signs of that demographic inflation which has recently been so widely and justifiably discussed. Population growth reached about 1.2 per cent, which, relative to previous change, constituted a marked acceleration. It was caused, as already noted, by a heavy fall in mortality due to medical progress and by a largely unchanged birth rate. Around 1950 the crude mortality rate was of the order of 25 per thousand.

Towards the end of the second world war a third phase began, marked by a genuine demographic inflation: the rates of growth of the non-communist under-developed countries, which were around 2 per cent in the first half of the 'fifties, exceeded 2.2 per cent in the second half of the decade, rose to slightly less than 2.5 per cent between 1960 and 1965, and a little over 2.6 per cent between 1965 and 1970. As we shall see shortly, it is probable that they will rise still higher in the years to come.

Population growth in Latin America has been noticeably higher since the very beginning of the period under consideration. In the early decades the difference was largely due to migrations, while in the more recent period larger available food resources probably account for the difference. At the present moment the population in that continent is growing at the rate of 2.9 per cent, as against 2.5 per cent for Africa and 2.7 per cent for Asia.

In the countries which began their development in the course of the eighteenth and nineteenth centuries, the forty or sixty years preceding the start of their industrial development experienced an average rate of population increase of less than 0.5 per cent per annum, while during the first sixty years of their 'take off' the rate was about 0.7 per cent per annum. There is thus a very wide gap between the rate of demographic growth of the developed countries at the time of their 'take off' and the rates experienced currently by the undeveloped countries. And to the extent to which such comparisons are valid, it is significant that the difference between the population growth of countries which had their industrial revolution in the eighteenth and nineteenth centuries and the present demographic inflation of the less-developed countries is quite wide — less than 0.5 per cent on the one hand and 2.6 per cent on the other.

B. Recent changes and future prospects

We have just seen that a very marked acceleration of population growth has recently taken place. However, when the earlier estimates are examined it will be seen that these tended generally to under-estimate population growth.

To illustrate this situation we shall take the case of the most populated of the non-communist, under-developed countries. From 1951 to 1961 the official estimates for India postulated a demographic growth of 1.4 per cent per annum. However, if we refer to the census of 1961, we find that the actual progression registered was 2 per cent.[4] The calculations of the Central Statistical Organization of India, made in 1959, anticipated a population of 480 million in 1966; new forecasts, made in 1962, gave a figure of 492 million.[5]

The same sort of under-estimation can be seen in most of the less-developed countries. However, it appears that the situation is slightly different in China (although the evidence is too unreliable for us to be able to pronounce confidently on this aspect of the problem) where population growth does not seem to have accelerated. As regards government policy, the following changes occurred; a violent anti-birth policy was succeeded in 1958 (after the Great Leap Forward) by a marked pro-birth policy: there was propaganda in favour of births, and there were perhaps even (although the facts are not very clear) measures in favour of large families. With the bad harvests of the years 1959–62 there was a return to an anti-birth policy which appeared to be still in force at the time of the cultural revolution. Information since then is not any easier to come by. Suffice it to say – and this does not indicate any change of official policy – that, according to visitors to the Canton fair,[6] the pill was on sale at a reasonable price in Chinese towns and villages and that it was manufactured locally.

However, demographic expansion in non-communist, less-developed countries does not necessary imply that no recent progress has been made in reducing fertility. Taking the present age structure of the Third World population, even a considerable reduction of fertility would not retard population growth in the short term. The lack of even relatively complete statistics of recent date certainly does not help one to form an objective appreciation of the situation. Even for crude birth rates regular annual data is available for only a few countries.

The absence of recent censuses in most under-developed countries makes the calculation of fertility rates even more hazardous. On the basis of statistics or estimates of crude birth rates, it would appear that a small number of countries have experienced reductions in this rate sufficiently important to establish the probability of a measurable reduction in fertility. But it has taken place only in small countries, such as Taiwan, Puerto Rico, Hong Kong, Mauritius, Trinidad and Tobago, etc, which have already benefited from some economic and social development and have received a large volume of aid. They have also undertaken birth-control campaigns of a thoroughness which would be out of the question in the larger countries. It is in these larger countries, of course, that the problem is really crucial, and it does not appear from an analysis of the crude birth rates that any significant progress has been achieved, since any plans for birth control have usually encountered many obstacles, particularly social ones.

The difficulties met with by campaigns to regulate births can be better illustrated by reports of actual experience than by global statistics. West Bengal, where the Indian authorities had made a special effort to promote a programme of fitting the intra-uterine device, will be taken as an example. According to the latest information this programme has largely failed. There has been a steady fall in the number of women accepting insertion. The number fell from 121,000 between October 1965 and March 1966 to 51,000 between April 1966 and September 1966, while it was only 72,000 for the whole of the following year, i.e. from October 1966 to September 1967.[7] This failure was mainly due to the fact that the effectiveness of the device was discredited through the personnel responsible not being sufficiently trained to deal with the many attendant medical problems. Even the vasectomy programme experienced a certain degree of failure in this region, because men undergoing the operation were not told that sterilization would not be effective until about three months afterwards. This was undoubtedly the cause of many births reported subsequently and it tended to throw doubt on what is otherwise a most reliable method.

These failures, or partial failures, are echoed from many directions and show us how urgent it is to speed up the search for a contraceptive method which is geared more closely to the economic, medical and, above all, social conditions of the under-developed countries. It is, in addition, most desirable that studies of the psychological aspects should be set in motion. Only when propaganda techniques are well attuned to local mentality will the introduction of family planning have a real chance of being effective.

The pessimism expressed in earlier editions of this book has been confirmed by the most recent population forecasts which are given below. The figures anticipated for the less-developed countries have had to be revised upwards once more.

If we confine ourselves to the short-term prospects we have to remember that even if these birth-control campaigns are successful they can influence population levels only very slightly, since growth in the foreseeable future depends much more on the age structure of a population than on changes in its fertility. As Henry and Pressat pointed out when speaking in 1956[8] of the demographic outlook for the Third World, the age pyramid has such a large base that if the population is not to increase there must be either an extremely low fertility rate or an extremely high death rate. This remark is even more pertinent now, when the changes which have taken place since the middle of the 'fifties have further enlarged the base of the Third World's age pyramid.

Allowing for this factor and assuming that the surpluses of western agriculture (and of North America in particular) would be capable of fending off for at least ten to fifteen years the risks of famine in the less-developed countries, we can expect with reasonable certainty that the rate of population growth of the Third World will increase in the course of the next ten years, probably up to 1980.[9] For this period we can assume as probable an annual rate of growth of around 2.8 to 2.9 per cent for the non-communist, under-developed countries, at least.

Table 2 *Projection of population for less-developed countries and the world 1970—2000*

	1970	*1980*		*1990*		*2000*	
	Population millions	*Population millions*	*	*Population millions*	*	*Population millions*	*
Medium variant							
Non-communist less-developed countries	1763	2329	2.8	3036	2.7	3828	2.3
Africa	324	430	2.9	579	3.0	770	2.9
Asia	1152	1517	2.8	1950	2.5	2397	2.1
America	283	377	2.9	500	2.8	652	2.7
Communist less-developed countries	801	943	1.6	1091	1.5	1231	1.2
Total less-developed countries	2564	3272	2.5	4127	2.4	5059	2.1
World	3632	4457	2.1	5438	2.0	6494	1.8
Non-communist less-developed countries: variants							
Low variant	1763	2272	2.6	2863	2.3	3475	2.0
Medium variant	1763	2329	2.8	3036	2.7	3828	2.3
High variant	1763	2375	3.0	3213	3.1	4243	2.8
Constant fertility variant	1763	2370	3.0	3280	3.3	4655	3.6

*Annual growth rate compared to the previous decade.
Sources: Derived from U.N. projections.

It will be noticed that the rates I have quoted relate to the non-communist countries only. For the communist countries it would be rash to make any forecast in view of the uncertainty of the past and present data. I have, however, reproduced in Table 2, for information only, the figures compiled by the United Nations experts which summarize the population forecasts made by them for the period 1970—2000. It should be noted that the future population growth rates I have retained (2.8 and 2.9 per cent) are a little above those derived from the medium variant of the United Nations projection (2.8 per cent). If we accept this medium variant the countries now reckoned as less-developed will account for 78.3 per cent of total world population by the end of the century. But if we postulate a constant fertility rate the figure rises to 82 per cent. In 1930 the under-developed countries accounted for only 63 per cent of world population[10] and in 1970 70.5 per cent (71.5 per cent if the more realistic figure for China is used).

It is only too obvious, therefore, that population growth has a burdensome part to play in the Third World problems to be discussed in the following chapters. Before this chapter closes attention must also be drawn to the recent emergence in certain quarters in the relatively under-populated countries of a sentiment hostile to the slowing down of demographic growth. This hostility usually results from a regrettable confusion between the pace of growth and population density. The real danger of demographic growth lies in too *rapid* an increase and not — at least not in every case, nor even in the short term — in the absolute level of population which that growth creates. It is true that for some under-developed countries it is possible and even probable that their present population density is not sufficient to permit a higher level of development.[11] But in seeking to achieve a higher density too quickly the very possibilities of development are themselves jeopardized.

2 *Agriculture*

INTRODUCTION

The importance of agriculture in the economy of the under-developed countries as well as in all traditional economies is such that a larger amount of space has been devoted to its study here than to any other topic. The crucial part played by agriculture in the economic life of the under-developed countries is revealed in two ways. Firstly, at the present time the sector occupies between 65 and 75 per cent of the total active population, provides about 35 per cent of the Gross Domestic Product and accounts for about 65 per cent of the foreign trade of these countries, excluding trade in oil.[1] Secondly, the importance of agriculture, spotlighted by the percentages quoted above, decrees that it must play a major role in the process of 'take off'. The latter would be inconceivable without the participation of such a substantial part of the population, who are, of course, also consumers.

The study of the industrial revolution[2] seems to indicate that it was this sector which gave the crucial impetus that started the western countries off on the road to industrialization. It is obvious, though, that structural conditions have since then been subject to profound changes which, on the one hand, make the 'take off' more difficult (for population growth is, after all, the special affliction of under-developed countries), while, on the other hand, allowing a degree of disengagement from agricultural determinism which, in the earliest phases of the industrial revolution, was almost complete. But the disengagement is in reality only partial and the momentum of demographic growth of a rural population alone makes a rise in agricultural productivity essential for growth in the economy as a whole. The dominance of agriculture which was paramount in western countries, will, in the course of this study, be shown to exist also in the under-developed countries, especially when we make comparisons between levels of agricultural productivity and growth of manufacturing industry.

Since in the last resort productivity is the best indicator of progress in agriculture, the main emphasis has been placed on this aspect. In the absence of comparable indices on an international level which would allow particular changes in one country's productivity to be compared with those of others, it has been found necessary to calculate[3] a special index of this kind for the twenty-four under-developed countries which represent 80 per cent of the Third World's population. The index is worked out for seven dates during the period 1909/13 to 1968/72, whereas the index numbers of production constructed by F.A.O. go back no further than 1934/38, and then only for a small number of countries.

The core of this subject will be the study of productivity, but I propose to preface it by a short analysis of the growth of aggregate agricultural output so as to complete my assessment of agriculture considered as a vital segment of the economy as a whole.

A. Agricultural production

For statistical reasons it is only possible to deal in detail with the changes in agricultural production after 1934/38 (see section II below). However, a relatively complete picture of changes occurring before that time can be sketched out briefly. For that period, even more than for recent years, it is preferable to treat subsistence cultivation and export cultivation separately. We have to remember that colonization usually endowed agriculture with a dualistic character: on the one hand there were the export crops generally, but not invariably, dominated by a plantation system employing advanced technology. On the other hand there were the subsistence crops, often excluded from the best land and almost always cultivated by methods which were both traditional and primitive.

I CHANGES IN PRODUCTION UP TO 1934/38
Let us see, first of all, what happened in the field of export crops in which there is an abundance of statistical data of a fairly reliable nature.

(a) Export crops

It should be remembered that since the sixteenth century differences in climate have made it possible to produce certain specialized South American crops at costs so low and profits so high as to bear the high transport charges. The fall in transport costs, the growing domination of Asia and Africa by colonial powers, and the industrial revolution, together made it possible to enlarge this system of exploitation considerably. The nineteenth century (especially the second half) saw a great expansion in the production and export of tropical commodities. Each year European markets absorbed an increasing quantity of sugar, coffee, tea and cocoa, as well as the more traditional spices and dyes. In the twentieth century the expansion even accelerated with other exotic goods, such as citrus fruits, bananas, rubber, oil seeds, etc., being added. Table 3 shows the increase in production of nine products, or groups of products, representing the most important export crops.[4] For comparative purposes the 1970 figures have been included.

Table 3 *World output of the principal tropical commodities from 1880 to 1970* (in thousands of tons: annual averages for quinquennia centring on dates in table, except 1970 where the average is for 1969—71)

	1880	1900	1910	1936	1970
Bananas[5]	30	300	1,800[4]	8,100	28,000
Cocoa	60	102	227	560	1,430
Coffee	550	970	1,090	2,110	4,420
Natural rubber	11	53	87	790	2,960
Cotton fibre[1]	950	1,200	1,770[4]	3,280	7,230
Jute[6]	600	1,220	1,560	1,960	3,290
Oil seeds[2]	—	—	2,700	12,060	22,400
Raw sugar cane[7]	1,850	3,340	6,320	14,200	41,100
Tea[3]	175	290	360	450	1,220

[1] Excluding U.S. and U.S.S.R.
[2] Ground nuts, copra, palm and palm oil
[3] Excluding U.S.S.R.
[4] 1911
[5] Before 1910: world exports
[6] And allied fibres (Kenaf and Congo jute)
[7] Centrifugal sugar

Note: Figures rounded up in units of ten to the nearest 1000 units.
Sources: 1880 Author's estimates based in general on various sources, but mainly the retrospective sections of the statistical yearbooks of France, and M. G. Mulhall, *Dictionary of Statistics* (London, 1899).
1900 to 1936 Mainly *Annuaire international de statistique agricole* of the International Institute of Agriculture, Rome, several years.
1970 F.A.O., and U.S. Dept. of Agriculture.

As can be seen, production of agricultural products for export grew very greatly before 1936. Weighting the volume of production by taking average export prices for 1926/29[5] we obtain annual rates of growth (based on five-year averages for the periods under consideration) for the nine export crops listed in Table 3 as follows:

1880—1900	2.6 per cent
1900—1910	4.2 per cent
1910—1936	3.6 per cent
1936—1970	2.7 per cent

According to F.A.O. figures the annual rate of growth of total agricultural production in the period 1936–1970 was 2.1 per cent, which confirms, if there is indeed any need to do so, that the products selected are representative.

(b) Subsistence agriculture

Information on the output of subsistence agriculture is much more fragmentary. On the basis of existing information it can be estimated that, between 1900 and the eve of the second world war, food production grew more slowly than population in these regions. But it is difficult to be more precise about the gap between the pace of growth. All that can be said is that it is not a large one – probably less than 0.5 per cent per annum – and that in 1934/38 the countries of the Third World still had a positive trade balance of cereals, i.e. as a whole, they exported more cereals on average each year than they imported. And this holds good even if we exclude Argentina, which in this respect, as in some others, is not really a part of the Third World. As we shall see later, in about 1936 this surplus (excluding Argentina and China) was of the order of 11 million tons of cereals, that is about 7 per cent of the production of such commodities by these countries.

Another point to be noticed is the more favourable growth of production in Latin America (and probably also in Africa) relative to that in Asia, a difference which is not wholly invalidated by the margin of error present in these figures. We shall now turn to changes in more recent years.

II CHANGES IN AGRICULTURAL PRODUCTION SINCE 1934/38

F.A.O. (Food and Agriculture Organization of the United Nations) calculate index numbers of agricultural production[6] for the principal under-developed countries (with, until very recently, the important omission of China, mainly because of the absence of complete statistics). The statistical services of this organization also calculate index numbers for the main geographical regions.[7] However, the F.A.O. index goes back no further than 1934/38.

(a) Changes in agricultural production by main geographical regions

In the tables below, in order to reduce the effect of fluctuations in yields, I have calculated five-yearly averages of the F.A.O. index numbers of agricultural production, as well as the annual rate of variation. As is indicated in Table 4 there are two series of index numbers, one relating to production of food and the other to total agricultural production. F.A.O. also calculates these same indexes per capita.

Table 4   *Agricultural production indices in less-developed*
            countries[1] *(1961—65 = 100)*

	Food products only		All agricultural products	
	Total	Per capita	Total	Per capita
1934—38	58	99	59	101
1948—52	66	90	66	89
1953—57	79	96	78	96
1958—62	92	99	92	100
1963—67	105	100	105	99
1968—72	121	101	121	101

[1]Excluding communist countries.
Sources: Derived from *Production Yearbook 1972* (F.A.O., Rome, 1973); *The State of Food and Agriculture 1970* (F.A.O., Rome, 1970), and *Monthly Bulletin of Agricultural Economics and Statistics* (F.A.O., various issues).
Except 1934—38: author's estimates on basis of F.A.O. regional data.

If we consider the entire period 1934/38—1968/72 it appears that the annual rate of growth of total agricultural production is around 2 per cent. The rate reaches or exceeds 2 per cent for Africa, Latin America and the Middle East, while it is about 1.9 per cent for Asian countries.[8] Growth in the African countries and the Middle East was slightly more rapid for non-food products, while the opposite was true of Latin America and the Far East. All the same growth was not uniform throughout the period. It was rather moderate from 1934/38 to 1948/52, more rapid during the following decade, while in the decade 1960/70 a slackening of overall growth can be detected.

If the periods of shorter duration are considered at a regional level, changes in the growth of agricultural production seem rather more homogeneous: slow growth from 1934/38 to 1948/52 (near 1.0 per cent), acceleration from 1948/52 to 1958/62 (near 3.5 per cent), then from 1958/62 to 1968/72 a slackening of the rate (about 2.5 per cent).

The high rate of population growth is responsible for absorbing nearly all this increment of production and even results in a lowering of per capita production. For Latin America this is relatively important since the figure fell by 0.3 per cent per annum from

Table 5   *Annual rate of growth of total and per capita agricultural production*
         (per cent)

	1934/38 to 1948/52	1948/52 to 1958/62	1958/62 to 1968/72	1934/38 to 1968/72
TOTAL				
Africa	1.7	3.1	2.5	2.4
Far East	0.3	3.3	2.5	1.9
Latin America	1.2	3.5	2.5	2.2
Middle East	1.0	4.0	3.1	2.5
Less-developed countries	*0.9*	*3.4*	*2.7*	*2.1*
PER CAPITA				
Africa	−0.2	0.8	*	0.1
Far East	−1.0	1.2	−0.2	−0.1
Latin America	−1.0	0.7	−0.4	−0.3
Middle East	*	1.4	0.3	0.5
Less-developed countries	*−0.9*	*1.1*	*0.1*	*

*Less than 0.05%.
Sources: See Table 4.

1934/38 to 1968/72. Only in the Middle East was a regression really avoided and slight progress registered. It is possible, of course, that these figures contain a margin of error, but the error would not be big enough to invalidate the changes described. The large number of countries involved would tend to reduce the margin of error contained in each of the indices taken individually.[9]

We shall now compare these rates with those of the western countries, firstly during their 'take off', and secondly at the present time. Because agricultural production is faced with structural rigidities more obdurate than those experienced by industry,[10] rates of growth in this sector were never very high. Thus, in England during the eighteenth century agricultural output rose at an average of 1 per cent per annum. The comparable figure for France was 0.6 per cent in the eighteenth century and 0.9 per cent in the nineteenth century, while in Belgium the rate was 1 per cent during the second half of the nineteenth century. The rate was higher in Russia and especially in the United States where it reached 2.5 per cent between 1870 and 1910.[11] In these two cases, of course, growth was due to the continuous colonization of new lands made possible by the influx of manpower. Thus, the rates of growth achieved by agriculture in the under-developed countries appear favourable compared to the rates of western countries during their 'take off' period. But the real difference between the performance of the two is caused by the growth of population which, as we have seen, was much lower in the western countries than in the under-developed countries. As for the present rate of growth of agricultural production in all the developed countries taken together, it is higher than that achieved in the course of the nineteenth century, as well as that in the under-developed countries in recent years. Thus, for the period 1948/52 to 1968/72 the annual rate of growth of total agricultural production was 2.9 per cent in Western Europe, 1.7 per cent in North America and 3.9 per cent in Eastern Europe and the U.S.S.R.

Therefore in this essential sector of the Third World economy the diagnosis of the level of production must be an unfavourable one: the speed of growth has been too slow, and generally slower than the growth of population. This negative diagnosis will be reinforced by the study of productivity; because, of course, if actual agricultural growth could have been accompanied by a growth in productivity, the global diagnosis would have been different. In fact, as we have seen, rates in absolute terms are not so low. If we look at global rates rather than per capita rates, they are slightly above those achieved by the developed countries at the moment of their 'take off'.

Before tackling the problem of productivity, however, we shall briefly examine the growth of agricultural output in some countries.

(b) Changes in agricultural production by countries

It is once again necessary to draw the reader's attention to the fragmentary nature of many statistics relating to the under-developed countries, especially with regard to agriculture. Anyone who is aware of the difficulties experienced by statisticians in this field, even in the developed countries with their relatively elaborate statistical organization, will accept this paucity of material as inevitable. All we can do here is to fill in for some countries the diagnosis already formulated for the larger geographical regions. In Table 6 five-year averages and the annual rates of variation have been calculated for three periods. Because F.A.O. has neither converted the pre-1952 figures to the former 1952/56 base nor to the new 1961/65 base for separate countries, I have been forced to make these calculations myself, which introduces an additional margin of error since these index numbers are in round figures.[12] For the annual rate of growth of agricultural production over a recent period for all countries for which F.A.O. calculates such an index readers should refer to the synoptic table in the Appendix.

Table 6 *Changes and annual rates of variation in the index of total agricultural production*

	Index 1961/65 = 100			Annual rate of variation	
	1934 1938	1948 1952	1968 1972	1934/38 1948/52	1948/52 1968/72
AFRICA					
Algeria	105	99	107	−0.4	0.4
Ethiopia	−	78[3]	124	−	3.1
Morocco	61	74	140	2.0	3.2
Tunisia	71	73	115	0.2	2.3
LATIN AMERICA					
Argentina	74	75	109	0.1	1.9
Brazil	49	58	129	1.2	4.1
Chile	61	76	114	1.6	2.0
Colombia	43	71	133	3.6	3.2
Cuba	56	88	111	3.2	1.2
Guatemala	−	56[3]	131	−	5.8
Mexico	33	51	124	3.2	4.5
Panama	−	62[3]	147	−	5.9
Peru	53	70	115	2.0	2.5
Uruguay	75	91	98	1.4	0.4
Venezuela	−	62[3]	139	−	5.5
ASIA					
Burma	86	75	108	−1.0	1.8
Ceylon	50	66	116	2.0	2.8
China (Taiwan)	56	61	156	0.6	4.8
India	68	69	117	0.1	2.7
Pakistan	71	75	128	0.4	2.5
Indonesia	74	76[2]	121	0.1	2.8
Malaysia (West)	54	74	149	2.3	3.5
Philippines	51	62	123	1.5	3.5
Thailand	36	44	130	3.0	5.5
MIDDLE EAST					
Egypt	57	66	124	1.0	3.2
Iraq	−	86[3]	143	−	3.4
Iran	−	74[3]	131	−	3.9
Syria	−	69[3]	102	−	2.6
Turkey	41	55	126	2.1	4.2

[1] For countries where there are no figures for 1948/52 the annual rate of growth is calculated for the period 1953/57 to 1968/72.
[2] 1951/53
[3] 1953/57
Sources: Derived from various issues of *Production Yearbook* and *Monthly Bulletin of Agricultural Economics and Statistics* (F.A.O., Rome).

So far as Africa is concerned long-term figures are available for only a few countries, none of which is part of Black Africa. In the Maghreb growth is very unequal: in Algeria regression is followed by stagnation; in Tunisia progress is limited and in Morocco expansion is relatively fast.

The rate for the whole of Latin America conceals a very wide variation between individual countries. Countries registering very little growth in output (less than 2 per cent) include Argentina, Cuba, Uruguay and Chile. On the other hand production in Brazil, Venezuela, Guatemala, Panama and Mexico has risen fast enough to overtake the increase in population. There is much less differentiation in Asia. Amongst the countries experiencing a favourable change are Thailand, Sri Lanka, the Philippines, Malaysia and Taiwan. But countries with an unfavourable change include three of the four largest in the continent: India, Pakistan and Indonesia. As we have seen, the F.A.O. does not calculate long-term indices for the fourth large country, China, but on the basis of the data collected for the remaining sections of this chapter, we may conclude that any change occurring has been more favourable than in most of the other Asian countries, particularly India, even according to western estimates.

As far as the Middle East is concerned, for the long-term index (1934/38–1967/71) we possess figures only for Egypt[13] and Turkey. The latter has during this period experienced a rise in agricultural production (3.3 per cent) which is noticeably faster than that of population. On the other hand, Egypt's rate of about 2 per cent has not kept pace with population growth. Other countries, apart from Syria, have experienced a relatively high and relatively homogeneous increase in the short term (about 3.5 per cent).

B. Agricultural productivity

As stated at the start of this chapter, the agricultural sector is of such importance that an index which would enable us to trace the growth of agricultural productivity in the various countries of the Third World would be well worth while constructing. In another study devoted to economic development in the nineteenth century[14] I was able to calculate such an index of agricultural productivity for twelve countries which are nowadays considered developed. An index for under-developed countries constructed by means of a similar method would have a double objective:

1. To measure and compare at an international level changes in agricultural productivity in the under-developed countries.

2. To compare the agricultural productivity of under-developed countries with that of developed countries before and during their 'take off' period.

I. METHOD OF CALCULATING THE INDEX OF AGRICUL-TURAL PRODUCTIVITY

One important preliminary remark must be made concerning the exiguous nature of the basic figures used in this study. I have already drawn attention to the substantial margins of error in Third World agricultural statistics. Within the limits of possibility some of the more obviously erroneous figures have been corrected by means of accepted statistical techniques, while some series are so fragmentary that they have been rejected altogether. But however much such statistical caution may have reduced the margins of error, they still remain considerable. We must accept the fact that errors are impossible to eliminate entirely, for if all quantitative material which included any margin of error were to be rejected this would lead to the rejection of almost all other data used in economic analysis, especially in such modern concepts as national product or income, capital output ratio, etc.

The index of agricultural productivity as it has been calculated here is in fact an estimate of the net agricultural production by male labour employed in agriculture expressed in 'direct' calories.[15] The exclusion of women from the population employed in agriculture is justified because the criteria used in different countries to determine their employment vary too widely. The stages adopted in calculating the index will very briefly be explained:

(a) Total production of gross calories
1. Vegetable products
The following crops have been taken into consideration: all cereals (including millet and sorghum), soya beans, manioc, potatoes (including sweet potatoes) and all dried vegetables. Calorific values have been obtained for each of these products and applied to output. An allowance has been made for the difference in calorific content between rice and other cereals so as to establish an average appropriate to each country as a function of the respective importance of the various cereals.

2. Meat

Statistics for meat production are practically non-existent for most under-developed countries, so, in order to make the series homogeneous, production had to be estimated. This has been done in the following way:

(a) The annual number of animals slaughtered for consumption at home and for sale has been estimated on the basis of total livestock existing at different dates. The coefficients used to determine the number of beasts slaughtered have been based on figures for countries with a similar or related structure for which valid statistics were available. I have also had to allow for changes over time, for as agricultural technique improves animals are slaughtered at a younger age. This means the coefficients must rise. I have, of course, used different coefficients for each kind of animal, country or group of countries, as well as for different periods. The averages for the different livestock species at the end of the period were as follows: oxen and cows 15 per cent; buffaloes 10 per cent; sheep and goats 22 per cent; pigs 70 per cent.

(b) Total weight for each species has been estimated on the basis of figures available for countries with a related structure (statistics in this field are actually more abundant). Here allowance has also been made for an increase in the average weight of animals.

(c) 2,300 calories per kilo have been postulated for all kinds of meat except pig meat, for which the figure of 3,200 calories has been taken.[16] However as these figures represent 'derived' calories, they had to be converted back into 'direct' or 'initial' calories. The choice of coefficients used (since, in fact, they differ widely between one kind of livestock and another) has posed problems of a technical and methodological nature.

Improvements in animal husbandry lead, in fact, to modification of these coefficients for, on the one hand (as pointed out above) the tendency to slaughter animals at an earlier age entails a reduction in the calories absorbed by 'animal maintenance', while, on the other, the improvement of breeds and techniques of animal husbandry lead to an increase in the energy yield (i.e. in the number of meat calories produced by a given quantity of forage and other feeding stuffs absorbed by the animal). Consequently as agricultural technique improves the coefficient in question is lowered. The problem of method which it poses is that of a choice between a variable or a fixed coefficient. A variable coefficient would be justified on the purely formal plane but it would lead to a considerable lowering of the effects of improvements, narrowly speaking, since for a given production of meat fewer and fewer vegetable calories are needed. But since the main object of this study is to measure changes and differences in productivity it seems as if the least inaccurate solution is to use a fixed coefficient.

As for the 'technical' problem, it is simply how to determine the average coefficients, since no work has been done in this field. Briefly, the following coefficients have been adopted here: oxen and cows 9 (nine vegetable calories to produce one meat calorie); buffaloes 12; sheep and goats 24; pigs 5.[17]

(b) Total production of net calories

The results of the calculations presented above provide an estimate of the production of gross calories, i.e. including seed.[18] These figures have been changed into net calories (excluding seed) by using for each period and country considered a different coefficient of correction. These coefficients have been estimated from yields per hectare of the various cereals under consideration and of the corresponding seed requirements, that is the seed-harvest ratio for the main cereal in each country. These coefficients have had to be adjusted for countries where manioc forms a large proportion of agricultural production because seed for this crop does not significantly reduce the harvest available.

(c) Male labour employed in agriculture

The total production of net calories obtained has been divided by the number of male workers employed in agriculture: as already stated, women have been excluded because there are important variations in the criteria used to determine their participation. Insofar as valid statistics from recent censuses are available, figures for the total number of male agricultural workers have been used. In all other cases this figure was estimated in the following way: on the basis of total male population the male working population was derived by using global activity rates extrapolated either from the same countries for dates where such figures exist, or from the activity rates in other countries at a similar level of development.

From this male working population the number employed in agriculture was estimated from information about the relative share of this sector. In many cases I have calculated these shares myself. I have then gone on to extrapolate on the basis of earlier known data and general changes in this field derived from information about other countries.

(d) Eliminating non-subsistence crops, particularly plantation crops
The fundamental difference between subsistence and plantation agriculture makes it necessary to exclude the latter when calculating our index of agricultural productivity.[19] Plantation agriculture should in fact be considered as totally outside the agricultural economy of most of the under-developed countries properly defined, partly because of the techniques employed and partly because of the nature of land-ownership. Excluding this sector of agriculture does not pose a problem from the production point of view, but it is much harder to separate employment in the two sectors. For all practical purposes statistics do not exist, so I have been forced yet again to make in each case an estimate based on the two following approaches, either together or separately.

(1) By using the various norms of labour required per hectare for each crop.

(2) By making an estimate of labour based on the value of production, on the average coefficient which labour represents in the cost price and on the average level of agricultural wages. Both these methods of estimating, especially the first, must be examined in a little more detail.

1. Norms of labour required per hectare
Very little work has been done in this field.[20] The only general study that I know, entitled *Normes de main-d'oeuvre pour les travaux agricoles au Congo belge*.[21] relates to the former Belgian Congo and refers mostly to tropical crops. On the whole we may accept these norms as valid if we treat them as general averages. A systematic search for norms in other periods or territories in studies dealing either with the products or the countries we are concerned with has resulted in some supplementary material.[22] It should be noted, however, that the figures calculated in the I.N.E.A.C. study on the Belgian Congo could not be used as they stood, because average norms had to be computed from figures relating to investment period, upkeep during the period when there was no yield, as well as the period of yield.

2. Estimate of labour's share in the value of production
From such fragmentary material as is available it is possible to establish that the average share of labour in the selling price of

plantation crops is about 42 per cent.[23] This is, of course, only a very rough figure, but the margin of error has, nevertheless, been kept to a minimum. From the ratio of the level of agricultural wages to the value of production of the crops under consideration, I have been able to form an estimate of labour requirements.

(e) Choice of countries: sources
The wide scope of this study[24] has rendered it impossible to make calculations for all the under-developed territories. It will be remembered how the fragmenting of former colonial empires has resulted in the creation of some 170 economic and political entities. In addition, satisfactory statistical information on agriculture for more than a small number of these separate entities simply does not exist. Consequently, I have been forced to use as my base here only the twenty-four countries which, it will be recalled, were selected according to three criteria, but which nonetheless represent 80 per cent of the population of the Third World. The fundamental figures of agricultural production are mainly based on information collected by F.A.O., either in the *Production Yearbook* or (for the most recent material) in *Monthly Bulletins of Agricultural Economics and Statistics*. For the period before 1946 the Year Books of the International Institute of Agriculture were used. Nevertheless for certain countries and certain products[25] additional research in the statistical year books of the countries, or in commodity studies, has been necessary.

II. PRODUCTIVITY THRESHOLDS
Before looking at the results of calculating our agricultural productivity index, I have attempted to give this index a slightly more realistic character. In addition to the information the index provides about the relative levels of individual countries, or of different economies, or about the changes which have taken place between different periods, we want also to be able to say that the agriculture of these countries has reached definite stages of development. With this object in view I have calculated a series of 'productivity thresholds' expressed in the same units which are used in the main index. The reader is reminded that the index of productivity is the average annual production of a male agricultural worker expressed in millions of net direct calories.

Approximately 0.9 units, or 900,000 direct calories, are needed annually to feed a man. This figure is based on a minimum of 2,100 calories per day[26] and allows on the one hand for an under-estimate, calculated as about 10 per cent, because certain products (milk, vegetables, oils and fruit) have been excluded and, on the other hand, for the fact that animal calories are here expressed as direct calories. On the basis of a working population representing 40 per cent of total population[27] and of a male working population representing 28 per cent of total population, we arrive at a figure of about 3 units as the minimum 'physiological productivity' required to support the entire population, assuming the total absence of other activities. By postulating a daily consumption of the order of 3,200 calories (which should be considered an optimum figure) — and also in the total absence of other sectors — the minimum productivity reaches 5.4 units (allowing for the rise in animal calories inherent in such a change). These levels are obviously purely theoretical, if only because they assume the total absence of other activities and because they omit losses and, above all, fluctuations in yields. It leads us on to calculate two, more realistic, thresholds of productivity in which these factors are accounted for.

The first, which can be called the 'physiological threshold', is also based on a daily consumption of 2,100 calories per head, which, as we have seen, implies a productivity of 0.9 units in the absence of other sectors. By postulating that the non-agricultural sectors represent 15 per cent of the working population[28] and that various losses (deterioration, waste through animal pests, milling, etc.) represent 10 per cent of production,[29] the physiological minimum amounts to 3.8 units. Therefore, at this level productivity can be considered sufficient to cover food requirements without noticeable quantitative scarcities.[30] But this threshold does not allow for a factor too often neglected in the diagnosis of the changes in agricultural economy: wide fluctuations in yields.

It is for this reason that I have thought it essential to define and calculate a second threshold which would give the average level at which agriculture can be considered to have surmounted the dangerline below which famines are still possible. It is true that in determining this threshold it would be necessary to take account of several factors which will be ignored here, especially the importance of animal husbandry as a buffer against the effects of fluctuations in agricultural yields.[31] In practice animal husbandry regulates the quantity of calories available for human consumption: during periods of good harvests the number of livestock is increased because of the surplus cereals available, while in years when harvests are insufficient or less good, animal slaughter allows food supplies to be increased not only by providing meat, but also by reducing the demand for cereals to feed livestock. However, it must be admitted that in general this mechanism is of little significance in under-developed countries because the low productivity of agriculture reduces the consumption of 'derived' calories. Consequently the second threshold, which I shall call productivity 'potentially free from the risk of famine', will take account only of fluctuations in yields.

Table 7 *Variations in yields (100 kg per hectare), 1947–1962*

Crop and country	Average yields (1947–62)	Lowest annual yield	
		Figure	Variation from the mean
RICE			
Ceylon	15.4	12.4	20%
India[1]	12.8	10.1	21%
Philippines	11.7	10.8	8%
Madagascar	14.2	12.6	11%
WHEAT			
Argentina	12.5	7.8	76%
Brazil	7.4	4.1	95%
Egypt	21.4	15.3	29%
Morocco	6.3	3.9	38%
MANIOC			
Brazil	13.0	12.4	5%
Indonesia[3]	8.2	6.7	18%
Peru	12.5	9.9	21%
Zaïre[2]	10.6	8.4	21%

[1] 1952–62
[2] 'village' output
[3] 1948–62
Sources: These averages have been calculated on the basis of material provided by the *Production Yearbook* for the years 1949–63 (F.A.O., Rome).

Table 7 shows variations in the yields of three food products which are important to the under-developed countries. It will be seen that within the period, according to produce and even country, there is a striking gap between average yields and lowest yields. The gap varies on average from about 20 per cent for rice and manioc to as much as 40 per cent for wheat. Bearing in mind that in under-developed countries both rice and manioc are of equal or greater importance than wheat we can roughly compute the probable average gap between average agricultural production and a very bad harvest as 25–30 per cent. This rate applies to gross production (including seed): the gap is even wider for net production, since it is obvious that the amount of seed remains the same no matter what the variation of yield within the country. Allowing for this factor, the gap can be taken as 30 per cent, which gives us a figure of about 4.9 units for the productivity threshold 'free from famine risk'. But once more this is only a theoretical figure, for it is clear that in the hypothetical case of a country where agriculture accounted for only a small fraction of total employment it could be much lower without being followed by a famine. Before examining the productivity index itself the different thresholds can be recapitulated as follows:

0.9 units: Food requirements per head on the basis of 2,100 calories per day.

3.0 units: Threshold of minimum physiological productivity for the whole population assuming the absence of other sectors.

3.8 units: Threshold of physiological productivity.

4.9 units: Threshold of productivity potentially free from famine risk.

III INDEX OF AGRICULTURAL PRODUCTIVITY: RESULTS AND COMMENTS

We shall briefly examine the results of the computations made according to the methods described above under the following three headings:

(a) Average levels (1960/64–1968/72)
(b) Changes between 1909/13 and 1968/72
(c) Comparisons with the developed countries, now and before their 'take off'.

(a) Average levels (1960/64–1968/72)

Although the indexes have been calculated for five-yearly periods, it seemed best, nevertheless, to use the average for the two recent periods when comparing levels of production, in order to eliminate as far as possible the effects of fluctuations due to variations in yields.

One preliminary conclusion springs to the eye immediately. This is the marked divergence between productivity in the Latin American countries and in the countries of Asia and Africa. The average for the former is around 10, for the latter 5, while the average for the Middle

Table 8 *Level of agricultural productivity: averages 1960/64—1968/72*

COUNTRY	Level of productivity	COUNTRY	Level of productivity
AFRICA		ASIA	
Ghana	3.9	China[2]	5.4/6.4
Kenya	5.3	Ceylon	5.4
Madagascar	10.6	India	4.0
Morocco	6.3	Pakistan	4.3
Nigeria	3.6	Indonesia	4.5
Tunisia	3.6	Philippines	4.7
Zaïre	5.5	Thailand	7.0
Weighted average[1]	4.7	*Weighted average*[1]	4.8
excluding Madagascar	4.5	excluding China	4.3
AMERICA		MIDDLE EAST	
Argentina[3]	75.6/38.1	Egypt	5.5
Brazil	11.9	Iraq	7.7
Chile	17.0	Turkey	11.3
Cuba	7.0		
Mexico	6.6	*Weighted average*[1]	8.6
Peru	6.6		
Venezuela	8.6		
Weighted average[1]	13.5		
excluding Argentina	9.8		

[1] Weighted according to the active male agricultural population employed in agriculture (excluding plantations).
[2] The first index number is based on western estimates of production, the second on information derived from the Chinese authorities.
[3] The second index number excludes stock-raising.
Sources: Author's estimates (see text for method of calculation).
Note: The small extent to which the figures have been rounded up does not imply any corresponding margin of error.

Eastern countries lies somewhere in between. It should be noted, however, that because Turkey is included, the Middle Eastern figure is not fully representative. Obviously within each group there are countries whose level of productivity differs considerably from the others and is nearer that of other groups, or even of the developed countries. Argentina is such a country. Argentina is usually included in the Third World because according to most classifications it is considered under-developed and because, together with Brazil and Mexico, it is one of what might be called the Big Three of Latin America. But it becomes more and more obvious that such a classification is wrong.[32] All classifications must be arbitrary to some extent and they can only be accepted if we recognize this fact.

But this said, the extremely high level of agricultural productivity in Argentina must surely exclude it from the list of those countries traditionally called under-developed.

1. Agricultural productivity and thresholds of productivity

All the countries included in the table are above the level of physiological productivity (3.8). But several of the African and Asian countries are below the productivity threshold (4.9) which marks the 'potentially free from famine' level: these are Ghana, Nigeria, Tunisia, India, Pakistan and Indonesia – to which we should add (always allowing for margins of error in the productivity estimates) the Philippines. Thus overall a large majority (nearly four-fifths) of the population of under-developed territories are supported on a level of productivity which still implies a risk of famine.[33] If we accept, as will be explained later, that China has been able to pass beyond this threshold, the proportion falls to about one-half of the entire Third World. Thus – as F.A.O. often declares through its directors, Mr Sen and more recently Mr Boerma – judged by the calorific value of available foodstuffs, the non-communist, under-developed countries, especially the countries of Asia, and to a lesser degree, of Africa, still live under a very real threat of famine. In Asia only a few restricted areas, such as Sri Lanka and Thailand, are free from this terrible risk. Even for those countries whose productivity has risen above the threshold, the threat of localized famine still exists, for the figures given here are national averages and there are very marked regional differences of productivity within countries, added to which difficulties of internal transport often hinder redistribution.

Consequently, for most under-developed countries, priority for agriculture is not so much a choice as a compelling necessity. The existence of an agricultural surplus in the developed countries (in particular in North America) has until now staved off a serious catastrophe. But stocks do not form more than a fraction of world production,[34] and it would only be necessary for a series of bad harvests to occur simultaneously in both developed and under-developed countries for the problem of famine in the Third World to become insuperable.[35]

It is obvious therefore that a rise in agricultural production beyond the threshold where the Third World would be potentially free from famine risk should be an absolutely essential objective. In this connexion I would like to discuss a factor which, so far as I know, has not been reckoned with in analysing development difficulties in those countries where religion requires its followers to practise vegetarianism. To help us understand this problem we should remind ourselves of the rôle livestock plays in reducing the fluctuations in available foodstuffs caused by variable yields. In good years a part of the surplus harvest is used to increase the numbers of livestock; on the other hand, after bad harvests, livestock is reduced and provides more food both through additional quantities of meat and through a fall in the quantity of cereals consumed by animals. But with a vegetarian population, in view of the high cost of food stocks, there is a much greater fluctuation in the quantity of available foodstuffs, with adverse consequences for the people's health. A vicious circle is thus set up, for bad health means a lowered capacity for work and thus a smaller agricultural output.

But more important still is the fact that a diet without meat inevitably lessens the incentive to increase agricultural productivity, since consumption soon comes up against a physiological barrier. In vegetarian diets the gap between average and maximum consumption of calories is fairly small, no more than about 20 per cent. In meat-eating societies the gap is much greater due to the fact that a calorie of meat needs about 7 vegetable calories for its formation. Thus, at present in developed countries the number of calories consumed daily can be as much as 9,000 while the maximum the body needs daily is approximately 3,500. Faced with such a small elasticity of demand, it is not surprising that vegetarian populations should make so little effort to increase their food supply.

Furthermore, by raising those animals which graze on vegetation which otherwise would be useless to man, total agricultural productivity is increased; these animals are in addition tended by members of the population (elderly people and young children) whose physical strength does not fit them to participate in agricultural production properly defined.

In view of all these factors it seems more than likely that vegetarianism has hitherto hindered development, and still continues to do so.

2. Agricultural productivity and availability of agricultural land
Allowing for inherent differences in the level of development, narrowly defined, there is also a correlation between the level of productivity and the agricultural area per male agricultural worker.[36] The level of productivity is higher where the availability of

agricultural land is greater. The correlation is not, of course, absolute, because several factors, such as soil fertility, type of crop or presence of irrigation, affect the relationship. The correlation coefficient of the two series in Table 9 is 0.92.

Table 9 *Comparison between agricultural productivity and availability of agricultural land*

Country	Level of productivity 1953/57–1960/64	Hectares of agricultural area[1] per male worker occupied in agriculture[2]
AFRICA		
Ghana	3.7	5.3
Kenya	5.0	4.2
Madagascar	10.5	43.2
Morocco	7.3	10.6
Nigeria	4.0	2.4
Tunisia	4.2	8.7
Zaire	5.7	20.2
AMERICA		
Argentina	64.4 (31.8)*	102.5
Brazil	10.9	13.0
Chile	15.0	9.8
Cuba	6.9	7.8
Mexico	5.9	16.7
Peru	6.7	12.2
Venezuela	7.5	26.6
ASIA		
China	4.8 (5.8)†	2.7
Ceylon	5.2	1.2
India	4.1	1.9
Pakistan	4.4	1.4
Indonesia	4.7	1.1
Philippines	4.9	2.6
Thailand	6.7	1.8
MIDDLE EAST		
Egypt	5.3	0.6
Iraq	8.1	13.6
Turkey	10.9	11.3

[1] Arable land; land under permanent crops; permanent meadow and pastures.
[2] In censuses taken between 1956 and 1962, except Cuba 1946, and China 1954.
*Excluding cattle farming   †Official estimates
Sources: Productivity, author's estimates; agricultural area derived from F.A.O.

The limited amount of agricultural land available in the Asian countries is certainly a major obstacle to any substantial increase in productivity. The figure of 1.8 hectares of agricultural land[37] per male agricultural worker (the average for Asia, excluding China) is of course very low indeed. As a matter of fact the figures for Asia (as can readily be seen from Table 9) are not only much lower than those for Africa and Latin America, but are also totally unrelated to those of the developed countries (France, 13.1; Belgium, 9.4; Italy, 5.8; U.S.S.R. 34.0) not to mention the North American and Oceanic countries of European settlement, where the figure is about 100 hectares (United States, 99; Canada, 90; New Zealand, 111; Australia, 1,100. The last figure is explained by the predominance of sheep farming). Furthermore, as we shall see in the comparative section, the amount of land available in the currently developed countries before their 'take off' was also higher.

3. Agricultural productivity and plantations
Productivity in subsistence agricultural is generally higher in countries where plantations are relatively unimportant. This situation is illustrated in Africa by Ghana and Nigeria, which both have a large number of plantations and where subsistence productivity is below that of the Congo and Kenya where plantations are fewer. There is the same difference in Latin America between Brazil and Chile and in the Middle East between Egypt, Iraq and Turkey. The difference is explained by the fact that plantations (or export crops) have monopolized the best land.[38] We should realize moreover that the more productive methods used on plantations do not seem to have had an apparent influence on subsistence agriculture.

4. Agricultural productivity and European settlement
The present point is particularly valid in Latin American countries. It is in just those territories where European settlement has been proportionately largest that agricultural productivity is highest, as is well illustrated in the cases of Argentina, Brazil and Chile. The difference is, of course, partly attributable to the influence of a population which has brought with it better techniques, but that is not the only explanation. Had the fertility of the land been low to begin with, or at least not obviously superior to the regions abandoned in Europe, the land would not have been settled.

5. Average productivity index for all under-developed countries
Finally, around 1970 the weighted average of the agricultural productivity index for all under-developed countries under consideration here is about 5.5 including China, according to the western estimate, and 6.1 including China according to the official estimate. Since these countries represent 80 per cent of the total population of the Third World and since, from the available information, the productivity of all the omitted countries together is probably a little lower than that of those studied, it is reasonable to set the average level of agricultural productivity of the whole non-communist Third World at about 5.4.

(b) Changes between 1909/13 and 1968/72
While a very great increase in agricultural productivity can be observed in the developed countries in the course of the seventy or so years which separate us from the beginning of the century (productivity increased more than five-fold during this period),[39] there has on the contrary been a falling off of agricultural productivity in the under-developed countries. This is especially true in the Afro-Asian countries. In Latin America there has been either a slight advance or at least a maintenance of the status quo. This is, of course, taking the region as a whole; there are marked differences between country and country.

Between 1909/13 and 1922/26, while there are divergences, the overall change in productivity is minimal. The Latin American and African countries experienced, on the whole, a moderate growth, but overall agricultural productivity in Asia suffered a slight regression.

Between 1922/26 and 1946/50 there was an almost general fall which was greater for Asia than for Latin America. Productivity fell in Asian countries by 19 per cent (that is 1.7 per cent per annum) from 1922/26 to 1934/38 and by 10 per cent (0.8 per cent per annum) from 1934/38 to 1946/50; while for the Latin American countries in the same period the decline was no more than 5 per cent (0.4 per cent per annum) and 6 per cent (0.5 per cent per annum). The change in Africa and the Middle East is less clear, although the indications are that the status quo was maintained on the whole, with only a slight tendency to decline.

From 1946/50 to 1953/57 the general tendency, with the exception of most African countries, was one of growth in productivity. For the whole of Asia growth was 17 per cent (2.3 per cent per annum); for Latin America 10 per cent (1.4 per cent per annum). and for the Middle East 38 per cent (4.7 per cent per annum). It is true that the classic problem of margins of error is still present: estimates of 'home consumption', which represents a major portion of agricultural production in these countries, are likely to have improved in accuracy. It is also possible that part of the growth registered should be imputed to progress in methods of estimating.

Table 10 *Weighted average[1] of index numbers of agricultural productivity*

Country	1909/13	1922/26	1934/38	1946/50	1953/57	1960/64	1968/72
AFRICA	6.9	8.7	7.1	7.3	5.2	4.7	4.6
AMERICA	11.9	13.3*	12.6	11.9	13.1	12.9	14.2
exclud. Argentina	7.2	7.6*	7.5	7.8	9.0	9.2	10.4
ASIA	—	—	4.2	3.7	4.4	4.7	4.8
China	—	—	4.4	3.7	4.4	5.1	5.6
ASIA excluding China	5.1*	5.0	4.1	3.7	4.3	4.4	4.2
MIDDLE EAST	—	—	6.0	6.1	8.3	8.4	8.8
Total for 24 countries studied	—	—	4.9	4.4	5.1	5.4	5.5
Ditto excluding China	5.9	5.9	5.3	5.0*	5.7	5.6	5.5

*After this date the number of countries included in the calculation of the weighted average is changed.
[1] Weighted according to the number of male agricultural workers occupied in agriculture, excluding plantation.
Sources: Author's estimates (see text for method of calculation).
Note: The small extent to which the figures have been rounded up does not imply any corresponding margin of error.

From 1953/57 to 1960/64 the general tendency was reversed and was once more a declining one, especially in the Afro-Asian countries, with the notable exception of China, to which we shall return later.

The under-developed countries of Latin America, due to the decline of Brazil (3 per cent, 0.4 per cent per annum) and the relative importance of that country, experienced a slight fall in the weighted average (1 per cent or 0.1 per cent per annum).

Finally, between 1960/64 and 1968/72 productivity rose again if only very slightly. For all under-developed countries taken together this growth was 0.2 per cent per annum. But if China is excluded there was a slight decline. In relation to the general average, the change has been relatively favourable for Latin America and the

Middle East, and unfavourable for Asia. On the basis of admittedly fragmentary information, agricultural productivity in China has grown by 1 to 1.5 per cent per annum. We shall have to return later to this. As far as the effects of the 'green revolution' are concerned, these will be discussed in section (c) below. Meanwhile let us examine the changes in some important countries.

For Latin America, stagnation in Brazil during the first half of this century should be noted and contrasted with the favourable changes taking place in Mexico[40] and Venezuela, even though the absolute level of productivity in these two countries still remains rather low.

In Asia the most significant phenomenon is of course the growth displayed since 1950 by China, a growth which contrasts with decline, or at least no major change, on the part of most other Asian countries. Even if we retain the western estimates, the annual rate of growth in productivity has been from 2.0 to 2.5 per cent per annum from 1946/50 to 1968/72, while the index of productivity rose from 3.7 to 5.6.[41] At this level China has broken through the barrier and is 'potentially free from famine risk'. It is, of course, probable that the harvests lie between the estimates based on western figures and those based on government information. It could then be postulated that the index of productivity around 1970 lies above 6. This would allow China to enter a process of wider industrialization, since at this level of productivity it is possible to free a significant proportion of the agricultural labour force from work on the land.

As far as the second Asian giant, India, is concerned, we are witnessing a deterioration in the level of productivity. It has at the present moment fallen to a level which is about 25 per cent lower than that of the period 1909/13 to 1922/26. With productivity at 3.9 India finds herself once more below the threshold of 'potential freedom from famine risk'.

The gap between the agricultural productivity of these two countries which have opted for such different modes of development is likely to have profound repercussions on the whole under-developed world, especially if the divergence continues in the future. A cautious extrapolation of the trends of Chinese growth and an assumption that India, contrary to past decline, will have a future growth of something like 0.5 per cent per annum, results in a prognostication that by 1980 there will be a difference of about 100 per cent between the agricultural productivity of the two countries.

No significant divergences can be observed for the African and Middle Eastern countries analysed here.

Table 11   *Index numbers of agricultural productivity by country*

Country	1909 1914	1922 1926	1934 1938	1946 1950	1953 1957	1960 1964	1968 1972
AFRICA							
Ghana	—	—	—	—	3.7	3.8	3.9
Kenya	—	—	—	6.1	4.6	5.3	5.3
Madagascar	9.7	13.8	11.1	11.9	10.0	11.0	10.3
Morocco	6.0	7.0	7.6	7.3	8.5	6.0	6.5
Nigeria	—	—	—	—	4.2	3.9	3.4
Tunisia	4.3	4.5	5.4	4.4	4.6	3.8	3.4
Zaïre	—	—	5.6	6.9	6.4	5.0	5.9
AMERICA							
Argentina	61.2	65.4	59.1	50.9	60.6	68.2	86.9
excluding cattle	33.8	37.0	36.1	24.3	30.0	33.3	43.0
Brazil	9.4	10.4	10.1	10.0	11.1	10.8	12.9
Chile	12.5	12.3	13.8	13.1	14.5	15.6	18.4
Cuba	—	—	5.6	6.5	6.7	7.0	7.0
Mexico	3.9	3.0	3.0	3.7	5.5	6.3	6.8
Peru	5.5	5.7	6.0	7.8	6.8	6.5	6.6
Venezuela	—	—	5.2	4.9	6.8	8.1	9.2
ASIA							
China (West. estim.)	—	—	4.4	3.7	4.4	5.1	5.6
China (Offic. estim.)	—	—				6.5	7.1
Ceylon	—	—	5.0	3.6	4.9	5.5	5.3
India	5.4	5.1	3.9	3.3	4.1	4.1	3.9
Pakistan	—	—	4.5	4.5	4.2	4.5	4.2
Indonesia	3.5	3.3	3.7	3.7	4.7	4.6	4.5
Philippines	—	5.5	4.7	4.5	5.1	4.8	4.6
Thailand	7.3	8.5	6.2	6.5	6.7	6.8	7.2
MIDDLE EAST							
Egypt	5.7	4.8	4.4	4.6	5.1	5.4	5.7
Iraq	—	—	8.9	7.6	9.2	7.1	8.3
Turkey	—	—	7.1	7.0	10.7	11.1	11.5

Sources: Author's estimates (see text for method of calculation).
Note: The small extent to which the figures have been rounded up does not imply any corresponding margin of error.

It is quite certain that the decline in agricultural productivity to be seen in most of the under-developed countries can be attributed largely to the population explosion. It has activated the old law of diminishing returns.[42] The number of male agricultural workers has, on average, more than doubled between 1900 and 1970. Such a growth, coupled with the low availability of land, whether of average or of low fertility, obviously poses almost insoluble problems. At this point it is useful to remember that agriculture during the industrial revolution developed with a relatively stable working population (see Table 12), the moderate increase in population (four or five times less than that of the under-developed countries) being relieved by the transfer of part of the working agricultural population into industry (see Chapter 9).

Table 12 *Change in the male working agricultural*
population (in round numbers)

Belgium		France		Great Britain	
Dates	*(1,000)*	*Dates*	*(1,000)*	*Dates*	*(1,000)*
1846	680	1815	4,500	1688	±2,000
1856	710	1830	4,800	1811	±1,600
1866	700	1856	5,150	1841	1,460
1890	640	1866	5,300	1861	1,820
1910	580	1896	5,750	1881	1,580
1930	500	1936	4,250	1921	1,390
1961	210	1962	2,650	1961	874

Sources: Population censuses of the respective countries and dates, except for France 1815–30; J. C. Toutain, *La production de l'agriculture française de 1700 à 1958* (Cahiers de l'I.S.E.A., **115**, 1961); and Great Britain: my own calculations based on G. King's estimates of the structure of the working population in 1688, and on the 1811 census (family results) and subsequent structural data.

The under-developed countries could not possibly benefit from the same relief because the required increase in the non-agricultural sector would need to be truly enormous to keep pace with the vast increases in population. On the basis of a population growth of 2.6 per cent per annum and of a non-agricultural sector of, say, 30 per cent of the working population, a stable number of workers in agriculture would assume an average growth of about 8 per cent per annum in the non-agricultural working population during the first ten years of such a change. Such a rate of growth assumes a pace of industrialization which would be quite impossible to achieve.

(c) Comparisons with developed countries at the present time and before the 'take off'

One of the aims of these estimates is to make it possible to compare the level of agricultural productivity in under-developed countries with that of the already developed countries before and during their 'take off'. In Table 13 I have adapted some features of my study on 'Levels of economic development from 1810 to 1910'. The data has been calculated by a somewhat similar method.[4][3] To provide reference points for the present time I have calculated levels for France and the United States for recent years on the same basis. In considering these cases it is clear that the methods of estimation of productivity devised for economies in an early stage of their development contain pitfalls if applied to more advanced economies.

Table 13 *Comparisons between levels of agricultural productivity*

Country and 'stage' of development	Period	Index number of agricultural productivity
DEVELOPED COUNTRIES		
Recent position		
France	1968/72	100.0
United States	1968/72	330.0
Position before or during 'take off'		
France	1810	7.0
Great Britain	1810	14.0
Sweden	1810	6.5
Belgium	1840	10.0
Germany	1840	7.5
Italy	1840	4.0
Russia	1840	7.0
Switzerland	1840	8.0
United States	1840	21.5
Spain	1860	11.0
LESS DEVELOPED COUNTRIES		
Recent position		
Africa	1960/64—1968/72	4.7
Latin America*	1960/64—1968/72	9.8
Asia	1960/64—1968/72	4.8
Middle East	1960/64—1968/72	8.6
TOTAL FOR ALL LESS-DEVELOPED COUNTRIES	1960/64—1968/72	5.5

*Excluding Argentina.
Sources: Author's estimates (see text for method of calculation).

It will be seen the level of productivity in European countries on the eve of the industrial revolution was about 7. This is below that of Latin American countries, about the same as that of the Middle East, but about 45 per cent more than that in Africa and Asia which are, from a demographic point of view, the nucleus of the under-developed world. A gap of about 45 per cent is sufficiently wide for us to be able to assert that agricultural conditions in the currently developed countries before the beginning of the industrial revolution must have been very different from those of the under-developed countries of Asia and Africa today.

A different picture emerges if we attempt a comparison between productivity in under-developed countries and developed countries before their agricultural revolution. By this 'revolution' we mean the rapid growth in agricultural productivity which, in most cases, preceded the industrial revolution by about fifty years and had itself been preceded, ever since the Middle Ages, by a very slow and irregular increase in agricultural productivity. It is estimated that in the forty to sixty years preceding the industrial revolution agricultural productivity had grown by about 40 per cent,[44] which means that the average level of agricultural productivity in the developed countries before their agricultural revolution was about 5 — a level which is still slightly above that of the Third World in Africa and Asia today. Given the essential rôle of agriculture, we can deduce that a similar gap also exists between the living standards of the under-developed countries and those of the developed countries before their industrial revolution.[45] This being so, the auspices for economic development appear to be very bleak even if we were to disregard the other adverse structural factors from which the countries of the Third World might suffer.

Figures of the availability of land have been compared with the index of productivity and here one should note that the figures for Asian countries, which are low in comparison with those for developed countries to-day, are also low if they are compared with figures for the latter at the beginning of, or before, their 'take off'.

It will be remembered that for Asia (excluding China) an average of 1.8 hectares of agricultural land per male agricultural worker has been computed. The corresponding figure for France at the beginning of the nineteenth century was 7.5 hectares, and at the beginning of the eighteenth century was probably nearly 9. For Belgium, a densely-settled country, the figure in 1846 was 2.7 hectares and at the beginning of the nineteenth century was probably more than 3 hectares.[46] For England at the beginning of the seventeenth century the figure was a little more than 5 hectares. As one can see, these divergences are very considerable and the gravity of the situation is certainly not lessened by the climatic conditions in most Third World territories, which tend to lower both soil fertility and human exertion.

Given the stagnation or decline in productivity in under-developed countries, on the one hand, and the constantly increasing productivity of the developed countries, on the other, the gulf between these two groups is now formidable. It can be seen from Table 13 that the productivity of a farmer in the United States is over sixty times that of an average Asian peasant. The comparison with France shows the gap to be less, but at a ratio of 1 to 20, it is still great. Furthermore, this index under-estimates the real state of affairs because it does not take account of the production of fresh vegetables, fruit and milk in the U.S. and France. These products play a much larger part in developed countries than they do in the Third World. Making allowances for this factor raises the index of productivity by about 15 per cent for the United States and by 10 per cent for France.[47] This adjustment makes American productivity nearly eighty times and French productivity over twenty times that of Asia. In this connexion it should be noted that the productivity of agricultural labour has increased very rapidly in the developed countries since 1940/50; indeed it increases noticeably faster than that of manufacturing industry — a total reversal of the secular trend. However, we shall return to this problem at the end of Chapter 6, where the terms of trade are discussed.

But the most significant comparison in our present discussion is that between the levels of productivity in the under-developed countries and the western countries at the period when the latter began to industralize. As we have just seen, the present average level of agricultural productivity in African and Asian countries (between them representing four-fifths of the Third World population) is 45 per cent below that reached by the developed countries at the start of the industrial revolution. In fact it is at the same level as that of the European countries before their agricultural revolution.

Now, most under-developed countries wish, consciously or un-consciously, to by-pass this stage just when other structural conditions of development are making a 'take off' more difficult than it was when most European countries and the United States were imitating England's example. What makes the failure to admit or even to recognize this problem all the more serious is that the problem itself is intractable. Leaving aside mental attitudes, land-ownership and political considerations, it cannot be stressed too forcibly that an increase in the area cultivated per agricultural worker is one of the essential conditions of an increase in productivity. But in view of the population explosion it is impossible to assume, even on most hopeful assumption, that the reduction in cultivated area per worker will be anything but slight.[48]

Of course, a consideration of present international economic conditions does brighten the picture a little. The western countries could not begin to industrialize without a growth in their own agricultural production because they relied on their own resources to feed the increasing number of non-agricultural workers — there being no other countries with a high enough level of development to be able to export large quantities of food continuously and profitably. But today surpluses produced by western agriculture, especially in North America, and the low costs of transportation, make it possible for the under-developed countries to count on imports of food. Although, before the war, the under-developed countries (excluding Argentina) had a surplus of about 11 million tons in their cereal trade, by the end of the war this had turned into a deficit which still continues to rise: from 6 million tons in 1950 to 16 million tons in 1960 and 25 millions around 1965. A few good harvests during recent years slowed down the increase in the deficit; it was around 29 million tons in 1972. But it is still too early to say whether a real reversal of the trend has occurred. The pre-war surplus represented a little more than 7 per cent of the total production of cereals, while the deficit in 1972 is more than 8 per cent. In spite of the fact that a significant share of imports of foodstuffs have been provided in the shape of gifts, or purchased at a reduced price and, in general, food prices have fallen, the cost of food imports has increased very rapidly, Thus, it is estimated that, expressed in value c.i.f., the imports of food by non-communist, undeveloped countries has risen from $4000 million in 1955 to $6000 million in 1962 and to $8000 million in 1970. This trend cannot continue for two reasons:

1. The resources of the developed countries are not unlimited. It is true that in most of these countries because agriculture regularly produces surpluses, laws attempting to restrict output are in force, thus making an increase in supply possible. But on the assumption that the Third World depends on foreign food, could supplies ever be sufficient to fulfil demand? It hardly seems likely. A simple computation based on a rather modest hypothesis (population growth lower than that expected; a lower level of consumption at the end of the period) will demonstrate the size of the problem. If we then suppose that from 1970 until the year 2000 the under-developed countries (including China) wishes to import foodstuffs amounting to one-third of their consumption, we find the answer to be one which would be impossible to achieve. Basing the computation on cereals alone, and assuming a per capita consumption of the

same order as in western Europe in 1900 (that is 500 kilos per head per year), and a demographic growth of 2.3 per cent per year from 1970 to 1990 and 2 per cent for the following ten years, consumption would reach 2,500 million tons, of which 800 million would have to be imported. This latter figure is about three times as much as the total production of the non-communist, developed countries and about thirty times more than the surplus (up to 1970) in these countries.

To satisfy internal and external demand over the thirty years from 1970 to 2000 (and taking into account the augmented internal demand which would result from a probable 35 per cent growth in population during this period) production in the developed countries would have to increase more than threefold, and thus grow at an annual rate of 4 per cent. Even if such a growth were technically possible, from a practical point of view it would seem quite unrealistic. Output in these countries during the last twenty years has only grown by about 2 per cent per annum, so that future growth would have to double.

2. Even if we assumed that growth in the western countries on such a scale *were* technically possible[49] there is another serious economic problem: that of the means of payment which might be available to the Third World to enable it to acquire this quantity of foodstuffs. It is absurd to imagine that exports of manufactured goods to developed countries could ever provide the means. It is not impossible, of course, that such exports might grow in the future, as they have done recently, but the cost of cereals, estimated above, is five times more than the value of the exports of manufactured goods from under-developed to developed countries in 1970, even based on present cereal prices. It is also obvious, assuming such an enormous increase in production, that land of lower productivity would have to be brought under cultivation entailing a rise in the cost of producing the cereals.

Where primary products and tropical agricultural products are concerned the possibilities are perhaps wider, but remain limited even so by the size of demand in the developed world. Recently, moreover, prices of these goods have suffered a sharp fall, clearly indicating that the present supply is already greater than demand can absorb. Indeed demand could hardly grow as fast as the export of agricultural products would have to do if the Third World were to be dependent on external agriculture. It should be pointed out that the cost of the quantity of cereals in our forecast is larger than the value of all exports from the under-developed countries.

It is clear from all this that the most important (although not the only) line of attack is to raise the level of agricultural productivity. How to do so is, alas, far from straightforward, as has been so amply demonstrated. As René Dumont puts it in his direct way, 'the real tragedy lies in the length of time it has taken the world to become aware of the gravity of the situation, and this does not mean merely ordinary people, but responsible administrators and politicians as well. But we must accept the absolute necessity for action if we are to face the austerity and arduous effort which will be required. The prospect of blood, sweat and tears is a disagreeable one.'[50] But he has also shown us that the problem is not technically insoluble. We must believe this, for otherwise past events might convince us that the outlook was hopeless.

C. Recent changes: A green revolution?

Recently there has been much talk of a new factor in the terrible equation of food versus population. This has been called by some people 'the green revolution', and even by some 'the green miracle', brought about by breeding varieties of high-yielding cereals adapted to conditions in the under-developed countries. The story of the green revolution is as follows.[51]

In 1944 the Rockefeller Foundation financed a programme in Mexico to select new varieties of wheat suitable for that country. It was originally intended to find a variety resistant to stem rust (blight). But in 1955 attention was directed also to yields. Norman E. Borlaug, the future Nobel Prizewinner, and his team developed several new varieties by crossing the dwarf Japanese wheat, Norin No. 10, with other wheats.

After being tried out in Mexico, where spectacular improvements in yields were achieved, the new varieties of wheat were successfully introduced in the 'fifties into the Middle East under the auspices of F.A.O. In 1964 India and Pakistan imported some Mexican seed to sow small areas. In 1968 India sowed 3.5 million hectares and harvested a total of 16.6 million tons, which was 50 per cent more than in 1963, while Pakistan, where 1.2 million hectares were sown with high yield varieties, the total wheat harvest at 6.5 million tons was 1.1 million tons more than the national objective. In 1971 the area sown in India rose to 59 million hectares and in Pakistan to 3.0 million. Other Asian and Middle Eastern countries followed suit, especially Turkey, Egypt, Afghanistan, Iran, Iraq, Kenya, Nigeria, Syria and Ethiopia, and several countries even developed their own varieties.

The adventure began somewhat later for rice, the basic cereal of so much of the Third World. In 1962 the Rockefeller Foundation and the Ford Foundation together founded the International Institute for Research on Rice at Los Baños in the Philippines. Research was concentrated on improving the type known as Indica. Within about one year the Institute developed IR-8, a variety resulting from a cross between an Indonesian rice called Peta with a dwarf Taiwanese variety, and this was christened the 'miracle rice' because of its fantastic yield. This variety and others, similar but more recent, were first sown on a large scale in 1966/67. It is estimated that by 1971 about 13 per cent of the area devoted to rice in southern and eastern Asia was sown with the new varieties of seed.

To begin with, therefore, progress merited the epithet 'miraculous', since new varieties of rice and wheat produced a great increase in yields, sometimes more than 100 per cent. The epithet was probably bestowed all the more readily since a combination of circumstances resulted in its total effect in the years 1967—8 being over-estimated. It will be remembered that in 1965 and particularly in 1966 agricultural production in the non-communist, under-developed countries had practically stagnated, mainly due to bad harvests in India, with a consequent decline in output per head. But in 1967, food production leapt ahead by nearly 5 per cent and much of this increase was attributed to the use of new seed varieties. It is certainly possible that the new seed played its part, but not to any great extent. The real impact is difficult to measure since there is usually rapid growth in output after a series of bad harvests when the land has had time to recover some of its fertility. This phenomenon together with more favourable weather would in itself bring a rise in yields, which, combined with stable or, more probably, increased areas under cultivation, would in turn lead to further rises in output. Similar, or even greater, increases had occurred earlier in the Third World countries, particularly in 1953, 1958 and 1962, to mention the period 1950/70. In spite of an extended use of new varieties of seeds, food production for all the non-communist under-developed countries between 1962/66 and 1971/75 improved only by a little less than 2.7 per cent per annum — a growth rate slightly above that of population and even below that of the 1952/56—1962/66 period (2.3 per cent). It is, therefore, obviously too soon to speak of a clear break with earlier trends.

Although it is true, as we have seen above, that new cereals can theoretically increase yields and productivity, experts warn us that the pace of dissemination is limited by the need to employ fertilizers and pesticides more intensively. In some cases also irrigation has to be extended. Furthermore, it is often hard to persuade the people for whom the new varieties are intended (and this applies particularly to rice) to make the necessary change in their traditional eating habits. The real problem, therefore, is not so much the *discovery* of new ways to increase output and productivity as the ability to *adapt* such discoveries rapidly and widely to the conditions of ecology and soil chemistry to be found in the different regions.

After all, in nineteenth-century Europe new methods of agriculture advanced by no more than a few miles a year. Modern communications should certainly help to speed the pace, and have already done so to some extent. But it must never be forgotten that country people to-day are still largely illiterate. For instance, if nearly 70 per cent of the total population of 14 years and over in India is illiterate, the level of illiteracy amongst the rural population would certainly be over 90 per cent. In such conditions the main problem is not the existence of innovation but how to disseminate knowledge of it.

Apart from this there are two other problems of a different kind involved in spreading 'the green revolution'. The first is one of social structure. It seems increasingly as if the introduction of improved seed only serves to accentuate the divergence of income between rich and poor farmers, since the larger landowners and well-to-do farmers can more easily use the new seeds and pay for the increased input needed. The increase in production resulting from the use of improved seeds leads, it is true, to a fall in cereal prices. But in the case of the larger farmers the increase in output generally compensates for the fall in the price per unit, while the poor farmers, not having the opportunity to use the new seed, do not obtain higher yields, so the fall in the price per unit goes with a more or less stable output. The rise in the total revenue of rich farmers, therefore, may be – and generally is – accompanied by a fall in the total income of the poorer ones.[52]

The second problem is perhaps even more serious because of the risks which it reveals. The new seeds are more vulnerable to disease, and as large numbers of local varieties are being replaced by single ones, the consequences of a new disease could be catastrophic.

For all these reasons it is much too soon to deliver a considered judgement on whether the experience has been a 'green miracle' or a 'green mirage'. Such a judgement will probably not be possible before the 1980s at the earliest. In the meantime the Third World, which by 1980 will have to feed nearly one-third more mouths than in 1970, still lives under the threat of severe famine.

3   *Extractive Industry*

This chapter and the next will be devoted to industrial activity, dealing respectively with changes in the extractive and in the manufacturing industries. Any such study must, however, start with a brief outline of the connexion between the two, since the extractive industries depend largely on the level of activity in manufacturing industries. I shall then enquire what changes have taken place in the exploitation of natural resources, and discuss the causes of growth. Finally I shall take a look at the consequences of this growth. I shall be dealing only with the non-communist, developing countries because the structural characteristics which interest us operate only in these countries. The output of extractive industries in non-communist, under-developed countries, as we shall see, is destined almost exclusively for export, which is not so in China or the other communist under-developed countries.

A. The connexion between the extractive and manufacturing industries

In a general, if somewhat simplified way, one could say that extractive industry exists to produce raw materials and energy intended almost entirely for manufacturing industry. If this view is accepted then extractive industry must be seen merely as a sector contributing to manufacturing industry with the latter determining absolutely the level and pace of its activity. But this economic determinism is affected by technological developments and, in particular, by two factors which modify the relationship between the two industries.

    1. Firstly there is the tendency of manufacturing industry to produce goods of a more and more complex nature. This is so obvious that we need not linger over it.

    2. Equally there are improvements in technique which lead to a better use of raw materials. This may be observed in several fields. Thus, taking coal as an example, we can see that technical progress has led to increased productivity from its use. At the end of the eighteenth century about six tons of coal were needed to produce a ton of cast iron, but now the corresponding figure is less than one ton (in some modern blast furnaces it is even less than 800 kgs,[1] although, of course, consumption varies according to the ore used

and its method of preparation). A similar improvement is apparent in the generation of electrical energy; thus, in Belgium, thanks to the increased efficiency of generating stations, net consumption in kilo/calories per kilowatt/hour has declined from 4.375 in 1939 to 4.033 in 1950, 2,995 in 1960 and 2.418 in 1970.[2] Technical progress has also led to larger yields of iron and electricity from lesser quantities of raw material, through the improved resistance of steel and the increased productivity of machines using electrical energy. One could, of course, quote many other examples of this kind.

In economic terms such changes in technology are generally accompanied, particularly in the developed countries, by a slower growth in the extractive industry relative to manufacturing industry. Thus, in western developed countries between 1958/60 and 1968/70 the annual rate of growth in manufacturing industry has been 6.0 per cent, while for extractive industry it has been no more than 2.7 per cent. This marked divergence is the result of a long drawn out evolution, as we can see in Table 14. The pace of growth in extractive industry at the start of the century was actually slightly above that of manufacturing industry, but the gap between the rates of growth in the developed countries gradually widened in favour of manufacturing.[3]

Table 14　*Annual rates of growth of output*

	Manu-facturing industry	Extract-ive industry	Ratio 2:1 %
United States			
1899–1914	5.5	6.0	109
1914–1924	4.3	4.3	100
1924–1929	4.8	3.7	77
1929–1951	3.4	2.4	71
Non-communist developed countries			
1938–1948	4.0	2.2	55
1948–1953	7.2	3.5	49
1953–1959	3.9	1.9	49
1959–1966	6.3	2.6	41
1966–1972	4.5	2.1	47

Sources: U.S. figures derived from *Historical Statistics of the United States* (New York, 1960); developed countries derived from various issues of *Monthly Bulletin of Statistics* (U.N.); recent figures derived from May 1974 issue.

What happened in the developing countries was exactly the opposite. Not only was the rate of growth in extractive industry higher than that in manufacturing industry, but the gap tended to increase. It is this phenomenon, as well as general changes in the extractive industry, which will be discussed in the following pages.

B. Changes in extractive industry: Causes and consequences

I. CHANGES IN OUTPUT

The statistical office of the United Nations calculates an index of production for extractive industries as part of their index of general industrial production. The latter, which does not go further back than 1938, is based on the aggregation of several national indices, and mainly because of this it does not adequately reflect changes which took place before 1960. The picture of the pre-war period is even more inadequate because very few of the developing countries possess indices going so far back. For this reason we have had to calculate our own index in a manner which will be briefly described. But the United Nations index is more accurate than this one for recent years because the statistical coverage has improved. For this reason I have retained my own calculations in the present edition only for the pre-1960 period, and have linked my index of earlier data with that calculated by the statistical office of the United Nations. This also gives readers an opportunity to update the figures.

(a) Method used to construct an index of production of extractive industries in the non-communist, under-developed countries
For the years 1900, 1913, 1926/28, 1936/38, 1948 and 1953 to 1965 total output in the non-communist, developing countries was calculated for the following products: coal and lignite, natural gas, petroleum; iron, copper, zinc, lead, tin, chrome, tungsten, nickel and aluminium (bauxite) ores; gold and silver. Two separate indices have been constructed, one for fuels (coal and lignite, natural gas and petroleum), the other for various minerals (i.e. all other products with the exception of those listed as fuels).

In the fuel index each of the three products has been weighted according to its calorific value. Natural gas and oil have been given an equivalent in coal on the basis of the coefficients adopted by the statistical services of the United Nations to determine the consumption of energy (1 ton of crude oil = 1.30 ton of coal; 1000 cu. m of natural gas = 1.33 ton of coal).

The ore index and the total index (fuel and ore together) are weighted according to the estimated value in 1963 of the output of each product on the basis of prevalent world prices.[4]

(b) Results and comments
Table 15 shows the results of these calculations: it attempts to provide an index of the mining output of the entire non-communist Third World.

Table 15   *Index of output of extractive industries of all non-communist, less-developed countries*
(1963 = 100)

	Fuel	Minerals	All
1900	0.9	9.1	1.8
1913	3.3	17.9	4.8
1926–28	8.3	30.6	10.6
1936–38	12.4	37.8	15.1
1948	25.2	37.6	26.5
1953–55	45.1	56.1	46.2
1958–60	69.8	79.3	70.8
1963–65	108.2	106.3	108.0
1968–70	173.7	132.3	162.7

Sources: Statistical office of the U.N.; and for figures up to 1958–60, author's estimates (see text).
Note: The small extent to which the figures have been rounded up does not imply a corresponding margin of error.

Here I must point out that there is a margin of error which, though not important, is nevertheless greater than the apparent precision of my decimal point might suggest. My intention in not rounding off the figures was to ensure as small a margin of error as possible in any calculations based on my indices that readers may like to make for themselves. The margin of error in the index is fairly small between 1948 and 1970. On the other hand, because the basic data is so much more unreliable, the margin of error in the pre-1948 indices (specially from 1900 to 1928) is larger, and therefore the figures should be taken merely as orders of magnitude. Furthermore for those years an additional distortion is introduced due to the weighting which is based on relative values of 1963. But on the whole the general trend which emerges from the index may be accepted as fairly realistic.

The trend of the global index between 1900 and 1970 reveals two distinct periods. The first, lasting from 1900 to 1948, shows a rate of growth of 6 per cent per annum in the extractive industries as a whole. Such a rate, in its historical context, may be considered very high, especially since it takes in the great depression of the 'thirties. An intensive exploitation of the mineral resources of the Third World thus began many years ago. However, another rapid acceleration occurred during the second period commencing about 1948. Between 1948 and 1970 annual rates of growth rose to an average of 9 per cent. There is no need to point out that such rates are extremely high.

Before proceeding to study the causes and effects of growth in the extractive industry, we must take a brief look at the component sectors. We can see that the most rapid expansion took place in the output of fuels, mainly oil, which by 1963 formed 67 per cent of the total. The annual rate of growth of fuel production was about 7 per cent between 1900 and 1948. But after 1948 this rate increased noticeably, reaching more than 9 per cent per annum between 1953 and 1970.

Where minerals were concerned there was an irregularly changing rate of growth from about 4.6 per cent per annum (for the period 1900 to 1927), to 2.1 per cent (1927 to 1937), to a stagnation (1937 to 1948), to 7.0 per cent (1948 to 1953), and to 8.0 per cent (1953 to 1957). Between 1957 and 1970 the changes were also irregular, alternating between years of regression (1958), relative stagnation (1961, 1962 and 1967), and heavy expansion (1959 and 1960). But on average the annual rate of growth between 1958 and 1970 was of the order of 6 per cent.

The trend of the index of mineral production conceals some very divergent movements in its component parts. Broadly, these movements can be separated into two periods with the years 1953/55 as the dividing line. Between 1900 and 1953/55 there was a vast expansion in the output of iron ore, together with copper, bauxite, tungsten and nickel ores; a more moderate expansion in the output of zinc, lead and chrome ores; and relative stagnation in the output of tin, gold and silver. From 1953/55 to 1970 there was also a vast expansion in the extraction of ores in the developing countries, but it was concentrated on iron and, until 1967, bauxite, with only a moderate expansion of copper and tin, coupled with stagnation, or even a fall, in the production of other ores.

From the geographical point of view, growth in output during the last two decades has been more rapid in the middle eastern countries and Africa, mainly because of the enormous expansion in oil production and (especially in Africa) iron ore. In Latin America growth has been slow, even slower than that of manufacturing industry.

II. CAUSES OF GROWTH IN OUTPUT

It must be emphasized that the enormous increase in the output of the extractive industries in the developing countries was in no way due to the demands of local industry. Indeed local industry absorbed only a fraction of production. For proof of this it is only necessary to compare – either globally or country by country – output with exports of the products of mining and extraction. Thus, for countries like Brazil, Chile, Liberia and Malaysia, exports of iron ore vary from 80 to 100 per cent of production. Further, while in 1970 the under-developed countries produced 39 per cent of world output of iron ore (excluding China and the U.S.S.R.), the same countries produced slightly less than 5 per cent of the world's steel. Thus, some 90 per cent of the iron ore mined in the under-developed countries goes to feed the blast furnaces of the developed countries. I say some 90 per cent despite the fact that the ratios (39 per cent and 5 per cent) produce an export rate of 80 per cent, since our calculations have to allow for the use of scrap iron.

Naturally we also find evidence of the process at the other end of the scale: for example between 1952 and 1970 the French iron and steel industry increased its consumption of foreign iron ore by about 2700 per cent. Starting in 1952 at 359,000 tons (that is 1.3 per cent of France's total consumption) by 1970 the figure had risen to 9,800,000 tons (21 per cent of her total consumption). In that year 2,240,000 tons of iron ore came from as far away as Brazil and a further 640,000 tons from Australia. Imports by all E.E.C. countries of iron ore originating in the under-developed countries rose from 15 million tons in 1960 to 46 million tons in 1970. Most of the other products of mining and extraction underwent a similar experience with the result that the share of under-developed countries in world output has gradually grown. In Table 16 changes in the share in world production of three minerals produced by the less-developed countries have been calculated.

Developments of this kind, moreover, tend to perpetuate themselves. The construction of larger and larger ore-carrying ships leads to a reduction in the cost of transport, while the relocation near the ocean of the iron and steel industry in the developed countries

Table 16   *Changes (1913–70) in the less-developed countries' share in world production of some extractive commodities* (in 1000s of tons)

	1913	1928	1948	1960	1970
IRON ORE (F.E. content)					
World production[1]	158,000[2]	73,000	87,300	172,300	285,000
Less-developed countries' output	4,000[2]	4,900	7,300	49,500	112,000
As % of total	3%	7%	8%	29%	39%
BAUXITE					
World production[1]	550	2,100	8,400	25,100	53,500
Less-developed countries' output	2	450	5,100	17,000	31,800
As % of total	0.4%	21%	61%	68%	59%
CRUDE PETROLEUM					
World production[1]	44,800	171,000	438,000	901,000	1,964,000
Less-developed countries' output	6,900	43,000	156,000	497,000	1,314,000
As % of total	15%	25%	36%	55%	67%

[1] Excluding China and the U.S.S.R.
[2] Weight of ore and not iron content
Sources: Derived from various numbers of *Statistical Yearbook* (League of Nations); *Statistical Yearbook* (U.N.), and *Eisen und Stahlstatistik* and *Petroleum Press Service*.

(which is both a cause and an effect of this change) merely hastens the tendency. The same development can be foreseen for oil tankers. In 1970 the largest tankers in service had a capacity of 325,000 tons (dwt), 16 times greater than the average tanker in 1958 (while needing a smaller crew) and about 150 times greater than the first tanker of 1868 (which, incidentally, was English). Tankers of 500,000 or even 1,000,000 tons are envisaged in the near future. In addition, speeds of navigation and of handling are also much greater. However, as a result, on the one hand, of recent discoveries of rich deposits of ores, oil and natural gas in the West (see below) and on the other of threats to the security of the supply lines created by the increased dependence of the western world on imported fuels, it is probable that the rapid growth of the Third World's share in world production will slow down. And it is not even impossible that the upward trend will be reversed, as has already happened in the case of bauxite mining.

For ores with a high specific value, the exploitation of mines located a long way from the site of conversion has been profitable for a relatively long period because transport costs, high though they may be, represent only a small part of prime costs. But for ores and fuels with a low specific value (like iron) the physical separation of mines and blast furnaces is only possible if the cost of transport is very low. The price of iron ore was, in 1965, about $10 a ton for ore of 50 per cent iron content. By way of comparison the price of Venezuelan oil was about $20 (also the average 1965 price in $ per metric ton); of zinc ore $70; of lead more than $100 (relative to its metal content, of course: in this case 30 per cent), and of tin about $2000 (for a metal content of about 70 per cent. Prices of tin ore fluctuate very widely and follow closely the price of the metal itself. In the course of 1964 the highest monthly average price was as much as 50 per cent above the lowest.)

It is not easy to determine average transport costs. Here too there are heavy fluctuations in prices. Even if annual averages are used, differences of the order of 50 per cent between one year and another are possible, and a difference of more than 250 per cent between maximum and minimum average annual prices has been known to occur within the space of five or six years. Furthermore, prices also vary according to the kind of contract (liner service, time charter, trip charter, etc) and the nature of the product. But to fix some sort of order of magnitude, we may accept that to move such products as ores or oil by sea a distance of 6000—8000 km (4000—5000 miles) in the mid-sixties would have cost about $6 per ton. By rail, assuming a complete trainload, the cost per ton per 100 km (60 miles) would have been $0.8.

Consequently while transport costs were high, long-distance movement of goods such as iron ore was economically impossible. Thus, in 1930, according to Ivar Hogbom's estimate[5] for the under-developed countries, maximum distances (allowing for transport costs) separating mineral workings from export ports were as follows: 'In normal circumstances', he says, 'coal, iron ore and phosphates can only be mined within a radius of 100 km (60 miles) and mineral oils within a radius of 250 kms (150 miles) of the coast. Manganese and chrome ores may be mined further from the coast than iron ore, and zinc and lead ores at an even greater distance. Nevertheless, the only common metals which can be mined economically anywhere in the world, that is a long way from the sea, are copper and tin.' At the present time, of course, taking iron ore as our example, the deposits being exploited in Mauretania lie 675 km (420 miles) from the port of export, i.e. seven times further than was considered normal before the war. The same applies to the deposits at Rourkela in India (720 km or 450 miles), at Cassinga in Angola (630 km or 390 miles), at Vale de Rio Doce in Brazil (560 km or 350 miles), at Knob Lake in Canada (570 km or 355 miles), etc.

The fall in transport costs, therefore, has given a powerful impetus to the growth of extractive industries in the under-developed world. But there are other factors, such as the gradual exhaustion of the richest and most profitable deposits in the developed countries and the design and production of efficient equipment for earthmoving and for public works, which, especially since the last war, has made possible the exploitation of mines and quarries and the building of transport lines in many under-populated regions, using small teams of technicians from the developed countries and local unskilled labour. This has been the case in Mauretania for example. But it remains nonetheless true that without low international transport costs the exploitation of minerals in the under-developed countries could not have been organized on such a scale and, most importantly, the output of such an expansion could not have been exported.

We must now analyse the consequences of these special circumstances of the mining and extractive industries.

III THE CONSEQUENCES OF GROWTH OF MINING AND EXTRACTION IN UNDER-DEVELOPED COUNTRIES
(a) Mining and manufacturing industries
The examination of the causes of growth in the extractive industries of the under-developed countries has revealed that one of the normally expected consequences of such growth (i.e. the creation of nearby industries to convert the minerals and ores into a more elaborate form) has not in fact occurred, since almost all output is exported. Additionally it appears that the great extension of mining, so far from encouraging the development of manufacturing industry, has actually hindered it. This conclusion emerges from an examination of the rate of growth in the two sectors. In fact, where one could expect to find a positive correlation between high rates of growth in extractive and manufacturing industries, brought about by the generally beneficial effects of the development of mining on the economy of Third World countries, one finds quite the opposite occurring.

For the period 1958–70, rates of growth in the manufacturing and extractive industries for nineteen under-developed countries for which relevant statistics are available have been compared. From an examination of these figures it is apparent that, among the countries registering a considerable expansion in the mining sector, most show only slow progress in manufacturing industry, and vice versa. Clearly, then, there is a correlation between high rates of growth in the extractive industry and low rates in manufacturing industry. Although it might be rash to assert that the development of mining and allied activities acts as a brake on the general growth of other sectors, it appears nonetheless from a comparison of the pace of growth that a rapid expansion of the mining sector is certainly not sufficient in itself to engender vigorous development in manufacturing industry.

To support this opinion I shall outline the conditions under which growth in mining might lead to regional development, and show how present circumstances in most under-developed countries prevent this from happening. I shall then briefly discuss the negative factors exhibited by the growth of extractive industries.

(b) Theoretical possibilities arising from expanding extractive industries

The discovery and exploitation of a source of raw materials opens up the immediate possibility of establishing secondary industries to make use of these materials. As we have seen, during the nineteenth century it was unthinkable in economic terms that raw materials should be processed at a site more than a short distance from the deposits themselves. In practice, therefore, mining was usually a prelude to the establishment of secondary industries. But when transport costs began to fall, geographical separation at once became possible, and today — as we have seen above — a large proportion of extractive industries in the Third World feeds secondary industries in the developed countries. A most important opportunity to prime the pump is thus lost.

But this is not normally the only opportunity theoretically provided by the development of mining. Broadly speaking other opportunities might arise in the following ways:

1. Induced effects of activities connected with the construction and equipping of the mine workings themselves.
2. Induced effects of activities connected with the transport infrastructure built to remove the output of the workings.
3. Local investment of profits accruing from mining.
4. Effects of aggregate wage outlay.

Each of these points will be dealt with in turn.

1. The induced effects arising from the construction and equipment of mine workings are, practically speaking, non-existent. Given

the low level of industrial technique in under-developed countries and the sophisticated nature of modern extractive enterprises, almost all the machinery needed must be imported from the developed countries. This also applies to almost all capital equipment, as we shall see in the chapter devoted to macro-economic data.

2. Induced effects of two kinds must be considered in connexion with the infrastructure built to remove production. The first is connected with the actual construction of the transport network. Here one limitation is immediately obvious: any such effects would be of short duration. But even if this aspect were disregarded, we should still be confronted on the one hand by the factors just discussed in the case of mining equipment, which apply equally to transport equipment, and on the other by aggregate wage outlay, the effects of which will be investigated below.

The second kind of induced effect is the more interesting. It arises from the use of the transport network once it is in being. The orientation of the lines of communication towards the export ports does not, in my view, produce positive effects. Quite the contrary, for it favours increased imports of manufactured goods from developed countries much more than it encourages the creation or development of undertakings serving local consumption. By lowering transport costs the infrastructure, intended to make mineral exports profitable, at the same time favours the import of industrial or agricultural goods coming from countries with a higher productivity. And this effect is even more pronounced since the availability of a return freight reduces still further the cost of transport in the direction of imports coming from developed countries.

3. The possibilities of investing the profits from mining and extraction. Without entering into a discussion of all the various cases (which would go beyond the scope of this study) I think it is obvious that in matters of investment both the nature of the firm and the policy of the government involved are of prime importance. In the present discussion we may generally assume that we are talking about countries dominated by foreign companies whose main aim is the realization, and especially the repatriation, of as large a proportion of the profits as possible. Such companies do not promote investment in an under-developed country except when by doing so they would earn profits higher than those produced by investing in a developed country — and high enough, moreover, to compensate adequately for the additional risks of nationalization and political troubles. The latter consideration also partly accounts for the reluctance of these companies to extend their activities into secondary industries, since

the under-developed countries offer no special comparative advantages in this respect. It is solely the wealth of their subsoil which offers such a high return and allows additional profitability on capital sufficient to compensate for the market being so far removed from the mines. There is therefore small likelihood that the proprietors of extractive enterprises would spontaneously diversify their activities outside the sector in which these countries present obvious natural advantages.

The only way to change such a situation would be to subtract somehow part of the profits in order to invest them locally. But it is obvious that whatever form such retention of profits took (e.g. royalties, or legal agreements requiring all or part of the profits to be invested locally) it could not be very substantial, since this would to some extent limit the profitability of the enterprise and thereby discourage investors. And even if profits were retained, the problem of how they were to be judiciously invested would remain. The example of oil royalties which have usually been invested in residential and administrative building, within and, particularly, outside the country, demonstrates that the problem is not simple.

These reservations apart, retention of profits in some form offers real possibilities for countries whose wealth lies in the subsoil. But it is essential that political conditions should be such as to make the imposition of such a policy practicable, and in most countries in which extractive industry (either oil or mineral) predominates this is far from being the case. But the success achieved for major oil producers by the Teheran Agreement of January 1971 is encouraging.

4. Aggregate wage outlay, i.e. the possible effects on development of an increase in demand resulting from wages spent. Here three factors combine to reduce the likely effects.

1. Employment in extractive industries (particularly in oil production) is generally not very substantial because only the most profitable deposits are exploited (Latin America, perhaps is an exception to this rule).
2. Skilled personnel is usually recruited in the developed countries, which has the effect of reducing considerably the demand for local consumption goods.
3. The advantage offered by return freight tends to favour goods imported from the advanced countries. What makes the advantage all the greater is that mines and oilfields are usually located far from the centres of agricultural production.

Finally, therefore, it seems that few of the factors which might, in the developed countries, aid development through the exploitation of natural resources play a similar part in the Third World. Furthermore to the lack of these positive factors must be added the existence of certain negative ones.

(c) Negative aspects of the development of extractive industries

By attracting a high proportion of qualified labour, already limited in such countries, mining severely restricts the opportunities for other sectors to recruit such labour. The same argument applies to capital in so far as local capital is to be found in such enterprises.

Lastly, and this is the most significant of the negative factors, mineral and oil deposits must to a great extent be treated as irreplaceable assets. And from this point of view the premature exploitation of the most profitable workings, whose output is exported, may profoundly handicap the country in question ten or fifteen years later, just at the moment when it might have been able to achieve the conditions necessary to process its own raw materials. At such a juncture, the earlier skimming off of the most important deposits will considerably reduce average profitability, and, consequently, increase the costs of production. Thus, just when the country might need raw materials at low cost to facilitate the launching of secondary industries it may no longer be able to lay its hands on them. In my opinion this factor is not sufficiently taken into consideration by local powers. Seeing that extraction by itself does not create conditions favourable for general development, it is dangerous to encourage too rapid an expansion in this sector without taking account of probable reserves and, above all, the economic value of those reserves. Thus, it may be assumed in general that far from creating favourable conditions, the expansion of extractive industries in under-developed countries, as carried out at present, produces an unfavourable rather than a favourable economic climate. Nevertheless the problem is far from simple, because rapid progress in developing and utilizing synthetic materials may mean that certain raw materials may lose their economic value in the future. Despite (and maybe because of) the recent debate on the energy crisis this may also be true of oil; indeed the fall in the cost of generating nuclear energy and the perfection of electric traction for motor cars, both of which are becoming increasingly feasible, may have substantially reduced the economic utility of oil reserves by 1980—90.

And this does not take account of growing competition in the foreseeable future from the expansion of reserves in the developed countries. In the East, Russia is beginning to have a surplus problem, thanks to a great expansion of oil production which between 1953 and 1970 multiplied more than six times, rising from 8 to 16 per cent of world production. The surplus is even more obvious in the field of natural gas, where output has multiplied more than thirty times between 1953 and 1970. In the West, natural gas from Europe is beginning to turn the whole structure of energy consumption upside down. French deposits at Lack, and others in the North Sea and in Holland are increasing prodigiously the volume of energy reserves available to the Old World, where the under-developed countries' principal customers for oil are at present to be found. Output has already reached an appreciable level. Thus, in the six principal producing countries, Germany, Austria, France, Italy, the Netherlands and Great Britain, production of natural gas has risen, between 1960 and 1972, from less than 12 to 126 thousand million cubic metres. In 1972 locally-produced natural gas contributed some 10 per cent of the total primary energy consumption of western Europe compared to one per cent in 1958. And this is no more than the start of an expansion which will accelerate enormously in the years to come. Furthermore, if recent indications are to be believed, we cannot exclude the possibility that the North Sea will prove to have very rich oil deposits as well.

It now seems probable that Australia will become an important oil producer in the antipodes, and elsewhere Alaska is in the process of becoming a new Texas. In general, undersea deposits are almost certain to augment the volume of reserves in the developed countries.

Thus, to repeat, the problem is certainly not straightforward. The margin between the danger of a premature exploitation, which might compromise the future chances of an easier industrialization, and a delay, which entails the risk of seriously reducing the economic value of the deposits, is both narrow and hard to determine. In addition, in many cases the interests of one country run counter to those of the larger region of which it is but a part.

4   *Manufacturing Industry*

INTRODUCTION

The subject of manufacturing industry is of particular importance because the development of secondary industries is the principal objective of all Third World policies aimed at economic growth. Moreover the degree of industrialization attained by under-developed countries is frequently used to mark the stages in their upwards progress from 'unindustrialized' beginnings.

This chapter is divided into three sections. The first examines rates of industrial growth (total, sectoral and by country) and compares these rates with those of developed countries at different stages in their growth. In the second section I shall try to define the level reached by industry in the main Third World countries and here again there will be an attempt at a comparison with the developed countries at various stages in their growth. The tentative nature of this exercise will become clear later when we see that precise definition of absolute, or even relative, levels of development is extremely difficult. The existence of structural variations and dissimilarities make realistic comparisons a matter of delicate judgement. However, by using six different indicators I hope to have reduced the margin of error to an acceptable scale. Finally, the third section will deal briefly with the problem of the relationship between levels of agricultural and industrial development, from the point of view of actual levels attained as well as that of changing economic conditions.

I originally intended to deal at length with changes in productivity, but the paucity of statistical material has forced me to abandon this project, because the results would be too limited and too tentative to provide valid conclusions. It should only be noted that, according to calculations by the statistical offices of the United Nations, the productivity of labour in manufacturing industry has grown more slowly in under-developed countries than it has in the rest of the world. Thus, between 1955 and 1970 productivity grew at the rate of 3 per cent per annum in the non-communist less-developed countries (3 per cent for Asia and 2.5 per cent for Latin America) compared to 4 per cent in western developed countries and 6 per cent in communist developed countries.

A. Rates of growth in manufacturing industry

In this section the pace of growth in manufacturing industry will be examined. The relevant facts, while not complete (many under-developed countries possess no indices of production in manu-facturing industry), are nonetheless sufficient to establish a valid diagnosis of the speed of growth in Third World countries in recent years. But, with few exceptions where figures go back to 1937/39, indices for individual countries are totally non-existent for earlier years.

To put alongside these indices for countries taken individually we also have, thanks to the U.N. statistical office, an index of production for groups of countries, as well as one for all under-developed countries taken together. It should, however, be noted that mainland China and the other communist countries are excluded from this index, as they are from most of the aggregates calculated by the U.N. The main reason for such an obvious omission is the lack of statistical material.

Because an index covering the whole of the under-developed non-communist world is available, the analysis will be made on two levels. First of all it will be made for all under-developed countries, and there will be at the same time an attempt to fit what we know about the pace of growth into the larger historical context. Then changes taking place in different countries will be examined.

1. ALL NON-COMMUNIST UNDER-DEVELOPED COUNTRIES
(a) The facts

The U.N. statistical office's index number of industrial production for all under-developed, non-communist countries is an arithmetical average of the indices for different countries by sector of activity, weighted according to the value added. However, because for many countries, especially in Africa, index numbers for manufacturing production do not exist, the index is incomplete from a geographical point of view. Nevertheless as it includes a number of countries, such as India, Pakistan and the big Latin American countries, with a large population, it is an acceptably faithful reflection of changes in under-developed countries taken as a whole. Moreover, I have tested the accuracy of the index by comparing it with the changes in energy consumption between 1950 and 1963 in non-communist, Third World countries. The United Nations in its estimates for geographical regions provides more comprehensive figures for energy consumption than for industrial production. As is well known, the connexion between industrial production and energy consumption is close, although energy consumption usually grows more rapidly — giving a difference of about 5 per cent between the curves of the two series.[1] As, therefore, energy consumption in under-developed countries between 1950 and 1963 rose by 7.1 per cent per annum, allowing for the above correction, the annual growth in manufacturing industry was 6.7 per cent. The U.N. index actually shows a rate of 6.9 per cent. This difference can attributed to the U.N. index omitting the African countries, because if we look at changes in energy consumption in all African under-developed countries, the conclusion is that these countries experienced a smaller growth in this field: i.e. not more than 4.6 per cent per annum.

Table 17   *Index and rate of growth of output of manufacturing industry in the less-developed countries* (excluding communist countries)

Index of output		Annual rate of growth %		
Year	1963 = 100	Period	Total	per capita
1938	29	1938—1950	3.5	1.8
1948	40	1950—1960	6.9	4.5
1950	44	1960—1970	6.3	3.6
1953	49			
1958	73			
1960	86	1938—1960	4.9	3.0
1965	118	1938—1970	5.3	3.1
1966	123			
1967	128			
1968	138	1950—1970	6.6	4.1
1969	149			
1970	158			

Sources: Derived from *The Growth of World Industry 1938—1961* (U.N., 1963); and *Monthly Bulletin of Statistics* (U.N.). For recent figures May 1973 issue.

The index of industrial production for all under-developed countries is, however, only calculated for 1938, 1948, and all subsequent years. It is thus not possible to indicate growth in this sector before 1938 by this means. Table 17 shows such indices as are available. We are immediately struck by the very rapid growth which took place after 1953. Thus, between 1953 and 1970, the annual rate of growth was 7.2 per cent (between 1938 and 1950 it was only 3.5 per cent). Even allowing for the large growth of population, the annual rate is still high, since it rose for the period 1950—70 by more than 4 per cent per capita.

Looking at changes over shorter periods, the following phases are apparent:

1938—48. This period must be considered as a whole since figures for intermediate years are not available. Only a modest development of manufacturing industry took place during these years, the annual rate of growth being 3.5 per cent, and the per capita rate being 1.8 per cent.

Between 1948—53 the pace of growth accelerated — 4.4 per cent or about 2.2 per cent per capita. It was, however, irregular, ranging from a maximum of 7.3 to a minimum of 1.5 per cent.[2]

Between 1953—56 the rate of growth was very high, reaching as much as 9.5 per cent (or 7.3 per cent per capita).

Between 1956—70 growth was again high, even though the rate was below that of 1953—56: 6.5 per cent, or about 4 per cent per capita for the whole period. But the pace was again irregular.

(b) Comparison with rates of growth in developed countries

The positive trend of growth rates in manufacturing industry in all the under-developed, non-communist countries is obvious from Table 18 where these are juxtaposed with data from selected developed countries for the modern period as well as for 'take off' periods in the eighteenth and nineteenth centuries. Indeed, it may be accepted that a per capita growth rate of 4.0 per cent in manufacturing is fairly close to that attained by the western countries since the end of the last war and during times between the wars when economic conditions were favourable. By contrast rates in the eighteenth and nineteenth centuries were lower, at about 2 to 3 per cent. This may appear surprising because there is a widespread belief that growth was more rapid during the earlier phases of industrialization.[3]

It should be pointed out, however, that a distinctly higher rate of growth has occurred in eastern European countries. This has been about 10 per cent per capita, but falling in recent years to 8 to 9 per cent. The same is also true in some other countries with uncentralized economies which began to industrialize towards the end of the nineteenth century. This suggests that industrial growth may be more rapid in countries where industrialization began later. The point is sufficiently important to warrant further examination before continuing the main exposition.

Table 18 *Annual rate of growth of manufacturing industry*

	Output manufacturing industry	Population	Output manufacturing industry per capita
Total non-communist, less-developed countries			
1938–1950	3.8%	1.7%	2.1%
1950–1960	6.9%	2.3%	4.5%
1960–1970	6.3%	2.6%	3.6%
Total non-communist, developed countries			
1938–1950	4.5%	0.7%	3.8%
1950–1960	5.0%	1.2%	3.8%
1960–1970	5.6%	1.1%	4.4%
Selected developed countries			
Great Britain			
1700/04–1760/64[1]	0.8%	0.4%	0.4%
1760/64–1800/04[1]	2.4%	0.8%	1.6%
1800/04–1850/54[1]	3.6%	1.4%	2.2%
1850/54–1900/04[1]	2.2%	0.8%	1.4%
1900/04–1910/14[1]	1.8%	0.8%	1.0%
1919–1929[1]	2.9%	0.4%	2.5%
1929–1938[1]	2.7%	0.4%	2.3%
United States			
1860/64–1880/84	6.9%	2.6%	4.2%
1880/84–1900/04	5.8%	2.1%	3.6%
1900/04–1910/14	4.7%	1.9%	2.8%
1919–1929	4.3%	1.5%	2.8%
1929–1938	−0.1%	0.7%	−0.8%
France			
1781/90–1803/12[1]	0.5%	0.6%	−0.1%
1803/12–1835/44[1]	2.7%	0.5%	2.2%
1835/44–1865/74[1]	1.9%	0.3%	1.6%
1865/74–1895/04[1]	1.7%	0.2%	1.5%
1895/04–1905/13[1]	2.0%	0.2%	1.8%
1920/24–1925/34[1]	4.4%	0.6%	3.8%
1925/34–1935/38[1]	0.5%	0.1%	0.4%

[1] Including extractive industry.

Sources: ALL DEVELOPED AND LESS-DEVELOPED COUNTRIES derived from U.N. statistics. GREAT BRITAIN derived from W. Hoffmann's Index (*British Industry 1700–1950*, Oxford, 1955), and K. S. Lomas, 'Production and Productivity movements in the United Kingdom since 1900', in *J. Roy. Stat. Soc.*, 1959 (cited in B. R. Mitchell, *Abstract of British Historical Statistics*, Cambridge, 1962); UNITED STATES calculated from several indices taken from *Historical Statistics of the United States*, New York, 1960; FRANCE derived from T. J. Markovitch, 'L'industrie française de 1789 à 1964'. *Cahiers de l'I.S.E.A.*, 163, July 1965.

(c) Period of industrialization and rate of growth of manufacturing industry

Table 19 gives us at least a partial answer to a whole series of interesting questions. The table gives the annual rates of growth for the periods 1928–57 and 1958–70 which I have been able to calculate from the index numbers of manufacturing industry. The character of these two periods in very different, but the starting and finishing points occur at 'moments' when conditions were rather similar. Growth rates have been calculated for two groups of countries, the first comprising those in which industrialization began early, i.e. approximately before the second half of the nineteenth century, and the second comprising several countries which came late to the process -- 'late' meaning after the second half of the nineteenth century. It should be observed that the under-developed countries have been excluded from this group but not from the table.

The countries have been divided according to the predominating economic system, and the order in which they are listed approximates roughly to the order in which the 'take off' occurred.[4]

The following are the most important points to emerge.

1. The growth rate in the second period (1958–70) is distinctly higher for the more recently industrialized countries than it is for the countries which developed earlier, irrespective of region or prevailing economic system.

2. Rapid growth in the newly industrialized countries is, however, a very recent phenomenon, since for the period 1928–57 (and for earlier periods not included in the table) their growth rates are very close to those of the older industrialized countries, with the notable exception of the U.S.S.R., the only country in the period 1928–45 to have a centralized economy.[5] Growth rates in this period for the older industrialized countries are much lower than those achieved in 1958–70. It should be noticed that, although the terminal years occur at 'moments' when conditions were rather similar, the period 1958–70, unlike the period 1928–57, did not include any major economic crisis nor any international war.

3. By comparing the results of Table 19 with those of Table 18 in which some growth rates achieved in the course of the nineteenth century are shown we can see that growth rates in manufacturing industry in the countries coming late to industrialization are higher for the last twenty years (but for no other period) than those of the older industrialized countries enjoying a similar level of development.

4. The recent development of under-developed countries would thus seem to proceed at the same pace as that of recently

Table 19 *Comparison of annual rates of growth in manufacturing output according to stage of industrialization and economic system*

	1928–1957			1958–1970		
	Output manufact. industry	Population	Output per capita	Output manufact. industry	Population	Output per capita
Early industrialized country:						
a) market economy						
Great Britain	2.4	0.4	2.0	3.6	0.6	3.0
United States	3.9	1.2	2.7	5.3	1.3	3.9
Belgium	1.1*	0.4	0.7	6.1	0.4	5.7
France	1.9*	0.3	1.6	6.0	1.0	5.0
West Germany	2.8*	0.3	2.5	6.6	1.1	5.4
Sweden	3.8*	0.6	3.2	6.3	0.7	6.2
b) centralized economy						
East Germany	–	–	–	6.8	0.0	6.8
Czechoslovakia	3.8*	0.0	3.8	6.8	0.6	6.2
Recently industrialized country:						
a) market economy						
Italy	2.9*	0.6	2.3	8.1	0.7	7.3
Spain	4.4[1]	0.9	3.5	10.4	0.9	9.4
Japan	3.8	1.3	2.5	15.9	1.0	14.8
Greece	4.0	0.9	3.1	7.6	0.7	6.9
Portugal	3.5[4]	0.8	2.7	8.1	0.8	7.2
Ireland	3.5[2]	−0.1	3.6	6.6	0.3	6.3
b) centralized economy						
U.S.S.R.	12.0*	1.1	10.9	9.0*	1.3	7.6
Bulgaria	–	–	–	12.5	0.8	11.6
Hungary	–	–	–	8.1	0.4	7.7
Poland	–	–	–	8.8	1.1	7.6
Roumania	–	–	–	13.1	1.0	12.0
Yugoslavia	–	–	–	9.7	1.1	8.5
c) non-communist less-developed countries	4.7[3]	1.8	2.9	6.8	2.5	4.2

Total industrial output
[1] 1940–1957 [2] 1929–1957 [3] 1938–1957
[4] Based on gross domestic product generated by manufacturing industry and in constant prices for the period 1948–1957.
Sources: Derived from *Statistical Yearbook* (U.N.); *Monthly Bulletin of Statistics* (U.N.); and statistical abstract of several countries.

industrialized countries, as far as growth rate is concerned. However, it seems that instead of an acceleration in the pace of growth, as happened in countries beginning their industrialization at the end of the nineteenth century, we may expect a slowing down. The reason for this is stagnation in the home market due to the slow growth, or even decline, in the purchasing power of the agricultural population, which, accounts at the present time for 70 per cent of the total active population. The relative unimportance of industrial output has prevented the expected factors from operating, because domestic production up to now has been a substitute for imports rather than an increase in local consumption, as is confirmed by various national studies[6] and by the figures for total imports in different regions. In Chapter 5, on foreign trade, we shall see how slowly imports of manufactured goods other than capital equipment have expanded. However, we must, as always, make allowances for regional differences as well as for changes at different periods.

Placing the growth rates of imports of manufactured goods by volume (excluding capital equipment and chemical products) alongside those of production and of estimates for local consumption of these commodities during the period 1955–70, it appears that import substitution grew more rapidly in Latin America than in Asia (considered as a whole). Within the period the growth of imports by volume expanded very rapidly between 1953–57 (8 per cent); stagnated between 1957–63; and finally expanded again between 1963–70 (9 per cent). Although such considerations as the availability of foreign exchange must have played an important part it is probable, nonetheless, that import substitution occurred mainly between the years 1956–57 and 1963–64. According to my estimates for all the under-developed, non-communist countries the relationship between the value of imports f.o.b. of manufactured goods (I.S.I.C. 6 and 8, i.e. goods other than capital equipment and chemicals) and the value added in manufacture changed as follows:

| 1953 | 37.5% | 1961/63 | 22.0% |
| 1955/57 | 38.0% | 1968/70 | 24.0% |

These percentages are clearly not a real index of the substitution of domestic production for imports, but they enable us, nonetheless, to plot the trend with a fair degree of accuracy. When discussing the problem, we must obviously allow, as always, for regional and national differences. Taken by itself this import substitution is clearly a positive factor, but if it is not accompanied by an enlargement of the local market the growth of domestic production will be held back by lagging demand. Given that rural population represents on average 70 per cent of total population, industrial expansion cannot keep up its current pace for long without an increase in rural consumption. If the decline in agricultural productivity (and, consequently, rural incomes) posited in Chapter 2 continues, we must expect a consequent slowing down in industrial growth, especially in those countries with a predominantly rural population.

I shall return to this problem later in the chapter, and also, partly, in the next section where differences in the growth rates of various sectors will be shown to confirm my hypothesis.

(d) Changes in manufacturing industry in all under-developed countries by sectoral activity

Table 20 sets out changes in the index of industrial output of the under-developed, non-communist countries since 1938 as seen in some of the main sectors of activity. It appears that heavy industry, and especially steel-making, has been the main cause of the immense growth in manufacturing industry. Between 1938 and 1970, rates of growth in heavy industry are more than 70 per cent above those of light industry — 7.4 per cent and 4.4 per cent per annum respectively.

Table 20 *Index of output in manufacturing industry of all non-communist less-developed countries* (1963 = 100)

	ALL			1970		
	1938	*1953*	*1958*	*All*	*Latin America*[1]	*E. and S. E. Asia*
Light industry	37	60	82	144	146	141
Heavy industry	18	39	67	179	185	175
Total manufacturing industry of which:	29	50	73	158	163	153
Food	36	63	83	146	144	148
Textiles	44	63	84	140	139	138
Clothing–footwear	53	65	80	133	144	123
Wood products	31	47	70	149	134	166
Paper, printing	11	35	69	157	161	154
Chemicals	21	41	70	174	178	172
Non metallic minerals	18	49	75	171	174	171
Basic metals	24	42	59	159	164	157
Metal products	14	33	61	193	203	182

[1]1969

Sources: The Growth of World Industry 1938–1961 (U.N., 1965), and *Monthly Bulletin of Statistics.* (U.N.) For recent figures May 1973 issue.

The gap is less evident for more recent years, although it still exists. The high rates of growth are due partly to the almost total absence of heavy industry in these countries before the war and generally before their political independence, and partly to the priority accorded to these sectors, with more or less justification, by those responsible for such decisions. The myth of the steel works as a symbol of independence and economic progress was widespread amongst politicians and even economists in these countries. The main cause of the enormous expansion of steel-making is the creation of centres of production in Asia. The conversion of other metals, although fairly rapid, has risen more slowly. There has also been a great expansion of papermaking, although, again, it is true that the original level was extremely low, production in under-developed countries in 1958 being only 4.4 per cent of world total. The creation and extension of oil refineries are responsible for the relatively high rates of growth in the chemical sector.

By contrast, the slow extension of light consumer industries, e.g. food and textiles, must be emphasized, especially in Latin America where this sector is hardly keeping pace with the growth in population. This is not unusual for these industries normally grow more slowly than other sectors, but even so the rates attained in Latin America are exceptionally low, especially when set alongside population growth.

These low rates of growth in sectors where the starting point is relatively higher than in other sectors, go some way to confirm the hypothesis propounded above that stagnation or decline in agricultural productivity in the under-developed countries must lead, in the medium term, to a decrease in industrial growth. And this is especially true because the practical limits in substituting domestic production for imports have, in many cases, almost been reached.

II RATE OF GROWTH IN MANUFACTURING INDUSTRY BY COUNTRY

We shall now examine changes in the manufacturing industries of different countries, including mainland China. Recent figures for the latter country, especially where growth rates are concerned, are not only exiguous but also contradictory. Here, as with all statistical material connected with China, we have two sets of data at our disposal: the first compiled from official figures and the second from estimates by 'western' experts, who are usually Chinese refugees working in the United States. These experts doubt the credibility of the official figures which they consider too optimistic, and attempt to re-evaluate changes on the basis of figures which are thought to be more realistic. We shall examine both series briefly,[7] but before doing so it should be noted that the index is one of total industrial production, i.e. it includes extractive industry and energy production, but excludes construction. As, however, the export rate of extractive products is very low, their inclusion does not distort the results and we may treat the index of Chinese industrial production as very nearly comparable to the indices of manufacturing in other Third World countries.

So far as the official figures are concerned it should be recalled that the Chinese authorities stopped issuing complete data in 1960: such information as they have provided is fragmentary and applies only to certain sectors. But the general impression for 1962 and 1963 is that production continued to grow, although total rates were not provided. For 1964 a total rate of 15 per cent was given, and for 1965 20 per cent. Matters are further complicated by the Cultural Revolution. According to the survey by Field,[8] based on very scanty information, official statements imply that average growth between 1957 and 1968 was about 9 to 10 per cent per annum. From the beginning of 1971 the quantity of statistical information put out by the Chinese government and officials markedly increased. This is probably because of the re-opening of China to the outside world accompanied by her admission to the United Nations, as well as because the end of 1970 marked the end of the third five-year plan, the quantitative aims of which, it will be noted, were never made public. In this connexion the dates of the previous five-year plans should be mentioned. The first plan covered the years 1953—57, the second the years 1958—62 and the third only began — after the economic re-organization resulting from the disturbances of 1961—62 and the break with the U.S.S.R. in 1960 — in 1966 and ended in 1970. The fourth plan will cover the years 1971—75. These plans, of course, never had the centralizing and coercive force of the Russian five-year plans.

Early in 1971, for the first time in ten years, China itself gave out some statistics of quantitative production, first in an interview which Chou en Lai granted to E. Snow,[9] but mainly by means of a study in *New China* which was completed by the traditional New Year editorial article.[10] The overall impression from these statements is one of industrial growth of the order of 18 to 20 per cent per annum between 1969 and 1971. If, from these incomplete figures, we may hazard an estimate of the approximate level of industrial production in 1970, this might be (taking 1963 = 100) about 200, as against 140 in 1959, 61 in 1957, 15 in 1950 and 11 in 1949. It is not, however, impossible that the authorities might claim an even higher level for 1970.

To turn now to the western estimates. Because complete official statistics after 1960 are lacking, most western experts terminate their series at 1959. For the period 1950—59 I have made a survey of the different estimates available,[11] which give for the years 1950 to 1959 an average annual rate of growth for industry of 15 per cent. For the years 1960—71 the material is even more fragmentary. The only western estimate for a long period at present available is, so far as I know, Field's,[12] which puts the level of industrial production in 1968 hardly above the level of 1959 at most and 11 per cent below that level at lowest, i.e. if we settle for the average, about 5 per cent below the level of 1959. It will be remembered that the latter date was the peak of the Great Leap Forward. On the basis of this material, supported by other figures for the years 1968 to 1970,[13] western estimates place industrial growth between 1959 (the peak of the Great Leap Forward) and 1970 at the annual rate of about one per cent, rising to 5 per cent if we take into consideration the years 1957 to 1970 which form a more significant period. It must be emphasized that this figure is no more than an indication and we must await the time when the Chinese authorities see fit to divulge fuller statistics before one can construct a more accurate estimate. When it comes to a choice between the merits of official figures and western estimates, we must accept that such a choice is, of course, no more than a very subjective one for there are as many opinions in this field as there are economists working on the problem. My own view is that the official figures certainly over-estimate growth and that some western estimates under-estimate it. The truth probably lies fairly close to the figures that we retained as an average of western estimates, with the probability that this is a slight under-estimate.

From the data on industrial growth in the under-developed countries presented in Table 21 the following conclusions may be drawn:

1. We find here a good illustration of the example given in courses of statistics about the uncertain nature of index numbers which relate to countries where the level of production is extremely low. An extremely high level of expansion may occur during a short period, as may be seen here to have been the case in Zaïre, Venezuela, South Korea, Pakistan and Taiwan. In some of these countries industrial expansion, having reached very high growth

rates, then falls. It must be remembered that this statistical distortion applies only to countries with a very low initial level, to small countries with an average level or, obviously, to countries which combine both elements, because, in such a situation, the establishment of a few modern units of production leads to a very great increase in the total production of the sector. China and Turkey are

Table 21 *Indices (1963 = 100) and rates of growth of manufacturing industry*

	Indices 1963 = 100				Annual Rate of Variation		
	1938	1950	1957	1970	1938 1950	1950 1957	1957 1970
AFRICA							
Algeria[3]	—	51	86	—	—	7.8	—
Kenya	—	—	77	168	—	—	5.1
Morocco	28	53	72	135	5.6	4.6	4.9
S. Rhodesia	—	—	80	163	—	—	5.6
Senegal	—	—	84[2]	115	—	—	2.6
Zaïre[3]	8	47	105	—	44.0	12.3	—
AMERICA							
Argentina	38	80	87	172	4.2	1.6	5.4
Brazil	15	34	57	164	7.0	7.5	8.5
Chile	31	47	70	121	3.8	5.7	4.3
Guatemala	—	61	78	129	—	3.6	3.9
Mexico	24	44	66	189	5.1	6.1	8.4
Peru	—	36	63	164	—	8.2	7.6
Venezuela	—	23	63	145	—	15.3	6.6
All Latin America	28	51	75	163	5.1	5.5	6.1
ASIA							
China (Taiwan)	—	8	57	342	—	15.9	14.8
China (official)[8]	—	15	61	190	—	22.0	9.1
China (western)	—	32	82	190	—	14.0	6.7
S. Korea	—	34[4]	56	390	—	10.5	16.1
India	36[1]	40	62	135	0.8	6.6	6.2
Pakistan	—	11	44	186	—	22.3	11.7
Philippines	—	44[4]	69	141	—	3.4	5.6
All Asia[9]	30	37	67	153	1.6	8.8	6.6
MIDDLE EAST							
Egypt	—	16[4]	33	123[7]	—	5.4	11.6
Syria	—	--	71[2]	244	—	—	10.8
Turkey	—	29	69	176[5]	—	13.1	8.8

[1] 1939 [2] 1958 [3] 1958 = 100 [4] 1953 [5] 1966 [6] 1967 [7] 1969 [8] General index of industrial output
Communist countries, Japan and Israel excluded
Sources: Derived from *Statistical Yearbook* and *Monthly Bulletin of Statistics* (U.N.); and *Statistical Yearbook* and *Monthly Bulletin of Statistics* of the countries concerned.

not included since in their case the starting level is not a dominant factor. Egypt is in a situation halfway between the two.

2. Where larger groups of countries are concerned, there are the following divergences: from 1938 to 1950 growth rates have clearly been higher in Latin America than in other groups.

But between 1950 and 1970 the situation is reversed, Latin America then experiencing a rate which is clearly lower than the average in other countries. The Latin American rate is strongly influenced by that of Argentina which occupies a leading place in the field of manufacturing. The recent very rapid growth of Brazil has not yet influenced the overall average of Latin America.

3. Where individual countries are concerned the following facts should be pointed out. In Latin America, the most developed country, Argentina, has since the war gone through a growth crisis. Chile is, to some extent, in the same position: her growth rate is lower than that of other countries, although her level of development is higher, as we shall see later. The rate of expansion in other countries (and especially Brazil) has been very rapid, around or above 8 per cent per annum, which, while allowing for a very high population growth, still gives an increase of about 5 per cent.

The most important and interesting question in Asia is the contrast between China and other countries, especially India, since the starting point of these two countries was close. When dealing with China the two sets of figures — the official and the western estimates — must be remembered. However, even if we take the western estimates, it seems that the Chinese growth rate has been definitely higher than that in India. The respective figures for 1950—57 are 14.0 per cent and 6.6 per cent and for 1957—70 5.0 per cent and 6.2 per cent. For the whole period 1950—70 the figures for China are 8.5 per cent and for India 6.0 per cent. In terms of the more significant per capita rates of growth the gap is even wider since India's population increased between 1950 and 1970 at an annual rate of 2.2 per cent while the comparable rate for China was probably below 2.0 per cent. If we take the official data for China, the figures for total growth are respectively 14.0 per cent and 6.0 per cent. In the confrontation between these two Asian giants all will ultimately depend on future events in China. If industrial growth recovers the pace of the years 1950—57 the advantage will incontestably lie with China. On the other hand, if the conditions that prevailed after the Great Leap Forward and during the Cultural Revolution recur the gap between the two countries will shrink. To judge from recent information the first alternative appears the more likely.

Pakistan, South Korea and Taiwan have experienced a growth rate close to, or higher than, that of China, but, as I have already pointed out, development in these countries started from a very low level.[14]

The somewhat laggard pace of the Philippines should be pointed out, at a time when industrial development in this country seems to be at a slightly higher level than in other Asian countries, China excepted. This is one more example of the problem of the relationship between the level of development and the pace of growth, to which attention has already been drawn in connexion with Argentina and Chile. Many of the factors involved (statistical bias due to low levels of production, effects of domestic demand, etc.) do not allow us to conclude positively that, having achieved a certain stage of development, under-developed countries experience as a result of this factor alone a slackening in industrial growth. In my view the essential factors here are the limits of import substitution and a weakening domestic demand arising from insufficient growth in agricultural productivity. This brings us to the problem of the relationship between industrial and agricultural growth, which will be the subject of a later section in this chapter. But before passing to it we must consider the problem of the level of development achieved by manufacturing industry.

B. Level of development in manufacturing industry

In this section I shall attempt to define the level of development achieved by manufacturing industry in the individual under-developed countries. Where agriculture is concerned we have seen that it is possible to measure, by means of productivity, both the changes taking place and the levels of development achieved in this sector, and also to make a comparison with developed countries in the present day and in the eighteenth and nineteenth centuries. This approach is feasible because we can reduce production in this sector to a common physical unit without relying on an expression of its monetary value. Unfortunately we cannot apply the same method to manufacturing industry. We shall therefore attempt to attain our objective by means of certain data on per capita output and consumption. For this purpose the following indicators have been used:

I. Two general indicators based on the relative position of manufacturing industry:
   (a) employment in manufacturing industry;
   (b) gross product generated by manufacturing industry.

Figures for China will not be included in either of the two indices because the data is too unreliable for comparisons to be valid, but I have tried to supply retrospective data for these two indicators in the case of the other countries.

II. Four particular indicators referring to per capita data:
  (a) energy consumption
  (b) steel output
  (c) industrial consumption of cotton
  (d) tonnage moved by railways.

It goes without saying that none of these indicators alone would be sufficient to reflect the level of development achieved in manufacturing, their selection having depended on available statistics.

However, all six indicators taken together permit a reasonably accurate diagnosis. Comparing the Third World with the developed countries at various stages in their industrialization is a very hazardous business, and the conclusions reached below should not be regarded as too precise.

I. GENERAL INDICATORS BASED ON THE RELATIVE POSITION OF MANUFACTURING INDUSTRY
For the first set of indicators, especially the relative level of employment, I have tried to assemble as long a series as possible, so that it is possible to make a diagnosis of economic conditions.

(a) Employment in manufacturing industry
Ever since Colin Clark and Fourastié published their studies, the structure of the working population has rightly been accepted as reflecting a country's level of development. Although classifying the active population into three sections is in some respects unsatisfactory, it does reflect fairly accurately changes resulting from the process of development. *A fortiori*, therefore, it is obvious that, in so far as it is an indicator of the level of manufacturing development, the proportion of the working population so employed can provide useful information about the early phases of development. The indicator based on employment data has the added advantage of providing longer and more extensive series for some countries than one which relates to output only. So far as the under-developed countries as a whole are concerned, changes in the active population engaged in manufacturing industry will be discussed in Chapter 9. But some details about individual countries are set out here.

able 22   *Percentage of the male working population occupied in manufacturing industry*

	1930–1946		about 1950		about 1960		about 1970	
	Date	%	Date	%	Date	%	Date	%
FRICA								
Algeria	—	—	1948	5.2	1954	5.6	1966	6.0
Morocco	—	—	1952	6.2	1960	7.0	—	—
Tunisia	—	—	—	—	1956	6.8	1966	7.7
Zaïre	—	—	1952	5.7	1955	5.7	—	—
MERICA								
Argentina	—	—	1947	20.3	1960	25.4	—	—
Brazil	1940	± 6.5	1950	± 8.5	1960	8.1	1970	±11.0
Chile	1940	±14.8	1952	17.1	1960	16.5	1971	23.4
Costa Rica	—	—	1950	10.1	1963	10.3	1970	15.3
Mexico	1930	±10.3	—	—	1960	14.1	1970	16.4
Peru	1940	±10.1	—	—	1961	12.1	—	—
Venezuela	1941	7.0	1950	9.4	1961	11.2	1971	19.2
SIA								
Ceylon	1946	± 7.3	1953	9.4	1964	9.2	—	—
India	—	—	1951	8.2	1961	10.1	1971	10.0
Pakistan	—	—	1951	6.2	1961	8.4	—	—
India & Pakistan	1931	10.1	1951	7.8	1961	9.8	—	—
Indonesia	—	—	—	—	1961	4.9	1965	4.7
Malaysia	1947	± 5.8	1957	7.0	1962	6.7	—	—
Philippines	1939	± 6.0	1948	± 5.7	1961	7.1	1970	7.6
Thailand	1937	± 2.1	1954	2.9	1960	4.1	1970	3.7
IDDLE EAST								
Egypt	1937	± 8.1	1947	10.3	1960	9.7	1966	13.2
Syria	1935	8.2	1950	± 9.9	1960	9.6	1969	10.3
Turkey	—	—	—	—	1960	11.0	1965	10.5

te: The ± sign represents an estimate based on the global figure for employment in manufacturing industry
us construction and, occasionally, electricity, water, gas and sanitary services; the categories have been deduced
means of an estimate derived from earlier or later data.
urces: Derived from *The Working Population and its Structure*, Vol. I of *International Historical Statistics*,
der the direction of P. Bairoch, by T. Deldycke, H. Gelders and J.-M. Limbor (New York and Brussels, 1968);
arbook of Labour Statistics, 1973 (I.L.O., Geneva, 1973).

Since the criteria defining an 'economically active person' fluctuate more for women than for men between one census and another, the data for individual countries relates solely to the male working population. Table 22 is therefore confined to percentages of the male working population engaged in manufacturing industry. These percentages show how unequal is the level of development achieved by manufacturing industry in the various under-developed countries, and further, how irregular is the rate of expansion in this sector.

We find almost the same differences here as in our survey of the level of agricultural productivity. The relationship which exists between these two aspects of development should lead us to expect this; unproductive agriculture cannot support much expansion of industry. As in the case of agriculture, the countries fall into three groups. The Afro-Asian countries, where employment in manufacturing, at less than 10 per cent of the whole working population, is very low (excluding China this makes an average in 1960 of about 9 per cent); the Latin American countries taken together, in which employment in manufacturing is slightly larger, the average being about 13 per cent; and, between these two groups, but nearer Asia, the Middle Eastern countries with an average of about 10 per cent.

Within these groups there are some marked differences. In Latin America we find once more that the proportion of workers in manufacturing industry in Argentina and Chile is noticeably above the average in the other countries. In the case of Chile we must also take note of the fact that an extremely high proportion, 4 per cent of all workers, is employed in mining. In Asia, although the gap is not large, India has a higher proportion of workers engaged in manufacturing than other countries in that continent as well as in most Middle Eastern countries. Table 23 allows us to compare the present level of manufacturing employment in the under-developed countries with that of the developed countries at various stages in their industrialization. It should be noted that because there are no statistics the precise percentage of the working population employed in manufacturing during the very early phases of industrialization in the developed countries cannot be determined. Nevertheless, it can be assumed from extrapolations and some fragmentary figures, that at the moment of 'take off' the percentage was between 10 and 12 per cent. The low level attained in under-developed countries in similar occupations today is thus all too evident. However, the differences between the two types of economies must not be forgotten: the productivity of the 10 per cent of workers engaged in manufacturing industry in present-day under-developed countries is probably much higher than that of an identical percentage in the traditional western economies before the industrial revolution, since, in the under-developed countries, a large proportion of the 10 per cent is employed in factories with a productivity similar, if not equal, to that of modern developed countries. This point will be raised later in discussing the other indicator when I shall attempt to assign the

Table 23 *Percentage of the male working population employed in manufacturing industry in some developed countries, 1841—1970*

GREAT BRITAIN		FRANCE		UNITED STATES	
Dates	Percentage	Dates	Percentage	Dates	Percentage
1841	35.7	—	—	1850	16.4*
1861	35.9	1856	20.6	1870	18.0
1891	34.2	1896	23.1	1890	20.1
1921	34.0	1921	25.3	1920	29.4
1951	37.2	1954	27.3	1950	26.3
1961	37.8	1962	28.3	1960	29.0
1966	37.0	1968	29.1	1970	29.1

*Total working population
Sources: Derived from *The Working Population and its Structure*, op. cit.; *Yearbook of Labour Statistics 1972* (I.L.O., Geneva, 1972).

relative levels of development reached in the Third World and the industrialized countries.

I am not going to discuss the changes in this index at length because the problem will be taken up again in the chapter on the active population and employment. Here it is only necessary to point out that before 1940—50 the proportion of the male population employed in manufacturing industry was generally declining and that progress since then has been far from uniform in all countries.

(b) The share of Gross Domestic Product generated by manufacturing
This indicator has the advantage over the one based on employment in that it embodies the notion of productivity. Indeed, assuming methods of estimating to be correct, the share of manufacturing in the Gross Domestic Product represents the relative share of this sector in final production, for the latter is roughly the sum of employment and productivity in the sector. Nevertheless, as it is here a matter of relative proportions (difficulties of conversion making comparisons between absolute values very uncertain), productivity in other sectors is also relevant. Thus, a country whose industrial sector is limited and productivity low, but whose agriculture is even less productive, could, because of this relationship, register in its Gross Domestic Product a higher relative share of manufacturing industry than could an industrially advanced country with a highly productive agriculture.[15]

Table 24　*Gross domestic product generated by manufacturing* (percentages in relation to total)

	1947–1949	1959–1961	1968–1970
AFRICA			
Morocco	–	13.5	13.8[1]
Nigeria	=	5.0	7.0[10]
Tanzania	=	3.2[2]	8.5
Tunisia[3]	–	14.0[2]	12.9
AMERICA			
Argentina	22.6[5]	32.3	28.0[10]
Brazil	20.3	23.6[4]	19.0[10]
Chile[6]	23.3	24.4	27.7
Colombia	15.8	17.0	22.2
Equador	16.0	15.4[2]	17.5
Mexico	17.9	26.3[1]	23.3
Peru	15.7	16.4	15.5[1]
Venezuela	8.9[5]	12.9[1]	20.0
ASIA			
Ceylon	4.2[5]	5.2	9.3
India[6]	16.2[7/8]	14.2[2]	13.3
Indonesia	–	12.8	9.5
Pakistan	7.8[9/8]	9.7	12.1
Philippines[6]	11.3	19.7	15.5
Thailand	10.4	11.0	15.5
MIDDLE EAST			
Iran	–	25.3	31.5
Turkey	10.6	12.0	14.4

[1] On the basis of constant price　[2] 1960–61　[3] Excluding basic metals
[4] 1959–60　[5] 1950–52　[6] Net domestic product for 1943 and 1961
[7] Including mining and construction　[8] 1948–49
[9] Including electricity, gas and water　[10] 1967–69
Sources: Derived from data collected in: *Yearbook of National Accounts Statistics*, 1961, 1964 and 1971 (U.N., New York); *Statistics of National Income and Expenditures*, 1954 (U.N.); and *National Accounts of Less Developed Countries* (O.E.C.D., Paris, 1968).

In Table 24, because of revisions in methods of estimating, the figures for 1947–49 are not in every case strictly comparable with the other two series. But if these limitations are accepted – and especially where they refer to a possibly over-hasty comparison with corresponding percentages for developed countries – it appears that the calculations made here confirm in general both the changes and the differences suggested by the indicator of employment (a) Nevertheless, it is worth underlining some of the differences and attempting to explain them.

In the Philippines 20 per cent of the Gross Domestic Product is generated by manufacturing industry, although this sector employs only 7 per cent of the working population. This situation is the result of an unproductive agriculture combined with a 'relatively' developed industry (relatively developed especially in comparison with that of India and Pakistan).[16] The divergence between India and Pakistan cannot be explained in the same way. Although the methods of estimation used for these two countries appear to be similar, it seems as if there must be a significant difference in the methods to account for the widely dissimilar results produced.

A comparison between Tables 22 and 24 confirms that there has been a general increase in productivity, as the share of manufacturing industry's contribution in G.D.P. has grown faster than the percentage of the male working population employed in the industry (see my final remark in the introduction to this chapter).

II. SIMPLE INDICATORS

Table 25 brings together indicators which are rather different, but which express in varying degrees the level of development achieved by manufacturing industry. The first (per capita energy consumption) is to my mind the most significant, although it is strongly biased in favour of certain countries, especially those producing oil, where the unlimited availability of the product encourages relatively high private consumption. This is the case in Venezuela, and to some extent also in Iraq and Iran. The second indicator (gross steel production per capita) is the least significant being of less value than that giving the consumption of cotton by industry and handicrafts. However, the reasonably good correlation between these two last series, and also between all four indicators, will be noticed. The fourth indicator (tonnage moved by rail) is more indirect. Yet, in spite of the distortions introduced by the difference in railway development, it seems to reflect the level of industrialization fairly faithfully, except in some unusual cases. While each of these indicators taken separately is not a sufficient measure of the level of development, yet all four taken together provide a valuable yardstick.

The discussion which follows will be conducted on two levels: we shall first consider the differences in the level of development reached by various under-developed countries and then try to establish an average for the various groups of countries and relate it to the level achieved by developed countries.

Table 25 *Supplementary indicators of the level of industrial development in the less-developed countries, 1970*

COUNTRY	ENERGY per capita consumption in kgs of coal equivalent	STEEL per capita output (kgs)	COTTON per capita consumption by industry and handicraft (kgs)	TRANSPORT per capita tonnage moved by rail (ton/kms)
AFRICA				
Algeria	462	2	0.2	98
Ghana	164	—	0.6	36
Madagascar	67	—	0.5	35
Morocco	194	—	0.5	171
Nigeria	45	—	0.1	29
Senegal	149	—	0.8	45
Tunisia	247	38	0.6	258
Zaïre	73	—	0.6	89
AMERICA				
Argentina	1,688	80	4.3	575
Brazil	472	58	3.1	280[1]
Chile	1,208	62	3.2	259
Colombia	578	11	3.3	55
Cuba	1,039	—	2.3	—
Mexico	1,205	78	3.0	466
Peru	609	14	1.4	43
Venezuela	2,498	89	2.1	1
ASIA				
China (official)	—	23	—	—
China (western)	526	22	2.1	—
Ceylon	156	—	0.2	29
India	191	10	2.0	223
Pakistan	98	1	3.3	66
Indonesia	111	—	0.3	3[2]
Philippines	279	—	0.1	3
Taiwan	925	21	9.3	187
Thailand	245	1	0.1	65
MIDDLE EAST				
Egypt	268	7	0.6	100
Iraq	597	—	0.1	241
Iran	939	—	0.2	96
Syria	483	—	0.3	16
Turkey	487	31	5.1	159

[1]1969   [2]1968

Sources: ENERGY: *Statistical Yearbook* (U.N.).
STEEL AND COTTON: Derived from U.N. data.
TRANSPORT: Derived from *Statistical Yearbook* and *Monthly Statistical Bulletin* (U.N.).

(a) Levels reached by individual countries

Once more the countries fall into the same three groups, with the Afro-Asian countries at the bottom of the ladder, the Latin-American countries at the top, and those of the Middle East in between. We shall not dwell on the divergences within these three groups, since these are clearly shown in Table 25. The most advanced countries in Africa are those in the Maghreb. And once again in Latin America the high level attained by Argentina, and to a lesser degree by Chile, is obvious. Indeed, to apply the adjective 'under-developed' to these two countries is hardly accurate.

The only point over which we shall linger, by reason of its implications, is the level reached by China, since no information about this country has been given for the two previous sets of indicators. If the level of industrial development achieved by China is set against that of other Asian countries, it is clear that about 1970 she easily surpassed the average, even by the lower western estimates. Her industrial level is clearly higher than India's, notwithstanding the fact that the starting levels of 1938–49 were about the same.[17] The divergence seems to justify those who attribute to China a higher rate of industrial growth than to India.

(b) Comparison with developed countries at different stages of industrialization

We shall now endeavour to make a comparison between the level reached by under-developed and developed countries at various stages in their industrialization. With this end in view identical indices for six developed countries were calculated and these countries have been divided into two groups; one (including the United Kingdom, the United States and France) representing the older industrialized countries, and the other (comprising the U.S.S.R., Italy and Japan) representing the newly industrialized countries. The choice of the two groups of countries was dictated by the opportunity thus offered of a more refined interpretation, based as it is bound to be, on a clearer definition of the level of development.

As far as the difference in the pace of growth between the earlier and the more recently industrialized countries is concerned, the figures in Table 26 confirm what has been said before, namely that until the post-war period one can see no obvious gap between the rates of growth as a function of the date of 'take off'. The countries which began their industrialization in the second half of the nineteenth century did not undergo, at least until after the 1939–45

Table 26 *Indicators of the level of industrial development of selected developed countries 1760–1970*

COUNTRY		ENERGY per capita consumption in kgs of coal equivalent	STEEL per capita output (kgs)	COTTON per capita consumption by industry & handicraft (kgs)	TRANSPOR per capita tonnage moved by rail (tons/kms)
Early industrialized countries					
Great Britain	1760	—	± 3*	0.2	—
	1810	± 600	± 20*	2	—
	1860	±2,600	130*	15	—
	1900	±4,200	220*	19	550[5]
	1929	4,110	210	15	660
	1950	4,420	330	9	710
	1960	4,920	470	5	580
	1970	5,360	500	3	480
United States	1760	—	±2*	—	—
	1810	± 250	8*	2	—
	1860	± 500	25*	6	1,090[2]
	1900	±3,900	190	12	2,720
	1929	6,570	470	14	5,400
	1950	7,510	580	13	5,670
	1960	8,010	500		4,650
	1970	11,140	580	8	5,440
France	1760	—	± 2*	0.1	—
	1810	± 200	± 4*	0.3	—
	1860	± 500	25*	3	85
	1900	±1,300	65*	5	430
	1929	2,420[3]	240	9	1,220
	1950	2,030	210	6	930
	1960	2,400	380	7	1,250
	1970	3,790	470	5	2,980
Recently industrialized countries					
U.S.S.R.	1860	—	5*	0.5	—
	1900	± 250	25*	2	—
	1929	± 400	35	3[4]	75
	1950	±1,300	150	5	3,300
	1960	2,850	300	6	7,020
	1970	4,450	480	7	10,270
Italy	1860	—	2*	0.2	—
	1900	± 200	1*	4	80
	1929	610	53	6	290
	1950	630	51	4	210
	1960	1,190	170	5	320
	1970	2,680	320	4	340

'able 26 *(continued)*

OUNTRY		ENERGY per capita consumption in kgs of coal equivalent	STEEL per capita output (kgs)	COTTON per capita consumption by industry & handicraft (kgs)	TRANSPORT per capita tonnage moved by rail (tons/kms)
Japan	1860	–	–	1[1]	–
	1900	± 150	1*	4	30
	1929	740	18	9	200
	1950	780	58	3	400
	1960	1,160	240	8	570
	1970	3,210	900	7	610

ig iron   [1]1850   [2]1882   [3]Including the Saar   [4]1913

According to G. Sundbarg's estimate (*Aperçus statistiques internationaux*, Stockholm, 1908), based on freight affic receipts.

urces: Pre-1929 data derived from material collected for my book, *Révolution industrielle et sous-veloppement* and my article, 'Niveaux de développement économique de 1810 à 1910'; data for 1929–70 rived from *Statistical Yearbook* and *Monthly Bulletin of Statistics* (U.N.) and statistical yearbooks and lletins of the respective countries.

war, a more rapid development than those which 'took off' earlier.

These levels of development will be compared to the average level of development in the main continental groups of Third World countries: Africa, Asia, Latin America and the Middle East. Such comparisons can only be tentative, but I think the attempt is of genuine interest.

Judging from the four indicators compiled here and, in part, from the two preceding ones, we can conclude that the African countries are at a lower level of industrialization than the western countries were when they were still in their 'traditional economy' stage. Present levels in Asian countries (excluding China) correspond to those in the developed nations in the first few decades of industrialization, i.e. about 1770–90 in England, 1800–10 in France and the United States, and before 1900 in the more recently industrialized countries. China's progress since 1952 places her at present approximately 15 to 25 years ahead of the average of the other Asian countries if we take western estimates, and 30 to 40 years ahead if we take the official figures. In Latin America Argentina and Chile have achieved an industrial development which corresponds to that of France in approximately 1900–10 or England 1850–60, while the other countries are another 20 to 30 years behind. The Middle East occupies an intermediate position, as it does where agriculture is concerned; somewhat closer to Asia than to

Latin America, i.e. about the level of France in 1840—50 or England, in 1800—10.

But, I repeat, these comparisons are only very approximate and consequently must not be taken too literally, although the margin of error is unlikely to exceed twenty years either way. Expressed in a time scale reflecting the rate of growth of the nineteenth century, the older industrialized countries of the West are more than two centuries ahead of Africa, about a hundred and fifty years ahead of Asia (an approximate average), fifty years ahead of Latin America and about a century ahead of the Middle East. But these comparisons do not take account of structural changes.

C. Agriculture and manufacturing industry

I do not intend to discuss the part agriculture played in the western countries while they were going through the industrial revolution, since it is not germane to the present study.[18] Suffice it to say that it was all-important in providing the initial impetus. Here I shall try to determine the present relationship between agriculture and industry in less-developed countries and compare this with the equivalent situation in the older industrialized countries. The relationship will be discussed briefly under two heads:

  I The level of development in both sectors.
  II The connexion between changing conditions in both sectors.

I   LEVELS OF DEVELOPMENT IN AGRICULTURE AND MANUFACTURING

The influence of agriculture was not limited to just the initial 'take off' period of industrialization, it also manifested itself in subsequent phases of industrial development. This is illustrated by the close correlation, during the nineteenth century, between agricultural productivity and industrial development in twelve of the advanced countries for which I have calculated figures.[19] If the coefficient of correlation between the two sets of figures is computed, the positive correlation is more than 0.9, and even more if agricultural development in one period is compared with that of industry in the following period.

It is probable that calculations for other developed countries in the modern period would produce a similar relationship. The situation in the under-developed countries is analagous. When we consider the larger geographical regions, the agricultural·productivity ratings (see Chapter 2) are reproduced in the level of industrial

Table 27   *Comparative ranking of the levels of industrial and agricultural development*

	1860		1880		1910	
	Agriculture	Industry	Agriculture	Industry	Agriculture	Industry
Germany	6—7	6—7	3	5	2	4—5
Austria	9	6—7	8	7—8	8	8
Belgium	4—5	2—3	5	2—3	4	3
Spain	4—5	9	9—10	9	10	9
United States	1	2—3	1	2—3	1	1
France	3	5	4	6	5—6	6—7
Italy	11	10—11	11	10	11	10
Japan	12	12	12	12	12	12
Great Britain	2	1	2	1	3	2
Russia	10	9—10	9—10	11	9	11
Sweden	6—7	7	7	7—8	7	6—7
Switzerland	8	4	6	4	5—6	4—5

Sources: P. Bairoch, 'Niveaux de développement économique de 1810 à 1910', *op. cit.*

development, the ratings for which are given in this chapter. Thus Latin America is at the top, followed by the Middle East, with the Afro-Asian countries coming last.

At the national level, the same correlation between agricultural productivity and industrial development, although not perfect, is once again evident. Thus, the two countries in Latin America with the highest level of agricultural productivity are Argentina and Chile. And amongst the seven Latin American countries for which calculations have been made the one in which agricultural productivity is lowest is also the one in which industrialization has advanced least, i.e. Peru. In the three Middle East countries for which calculations of agricultural productivity have been completed, both agricultural productivity and industrialization are highest in Turkey. In the Afro-Asian countries the relationship is not so obvious, since the differences between countries, both in agriculture and manufacturing, are not so great. However, we can see a correlation in at least a few instances. In Asia, amongst the big four — China, India, Pakistan and Indonesia — it is China, with the highest agricultural productivity which also has the most developed industry. In Africa, Tunisia proves rather an exception to the rule, with a low level of agricultural productivity and a relatively high degree of industrialization. But in Morocco, and most of the other countries, the relationship between these two sectors accords more nearly with what has been observed before.

II CHANGING CONDITIONS IN AGRICULTURE AND INDUSTRY

In a closed economy dominated by agriculture it is natural that industry should be strongly influenced by changes in agricultural conditions, for a decline in agricultural production reduces the outlets for industrial production through a general fall in purchasing power.[20] A situation of this kind occurred in most European countries in periods when their industrialization had not proceeded very far. Thus in France, right up to 1870, every bad harvest was followed by an industrial crisis. The various statistical series by which the parallel movement of the curves of agricultural and industrial output can be demonstrated will not be given here, but figures taken from Professor Marczewski's interesting and suggestive study of the quantitative aspects of French economic history (Table 28) show the close relationship between the two sectors.

Given the part played by industrial imports in under-developed countries and assuming also that the growth of local production has hitherto been based largely on import substitution — imports being much more sensitive to economic fluctuations than is production when it forms so small a part of consumption — it is difficult to find a significant correlation between agricultural and industrial produc-

Table 28   *Comparison between the growth of purchasing power generated by agriculture and the industrial output in France* (annual averages in millions of current francs)

Period	Growth in absolute value in purchasing power generated by agriculture	Growth in absolute value of industrial output
1781/90—1803/12	797	1,090
1803/12—1815/24	464	208
1815/24—1825/34	577	1,072
1825/34—1835/44	159	1,444
1835/44—1845/54	793	948
1845/54—1855/64	2,076	1,824
1855/64—1865/74	1,024	1,031
1865/74—1875/84	−566	451
1875/84—1885/94	−609	227
1885/94—1895/1904	324	1,274
1895/04—1905/13	2,730	3,809

Sources: Jean Marczewski, 'Le produit de l'économie française de 1789 à 1913 (comparaison avec la Grande Bretagne)' in *Cahiers de l'I.S.E.A.* AF 4, no. 163, Paris (1965), p. lxvi.

tion. Moreover as the available series are so few and cover so short a period it is improbable that we should be able to fine one. For these reasons I have endeavoured to establish the influence of agriculture on industrial conditions by comparing the change in the gross product generated by agriculture with that generated by manufactures.

This comparison clearly shows a strong relationship between the two sectors in under-developed countries: the curve of agricultural output powerfully influences that of manufacturing industry. The U.N. statistical services calculate index numbers of gross agricultural product and gross industrial product (manufactures) for the continents of Latin America and non-communist Asia (excluding Japan). The movement of these curves is evidence of agricultural influence and the correlation coefficient between the two series reveals very high ratios: 0.99 for Latin America and 0.97 for Asia. It should be noted, nevertheless, that the real correlation is over-estimated due to the progression of the two curves.

But the examination of the correlation for individual countries is far more illuminating. The curves of the two series have been examined for forty under-developed countries between 1950 and 1970. The correlation is clear for nearly all the countries with a relatively important manufacturing sector. Each decline in, or slowing down of, agricultural production is followed by a similar movement of manufacturing output, and similarly each acceleration in agricultural production leads to an acceleration in industrial growth. In most cases a delay of approximately one year separates the two curves, which, since harvests occur mostly in mid-year, is what might be expected. I have attempted to verify the relationship by comparing the curve of imports of manufactures with that of agricultural output (F.A.O. figures) for Asia, Latin America and the Middle East. The trend of these two curves indicates the influence of agriculture on imports of manufactures in the case of the two first groups of countries. But the figures for the Middle East are less clear cut because receipts from oil exports distort the relationship.

Thus, as we might have expected, given the proportionate size of rural population, it is quite clear that agriculture strongly affects the development of manufacturing industry and economic conditions generally in the Third World countries, as it did in the western economies at the time of their 'take off'. I shall leave further discussion of this most important aspect of economic development to the concluding chapter.

5   *Foreign Trade*

INTRODUCTION

I shall devote two chapters to the foreign trade of the Third World, the first dealing with general quantitative aspects and the second focussing on the problem of terms of trade, where, I shall attempt to show the real changes which have taken place in these over the whole period 1870–1970.

For the purposes of the present study it is unnecessary to analyse the pattern of foreign trade for each individual country, as complete and reliable statistics are available for the Third World taken as a whole. However, the reader will find in the appendix a synoptic table of figures relating to 1970 imports and exports (and the annual rate of variation of exports between 1960 and 1970) for most of the under-developed countries.

Literature on the problems of foreign trade abounds,[1] so I shall make my commentary brief. Of the four sections in this chapter the first three deal with the non-communist, under-developed countries and the fourth with China, under the following headings:

A. General changes in foreign trade
B. The pattern of foreign trade by commodities
C. The geographical pattern of foreign trade
D. A note on the foreign trade of China

A. General changes in foreign trade

Thanks to the statistical office of the United Nations we have at our disposal tables which assemble data about the foreign trade of the entire under-developed world from 1938 onwards, excluding only the communist countries. The omission of the latter is of no significance for the present study since their foreign trade is very limited. Thus, while the communist under-developed countries have a population nearly half the size of the under-developed non-communist countries, their share in terms of exports is no more than about 4 per cent. Their omission can also be justified on methodological grounds, for foreign trade in the so-called 'market' economies plays a totally different rôle to that which it plays in most communist economies – and especially in China. (For a brief summary of Chinese overseas trade the reader should turn to the end of this chapter.)

92

I have supplemented the United Nations series for the period 1900—28 from the figures of the individual countries. It should noted that the United Nations statistical office counts Turkey as a developed country in all their trade data (total trade, geographical structure, price, etc.) while in reckoning other aggregates, that country is usually considered part of the Third World. But these figures have not been adjusted for two reasons. The first and the most important is that the overseas trade of Turkey represents no more than one per cent of the total for the whole non-communist, under-developed world (and less than 0.3 per cent of that of the non-communist world). The second reason is that these very minor corrections might confuse any one wishing to update my figures by reference to published data. The reader should also bear in mind that in this chapter, unless otherwise indicated, amounts are expressed in current U.S. dollars.

Table 29 *Foreign trade of less-developed countries*[1] *1900—1970*

	IMPORTS c.i.f. in millions US dollars	EXPORTS f.o.b.		BALANCE OF TRADE	
		in millions US dollars	as percent of world exports	in millions US dollars	as percent of imports
1900	1,600	1,600	16.0	—	—
1913	3,500	3,800	19.0	+ 300	+ 9
1928	6,500	7,600	23.0	+1,100	+17
1938	5,800	5,900	25.0	+ 100	+ 2
1948	18,600	17,100	29.7	−1,500	− 8
1950	17,500	18,900	31.0	+1,400	+ 8
1953	21,500	21,100	25.5	− 400	− 2
1958	27,800	24,800	22.9	−3,000	−11
1960	30,200	27,300	21.3	−2,900	−10
1963	32,900	31,500	20.4	−1,400	− 4
1965	38,000	36,400	19.5	−1,400	− 4
1968	46,000	44,100	18.4	−2,200	− 5
1970	57,600	55,600	17.8	−2,000	− 4

[1] Excluding communist countries
Sources: 1900—28, author's estimates; 1938—70 derived from *Yearbook of International Trade Statistics* (U.N.), various issues; recent figures from *Monthly Bulletin of Statistics* (U.N.), May 1973.

Long-term changes in the foreign trade of the under-developed world, i.e. since 1900, can be divided into three fairly distinct periods. The first — which to all intents and purposes began in the mid-nineteenth century and ended in 1950 — saw a gradual growth in the importance of the foreign trade of these countries in the world economy. In 1900 their overseas trade formed about 16 per cent of world trade: by 1913 the figure had reached 19 per cent: by 1948 30 per cent. The period was also characterized by favourable trade balances since exports easily outpaced imports (in spite of the fact that, as is the general custom, exports are expressed in f.o.b. prices, while imports are expressed in c.i.f. prices).[2] But, in fact, the term 'trade balance' is hardly applicable to the countries we are considering since most of them were still part of a colonial system.

The second period ran from 1950 to 1962 and saw an overall reversal of the trend established between 1900 and 1950. There are three points to be made about the general development of the foreign trade of the Third World during this period.

1. Although in absolute volume the overseas trade of the under-developed countries had definitely increased, the rate of growth was nevertheless lower than that of Gross Domestic Product. Thus, taking 1950 = 100, exports were 148 in 1962, while the index number of the G.D.P. was 174.

2. The foreign trade of the developed countries grew much faster than that of the Third World, thereby bringing about a continuous and significant reduction in the latter's share of world trade. Thus, Third World exports which in 1948 had formed 30 per cent of the world total, had fallen to only 20 per cent by 1962. The setting up of the Common Market and, to a certain extent, the European Free Trade Association, by favouring trade between their members, helps to explain this development. However, the foreign trade of industrialized countries who were not members also grew faster than that of the under-developed countries.

The deterioration in the terms of trade of the under-developed countries (to which I shall return in the next chapter) obviously played a part in reducing the momentum of their international trade. Indeed, if expressed in current prices with the level of 1950 as 100, the index of their exports in 1962 was 148, whereas expressed in constant prices it was 156 (the index number of the unit value of exports having fallen from 100 in 1950 to 95 in 1962). As we shall see in the next chapter, this worsening of the terms of trade occurred mainly between 1955 and 1962.

It must be emphasized that without an increase in the volume of oil sales (and in spite of the intervening fall in prices) the Third World's trade would have suffered even more. I shall return to this point later when discussing the structure of foreign trade. The marked falling off is mainly evident after 1954.

The whole question of the under-developed countries' position in world trade, especially in that of the western world, has sufficiently important implications to merit separate discussion (see below, section C,II).

3. The period is marked in general by a relatively large deficit in the trade balance of the under-developed countries. This deficit reached and even, during some years, exceeded 3 billion dollars (i.e. 10 to 11 per cent of imports), thereby reinforcing the necessity for financial aid. I shall return later to the problem of the trade deficits.

The third period began about 1962 and lasted until after 1970. Its essential characteristic was a much faster expansion in both the value and the volume of exports. While from 1950 to 1962 exports in current values increased at an average annual rate of 3.4 per cent, from 1962 to 1970 the rate more than doubled, reaching 8.4 per cent. This acceleration is linked with a halt in the fall in unit prices of exports (measured by volume, the respective rates of expansion are 4 per cent and 7 per cent) and with the generally expansive movement in international trade which was characteristic of the 'sixties. Indeed during those ten years and especially after 1959, the expansion of international trade was quite unique: never before had there been a continuous upward movement of such amplitude. From 1958 to 1970 the value of world exports leapt from 108 billion dollars to more than 312 billion dollars, which represents an annual rate of growth of some 9 per cent. The expansion of exports measured by volume was slightly less — about 8.5 per cent[3] — but even so it was remarkably high, representing as it did a doubling of volume every nine years.

Another cause of the rapid growth in the Third World's exports was the great increase in their sales of manufactured goods, especially after 1963. Between 1962 and 1970 sales practically tripled, and I shall have to return to this important aspect of foreign trade below (section B).

However, even after 1962 world international trade grew faster than the foreign trade of the under-developed countries; so their share of exports in the world total still fell, although more slowly than formerly, from 20 per cent in 1962 to 19 per cent in 1966 and 18 per cent in 1970. The figure for 1970 is close to that for the beginning of the century. The peak of 31 per cent had been reached in 1950, this percentage being exceptionally high because the prevailing prices of tropical commodities were also high, so that we should perhaps consider the maximum 'normal' share of the less developed countries in the world total of international trade to be about 25—28 per cent — what it in fact was around 1950.

A slower growth of imports in relation to exports, especially after 1963, led to the gradual reduction of trade deficits which appeared after 1948. If we ignore the distortion introduced by the difference between c.i.f. values of imports and f.o.b. values of exports this trade deficit has practically disappeared in recent years. When the figures are corrected to take account of this difference[4] there is even a slight surplus in trade balances from 1963 to 1970. However, since the foreign trade of the under-developed countries is carried by merchant shipping of the developed countries,[5] the difference between c.i.f. value of imports and f.o.b. value of exports, which is essentially the cost of transport, is not recovered by the under-developed countries. This is why, when considering resources created by exports, we should only take account of f.o.b. values. This particular equilibrium is only valid for the under-developed countries taken as a whole, for there are obviously substantial variations between individual countries (see synoptic table, Appendix p. 244) and groups of countries. It must also be emphasized that equilibrium was only achieved through the increasing volume of oil exports which, by 1970, formed more than 33 per cent of exports as against only 20 per cent in 1953. Thus, for example, the trade deficit for the years 1969 and 1970 for all the under-developed countries together was about 2 billion dollars, i.e. 3.6 per cent of imports, but if we were to exclude the main oil-producing countries, the deficit would rise to about 10 billion dollars, i.e. 20 per cent of imports. This is even more striking when we consider that the countries exporting oil have less than 3 per cent of the total population of the Third World. The deficit of 10 billion dollars is a record, the more normal figure between 1957 and 1966 fluctuated around 6 billion, but in relation to imports the deficit (20 per cent of imports) is not so exceptional, for it was 21 per cent on average between 1957 and 1966, rising to a peak of 24 per cent in 1961.

Before discussing the structure of foreign trade, the changes in the trade balances of the main geographical areas since 1913 will be briefly examined.

Latin America had a positive trade balance for the whole of the period up to 1967, except for a few untypical years. Since the end of the war the surplus has been due in large measure to Venezuelan exports of oil. Yet, in spite of the Venezuelan contribution, there has been a growing deficit since 1968.

Similarly oil exports are responsible for the very great surplus in the trade balance of the Middle East which began to manifest itself in the 'fifties and which, by 1970, formed nearly 60 per cent of imports. In that year the surplus was about 4.2 billion dollars, although without the oil trade, of course, there would have been a deficit of about 7 billion dollars.[6]

The rest of Asia suffered a rude reversal of its trade balance, which until the war had been a strongly favourable one (24 per cent in 1913 and 26 per cent in 1928); after the war the balance swung almost equally far in a negative direction. The trade deficit, which was less than one billion dollars up to 1953, reached 1.8 billion dollars in 1958 (22 per cent of imports), 2.2 billion dollars in 1960, 3.5 billion dollars in 1965 and close to 4.5 billion dollars in 1970 (i.e. 23 per cent of imports).

Lastly, Africa's deficit fell steadily, though intermittently. In 1913 it formed a quarter of its imports; but since 1964 the trade balance has been either in equilibrium or very slightly in surplus.

Table 30   *Change in foreign trade and trade balance of non-communist, less-developed countries according to geographical regions* (in millions of dollars)

	1913	1928	1938	1948	1953	1960	1970
LATIN AMERICA							
Imports	1,450	2,450	1,540	6,180	6,530	8,350	18,920
Exports	1,600	3,100	1,710	6,520	7,620	8,560	17,180
Balance	+ 150	+ 650	+ 170	+ 340	+1,090	+ 210	−1,740
as %age of imports	+ 10.3	+ 26.5	+ 11.0	+ 5.5	+ 16.7	+ 2.5	− 9.2
ASIA							
Imports	1,250	2,500	2,370	6,010	7,010	9,830	18,770
Exports	1,550	3,140	2,650	5,200	6,050	7,630	14,430
Balance	+ 300	+ 640	+ 280	− 810	− 960	−2,200	−4,340
as %age of imports	+ 29.0	+ 25.6	+ 11.8	− 13.5	− 13.7	− 22.4	− 23.1
MIDDLE EAST							
Imports	410	630	720	2,230	2,500	4,520	10,150
Exports	330	630	550	2,060	2,810	5,130	14,300
Balance	− 80	−	− 170	− 170	+ 310	+ 610	+4,150
as %age of imports	− 19.5	−	− 23.6	− 7.6	+ 12.4	+ 13.5	+ 40.9
AFRICA							
Imports	330	690	670	2,750	3,750	5,320	8,840
Exports	250	590	660	2,260	3,290	4,440	9,030
Balance	− 80	− 100	− 10	− 490	− 460	− 880	+ 190
as %age of imports	− 24.2	− 14.5	− 1.5	− 17.8	− 12.3	− 16.5	+ 2.1

Sources: 1913−28, author's estimates; 1938−70 derived from *Yearbook of International Trade Statistics* (U.N.), various years, and *Monthly Bulletin of Statistics* (U.N.).

B. The pattern of foreign trade by commodities

Only since 1955 have we had a homogeneous series of statistics enabling us to study the structure of foreign trade in the Third World as a whole. This account of changes in the composition and direction of trade commodities is based on the information given in these statistics (prepared by the U.N. statistical office).

In the first place the percentage distribution of the various products confirms the lowly position of industry in the under-developed countries. In 1970, in spite of tremendous growth in recent years, manufactured goods formed only 23 per cent of exports while forming 69 per cent of imports. By way of comparison, in the same year manufactured goods formed 76 per cent of the exports from developed countries. Though we may not find this difference surprising yet we should remember that the industrialized countries of the present-day had, at the outset of their 'take off', a very different pattern of foreign trade to that now prevailing in the Third World, with manufactured goods forming a much greater proportion of their exports.

Thus manufactured goods formed about 43 per cent of French exports in 1715; 45 per cent in 1787; 56 per cent in 1798—1800 and 70 per cent in 1827—30.[7] In other countries the pattern was similar. However, these statistics must not be taken to mean that the difference between the levels of development attained by the developed countries then and the Third World now, was correspondingly great. In the past exports formed a very small part of Gross Domestic Product (in the traditional western economies before industrialization it was probably around 3—5 per cent) whereas in the under-developed countries of today exports can in some countries be as much as, or even more than, 30 per cent of G.D.P. (1970). For all under-developed, non-communist countries the average percentage of exports in G.N.P. for 1970 was 15 per cent; in the early 'fifties it was about 20 per cent; while at the beginning of the century it had already reached the level of 15—17 per cent. Thus on average and overall the relative share of exports in the G.N.P. is three to five times greater in the under-developed countries in this century than it was for traditional economies before their industrialization. These statistics help to explain, at least partially, the startling difference in the distribution of export commodities outlined in the previous paragraph.

To return now to a more detailed examination of the structure of the foreign trade of the under-developed countries and the modifications it has undergone. As has already been emphasized, manufactured goods form an important share of imports, but only a minor share of exports. Nevertheless changes in this field between 1955 and 1970 have been favourable. Although the percentage of manufactured goods in the total imports has increased from 59 to 69, this was due mainly to imports of capital goods; the absolute growth in the value of other manufactured goods imported has not kept pace with the growth of total imports. We have already seen in an earlier chapter that import substitution resulting from the relatively fast development of manufacturing industries can account for this decline.

In the field of exports, rapid growth in two groups of products must be singled out: fuels and manufactures. Where fuels are concerned, growth began well before 1955, but the changes in production of manufactured goods have been much more recent. Until 1962 sales of manufactured goods increased at nearly the same rate as total exports; but between 1962 and 1970 a most spectacular expansion occurred — the value of these goods rising from 4.3 billion dollars to 12.7 billion dollars, i.e. an annual average increase of 14.5 per cent.

The incidence of benefits arising from these changes needs close inspection. The expansion in exports of manufactures has actually

Table 31 *Foreign trade by commodity classes of non-communist, less-developed countries*

	IMPORTS			EXPORTS		
	1955	1960	1970	1955	1960	1970
TOTAL (in billions of US$)	23.1	29.1	57.7	23.7	27.4	54.3
Distribution of products as percentage of total						
Food products	15.4	16.2	12.9	32.5	29.6	24.3
Primary products	8.1	7.4	6.2	29.4	27.9	18.2
Fuels	11.8	10.0	8.0	25.2	27.9	33.3
Chemicals	7.0	7.5	8.9	1.0	1.1	1.5
Machinery & Transport	23.3	27.6	33.4	0.5	0.7	2.4
Other manufactures	29.0	27.8	26.4	11.4	12.4	19.5
−3 Raw materials	35.3	33.6	27.1	87.1	85.4	75.8
−6 Processed goods	59.3	62.9	68.8	12.9	14.2	23.4

Note: The above totals are not strictly comparable with total imports and exports quoted elsewhere since no account has been taken of ships' stores, bunkering fuel and other special types of merchandise, figures for which are not available. In addition the figures for imports are based on world exports destined for these countries which, consequently, implies that the values are f.o.b.

Sources: Derived from the Statistical Office of the U.N. (revised series in roneo form) and *Monthly Bulletin of Statistics* (U.N.), July 1972.

taken place in a few countries with small populations: thus the share of these goods exported from Hong Kong, Nationalist China (Taiwan), Israel and the Republic of Korea combined, has risen from 29 per cent of the total Third World exports of these goods in 1959 to 42 per cent in 1968. In 1968 these countries provided only 8 per cent of the total exports of the under-developed world and formed only 3 per cent of its population.[8]

Hong Kong's case, which is often taken as an example of the possibilities theoretically open to under-developed countries in the export of manufactures, can serve to illustrate the limits to such development. Simple arithmetic will show us that if the under-developed countries (always excluding the communist countries) had exported in 1970 as many manufactured goods per capita as Hong Kong did, these exports would have risen to $1040 billion, i.e. nineteen times more than the total Third World exports and over three times more than total world exports.

Exports of 'fuels' — almost entirely oil — grew from 6 billion dollars in 1955 to 18 billion dollars in 1970 (in spite of the fall in prices already mentioned above) which pushes up the relative percentage of this sector from 25 per cent of exports to 33 per cent.

These two groups of products together form more than half the total exports of the Third World (55 per cent). The remaining exports are composed of a huge assortment of primary and agricultural products. Around 1970 the two principal commodities were coffee and copper, each with about 5 per cent of total exports, followed by sugar, cotton, oilseeds, cereals and rubber, each with about 3 per cent, while tea, cocoa and meat formed no more than one per cent each.

To sum up, though it may seem as if, overall, the structure of foreign trade in the Third World reflects the condition of under-development, yet changes occurring since 1955 have been favourable, with imports of capital goods increasing while those of other goods decline relatively, and exports of manufactured goods expanding rapidly. These changes confirm the diagnosis I made when discussing manufacturing industry, when I pointed out the favourable movements in this sector, noting at the same time that this positive development might be short-lived because industrial production has been out-stripping domestic consumption — the latter being relatively sluggish because agricultural productivity is stagnating if not actually declining. Industrial expansion has so far been sustained by the substitution of home-produced goods for imported ones.

Before going on to examine the geographical structure of foreign trade a few words must be said about the concentration of commodity-export in under-developed countries and about fluctuations in export prices. Extreme cases of concentration of commodity-export in many Third World countries have been the subject of much discussion, and I shall limit myself here to estimating its importance for the under-developed world as a whole. To this end I have calculated a weighted average (by dollar value of exports) of the share of a principal product relative to total exports. In 1963, for the entire Third World, 55.6 per cent of all exports consisted of goods which were at the top of the list in individual countries; in the developed countries the proportion was only 18.5 per cent. It is obvious that this difference is crucial and that diversification of foreign trade should be one of the objectives of economic policy in the under-developed countries, although naturally it must depend to a great extent on industrialization. Diversification will also help to resolve the problems caused by excessive fluctuations of export prices in under-developed countries, since such fluctuations arise mainly from the predominance of a small number of agricultural and mining products.

C. The geographical pattern of foreign trade

I GENERAL CHANGES
In Table 32 I have calculated the geographical distribution of the foreign trade of the non-communist, under-developed world on the basis of U.N. statistics. The figures upon which these percentages have been based are not strictly comparable to those which will be found in preceding tables. The differences are due to the fact that while the data is assembled from the figures of exports classified by destination (imports therefore being expressed in f.o.b. prices), it has remained impossible to treat *all* figures according to this classification, as the destination of some exports is not specified. Additionally, some figures are revised less frequently than the totals, which also affects the results. It is impossible to eliminate these differences, but they are not important enough to introduce significant bias into this table. Scrutiny of this table immediately reveals one important point: the very minor role played by trade between the under-developed countries themselves. Indeed such exchanges formed less than 20 per cent of the total foreign trade of the Third World in 1970. The percentage has tended, moreover, to fall. In the neighbourhood of 25 per cent before the war, it rose to 30 per cent immediately afterwards due to the relative decline in the

foreign trade of the European countries; but by 1953 it had fallen back again to 25 per cent and by 1965 it was about 21 per cent. Thus the overseas trade of the non-communist Third World is conducted mainly with the developed countries, and more especially with the western developed countries. Their exchanges with the communist countries, although they have strongly increased recently, still remain very limited.

Table 32 *Changes in the regional origins and destinations of the foreign trade of the non-communist less-developed countries, 1938–1970*

	Origin of imports into less-developed countries (percentage)				Destination of exports from less-developed countries (percentage)			
	1938	*1948*	*1960*	*1970*	*1938*	*1948*	*1960*	*1970*
DEVELOPED COUNTRIES (non-communist)	**68.0**	**67.4**	**74.8**	**72.7**	**71.9**	**66.6**	**72.3**	**73.5**
North America	17.2	32.1	25.8	23.9	17.1	23.9	23.6	21.7
Common Market	20.7	12.8	23.0	20.0	23.6	16.9	22.8	25.4
E.F.T.A.	17.4	17.7	15.6	11.2	20.3	19.8	16.2	12.3
Japan	10.7	0.9	7.0	13.4	8.1	1.0	5.1	10.6
Oceania	1.2	2.8	1.2	1.8	1.9	2.6	1.9	1.3
LESS-DEVELOPED COUNTRIES (non-communist)	**25.2**	**30.0**	**20.9**	**18.4**	**21.7**	**29.1**	**22.3**	**19.5**
COMMUNIST COUNTRIES	**6.6**	**2.6**	**4.2**	**8.9**	**3.1**	**2.7**	**4.5**	**5.7**
Europe & U.S.S.R.	4.2	1.2	2.8	6.9	1.4	1.8	3.5	4.9
Asia	2.4	1.4	1.4	2.0	1.7	0.9	1.0	0.7
TOTAL	**100.0**	**100.0**	**100.0**	**100.0**	**100.0**	**100.0**	**100.0**	**100.0**
in millions $ (f.o.b.)	5,070	16,800	29,140	57,790	5,900	17,300	27,340	54,29●

Sources: Derived from *Yearbook of International Trade Statistics*, (U.N., 1963) and *Monthly Bulletin of Statistics*, (U.N., June, 1972). See text for differences in comparability between this table and preceding ones.

If the share of all the developed countries in the overseas trade of the Third World has not, in global terms, altered very profoundly (rising from a total of 70 per cent in 1938 to 73 per cent in 1970), there are nonetheless some individual changes to be observed. North America, which in 1938 had a smaller volume of overseas trade than either the Common Market or E.F.T.A. countries as a group, overtook them after the end of the war, especially where imports coming from the Third World were concerned. The real reasons for this changeover were firstly the enormous increase in sales or gifts of American agricultural produce, and secondly (and this is also true for foreign trade as a whole) the isolation of Europe during military hostilities so that world trade turned towards the United States, where the immense growth in output in the war period favoured trade with the less-developed countries who remained outside the grip of the Axis powers. But gradually continental Europe is regaining and even superceding its former importance in Third World trade.

Contrary to what might have been expected from its geographical location in the western hemisphere, Latin America's share in U.S. trade with the Third World is not really predominant. Thus, in 1970 U.S. trade with Latin American countries formed only 51 per cent of American exports destined for under-developed countries and 53 per cent of imports thence. It was only in the few years immediately after the war that these currents of trade assumed great importance; in 1948 they formed some 65 per cent of the trade between the U.S. and the under-developed countries.

In western Europe the experiences of the Common Market and E.F.T.A. countries were divergent. In 1938 trade between these two groups and the Third World had been at a very similar level but the E.F.T.A. countries gradually lost ground in spite of the smaller impact of the war on their economies. By 1970 their share of trade was no more than 12 per cent compared to about 19 per cent in 1938. The Common Market countries, whose trade had been so much reduced by the war, experienced a marked revival and the relative level reached by 1970 was about the same as that of 1938. Decolonization does not appear to have entailed a significant re-orientation of trade, especially if the Common Market and E.F.T.A. countries are taken as a whole. On the other hand, in the case of individual countries, changes usually meant a reduction in the part played by the principal trading partner.

Japan, which by the end of the war had lost its place in the markets of the under-developed countries, gradually recovered her position. Thus although in 1948 she had only one per cent of Third World trade as compared to 9.5 per cent ten years previously, by 1965 her share was nearly 10 per cent again and in 1970 it had risen to 12 per cent.

Eastern Europe's volume of trade with the Third World was much reduced by the war and by the subsequent communist takeovers. Not until after Stalin's death, and the changes in economic and foreign policy which followed, did these countries begin to assume a more important, though still limited rôle, as trading partners. In 1954 the volume of their trade with the Third World increased by 70 per cent compared to the level of 1953. The increase has continued, though the rate has hardly been maintained, and these countries had regained their pre-war share by 1960. In 1970 the European communist countries took over 5 per cent of all trade with the under-developed countries: little enough compared to the western countries, but, even so, three times more than the pre-1953 figure. A similar change in the trade between the Asian communist countries and the under-developed world is evident, although the volume remains very low — about 1.5 per cent of total trade in 1970.

In conclusion the following two points deserve re-emphasis:

1. The very small amount of trade between the under-developed regions themselves. Obviously the principal reason for this is that their economies are not complementary. But as this is also due to the patterns of trade established by colonial and neo-colonial domination[9] a partial re-orientation is certainly possible as well as desirable.

2. The pre-dominance of the western and European countries in the trade of the under-developed countries.[10]

II THE PLACE OF THE UNDER-DEVELOPED COUNTRIES IN THE FOREIGN TRADE OF THE WESTERN DEVELOPED COUNTRIES

We have just seen that the western developed countries are taking a growing and largely dominant place in the foreign trade of the under-developed countries, since at present some 73 per cent of the latter's trade is with them. Consequently, it would be interesting to see if the place of the under-developed countries in the foreign trade of the developed countries is equally important and if it has moved in the same direction.

The answer is in the negative. The relative dimensions of the two elements are quite disproportionate and the trend of change is divergent. Indeed in 1970 the under-developed countries took no more than 19 per cent of the total exports of the developed countries, and this percentage has for some years shown a distinct tendency to fall, especially since 1958, at which time it was still nearly 28 per cent. In 1938 the under-developed countries provided 23 per cent of the developed countries' foreign markets; in 1948 the percentage was 31 and remained approximately the same until 1958. But the decline began in that year and continued until 1970, when, as we have seen, it was no more than 19 per cent. The share of imports from Third World countries in total imports of developed countries is very similar.

Thus we are confronted with a pattern which, in global terms, places the under-developed countries in an unfavourable situation, for although the western market is of prime, even vital, importance to them, the place of the under-developed countries in the trade of the western world can by contrast be considered if not exactly marginal, then certainly far from being of major importance. And if the share of the developed countries' exports to the Third World in 1970 is expressed as a percentage of their Gross Domestic Product the figure is no more than 2.0 per cent (see Table 34) — hardly a substantial figure. In 1958, the figure — at 2.5 per cent — was slightly higher, but it has certainly never reached 3 per cent. On the other hand, if we express the exports of the under-developed countries destined for the developed countries as a percentage of their G.D.P., the figure for 1970 is about 11 per cent (Africa and the Middle East, 22 per cent; Latin America, 8 per cent; and Asia, 5 per cent). The size of this divergence helps explain many of the 'domination' effects of the developed countries on the Third World.

The share of the under-developed countries in the foreign trade of the developed countries obviously varies from sector to sector and from country to country. Given that manufactured goods form the larger part of it, the volume of these goods exported to the Third

Table 33 *The share of the less-developed countries in the exports of the developed countries as a percentage of total exports of the various products*

		1955	1960	1970
1.	Food products	21.3	25.0	18.3
2.	Primary products	7.7	8.4	9.1
3.	Fuel	15.6	15.8	8.0
4.	Chemicals	36.8	30.8	22.7
5.	Machinery and transport	35.5	31.8	21.3
6.	Other manufactures	29.5	24.6	16.1
	TOTAL	27.7	25.5	18.1
1—3.	Raw materials	14.9	16.6	13.3
4—6.	Processed goods	32.6	28.3	19.2

Sources: Derived from information about the 'special feature' of the *Monthly Bulletin of Statistics* (U.N.), various numbers; recent figures in the number for July, 1972.

World by developed countries is proportionately more important but still not dominant. Thus, exports of manufactured goods to under-developed countries in 1955 formed 33 per cent of total exports of these goods.

But it can be seen that between 1955 and 1970 the Third World considered as a market for the developed countries declined rapidly in importance both for manufactured and for capital goods. For while in 1955, for example, it absorbed more than 35 per cent of total exports of capital equipment from the developed countries, the rate has since dwindled steadily, being no more than 32 per cent in 1960 and only 22 per cent in 1970. A similar change occurred where fuel, chemicals and other manufactured goods were concerned. The trend is obviously at least partly the result of the phenomenon discussed earlier: i.e. import substitution has caused an expansion of manufacturing in under-developed countries. But the main reason has surely been the immense increase in the trade of the developed countries among themselves resulting from their rapid economic growth and the treaties of economic integration such as the Common Market and E.F.T.A. Thus, for example, from 4 billion dollars (4.9 per cent of world trade) in 1953, inter-community trade between Common Market countries rose to 6.9 billion dollars in 1958 (6.4 per cent of world trade) and 43.3 billion dollars (13.9 per cent of world Trade) by 1970.

To turn now to the Third World's share in the developed countries' imports. The only sector which is a really dominating one, and increasingly so, is that of fuel (in 1970 fuels originating in the Third World formed 64 per cent of total imports of these products). Where other products are concerned the imports of the developed countries have declined. In 1970 only 32 per cent of total imports of foodstuffs and less than 29 per cent of imports of primary products came from under-developed countries. The rapidly growing exports of manufactured goods has led, since 1963, to a slight increase in the Third World share in total imports of these products by developed countries — a rise from 6 per cent in 1963 to close on 6.5 per cent in 1970. But, as we have seen, this growth profited only a very small part of the Third World.

In Table 34 I have worked out, for the principal countries and groups of countries, the 1970 percentages of exports destined for the Third World, compared to total exports and to G.D.P. The estimate for the eastern European countries contains a margin of error which, however, is not more than that which would result from rounding up the figure.

Table 34 *Exports from developed countries intended for the*
non-communist Third World in 1970 compared to total
exports and to G.N.P. at market prices

	Exports Destined for Less-Developed Countries		
	In millions of $	*As percentage of total exports*	*As percentage of GNP*
United States	12,600	30	1.3
Canada	1,200	7	1.6
Common Market	11,500	13	2.4
Germany	4,200	12	2.3
Belgium & Luxembourg	900	8	3.6
France	3,700	20	2.5
Italy	1,900	14	2.0
Holland	1,100	9	3.5
Free Trade Area (E.F.T.A.)	6,500	15	2.8
Great Britain	4,000	20	3.3
Sweden	600	9	2.0
Switzerland	800	16	4.0
Japan	7,700	40	3.9
Australia, N. Zealand	1,100	19	2.6
All western countries	41,900	19	2.0
East European countries (including U.S.S.R.)	4,000	13	0.7

Sources: Author's estimates (see text).

Although, compared to total foreign trade, the share claimed by
the under-developed countries varies considerably it will be noticed
that, when expressed as percentages of G.D.P. the differences are
much less evident. The share of exports directed towards the Third
World lies between a minimum of 1.3 per cent and a maximum of 4
per cent of the Gross Product of the industrialized countries, which
is, even at maximum, a very small proportion. In 1970 exports
destined for the non-communist Third World from all industrialized
countries taken together formed, as we have seen, 19 per cent of
their total exports and 2.0 per cent of their Gross Domestic Product.

If we look at the larger groupings of countries or the great
economic powers, we shall find that the Third World, relatively
speaking, is the most important outlet for Japan (40 per cent of
exports and 3.9 per cent of Gross National Product). Japan is
followed by E.F.T.A. (15 per cent of exports and 2.8 per cent of
G.N.P.) and then by the Common Market (13 per cent of exports

and 2.4 per cent of G.N.P.). Although the under-developed countries absorb 30 per cent of total United States exports (a quarter of which are foodstuffs) these exports do not form more than 1.3 per cent of American G.N.P., owing to the low export rate of the American economy.

*   *   *   *   *

This chapter lacks an analysis of the relationship between foreign trade and economic development. I started a study of this problem after the first edition of this book was published, but the present state of my researches does not allow me to provide more than a few general and provisional conclusions.[11]

From an analysis of the period 1950—70 it is apparent that, contrary to what occurred in the industrialized countries, there was almost no relationship between the rate of growth of exports and that of G.N.P. This holds good both for individual countries (with a few small and isolated exceptions) and for the Third World taken as a whole, even though in 1950 the latter's exports formed about 19 per cent of G.N.P. Moreover, in the years 1962—66, which were the best ever experienced by the Third World until 1968 as regards the value of exports, the G.N.P. grew more slowly than it had done since 1950. This resulted, of course, mostly from the fall in agricultural production, itself largely attributable to unfavourable weather conditions in India. But the limited connexion between exports and the rest of the economy was above all due to the fact that most goods exported by the under-developed countries were produced in what one might call economic 'enclaves' (either plantations or mines) which had only a tenuous relationship with the rest of the economy and whose effects on the economy as a whole were consequently very limited.

Furthermore these export sectors employed only a small part of the working population. Rather crude estimates of my own reveal that for non-communist, under-developed countries 5—7 per cent of the working population produce goods of which some 90 per cent are exported while the other 93—95 per cent produce goods of which only 1 per cent is exported. Such a total lack of symmetry is never found in industrialized countries. The most extreme case is that of oil production which, in 1970, formed 33 per cent of total exports from the under-developed countries and yet provided no more than 0.02 per cent of total employment. This, of course, is the main explanatory factor in the conclusions of MacBean's study, which are at first sight so paradoxical. Taking as a working hypothesis the commonly-held view that annual fluctuations in export receipts have a negative economic influence, he has sought to measure the effects of these fluctuations on some individual countries, and has concluded that there is no direct link between fluctuations in export receipts and those of the economy as a whole.

If I have stressed the limited degree to which foreign trade can influence the economic life of most Third World countries, it is because there is a large body of opinion which tends to exaggerate the possibilities. But we must beware of falling into the opposite error. Foreign trade fulfils many important functions. At the most obvious level, export receipts are needed to pay for a whole range of commodities which could never be produced locally in the early phases of development, but which are nonetheless absolutely essential for this development. About 70 per cent of total external receipts of the Third World come from exports. Furthermore, because many Third World countries are so extremely small, foreign trade is their sole avenue to development. Seen from this angle regional integration becomes, for a large part of the Third World, an absolute imperative.

D. Note on the foreign trade of China

The first thing to be said about China's foreign trade is that the enormous size of the country combined with the comparatively recent and far from complete penetration hy western traders has meant that trade, even before the advant of the present regime, had always been limited. Thus, in 1900 Chinese exports were 0.3 dollars per capita as against 1.2 dollars in India, and 3.7 dollars in the rest of the under-developed countries. This ratio was not altered by subsequent events since as the Chinese share in the total foreign trade of the Third World remained stable, which it did until the outbreak of the second world war. Chinese exports were worth in current values about 120 million dollars in 1900, 290 million in 1913, 720 million in 1928 and 420 million in 1938.[12]

Before the Japanese occupation of Manchuria began in 1931, the principal exports were leguminous plants, especially soya beans (about 20 per cent of total exports), followed by raw silk (slightly less than 20 per cent). Manufactured silk goods formed less than 5 per cent, as did also tea, while the balance consisted of other agricultural products and some minerals, particularly coal.[13] Japan had increasingly become China's main trading partner, closely followed by Hong Kong and the United States.

Passing over the troubled years of 1945—49, in which exports stagnated at no more than a few hundred million dollars, we come to the period 1950—70. These decades can be divided by the break with the Soviet Union into two periods of equal duration.

The characteristic of the first period was a renewal and rapid development of China's foreign trade, in which exports rose from 620 to 2,205 million dollars[14] between 1950 and 1959, or from 0.8 to 1.9 per cent of world exports. This, of course, was still a minute proportion, although it was not far short of the 1928 figure of 2.2 per cent. During this first period a little more than two-thirds of the trade (exports as well as imports) was conducted with other communist countries, especially the Soviet Union. Concerning the pattern of exports, there was an increase in the sales of manufactured goods which in 1959 formed 33 per cent of total exports.

The second period (1960—70) was marked, until 1962, by a slump in foreign trade. During 1962 exports amounted to no more than 1,525 million dollars (1.1 per cent of the world total). This recession was due to a fall in the trade with most of the communist countries. From 1963 onwards a slow revival got under way, thanks largely to a rapid increase in trade with western countries (which doubled between 1962 and 1965), while trade with the communist countries continued to decline. By 1970 the 1959 level had once again been attained and even slightly exceeded: Chinese exports in that year can be estimated at 2,100 to 2,300 million dollars, i.e. 0.7 per cent of world total. Or, in other words, slightly less than $3 ($2.7) per capita compared to $31 for the whole of the non-communist, under-developed world (but only $3.7 for India), $311 for the western countries and $89 for the East European countries.

By 1970 the geographical pattern of trade was very different to what it had been before 1960, for only a third of the trade was conducted with communist countries. The principal trading partner was Japan (about a fifth of total trade), followed in order of importance by Hong Kong, West Germany, Great Britain, Australia and Canada.

The principal exports in 1970 were foodstuffs, (about 30 per cent of the total) and, close behind, textiles and clothing (slightly less than 25 per cent). Amongst imports first place was occupied by metals (about 25 per cent), followed by cereals (about 15 per cent, but the level fluctuated wildly from one year to another), machinery (about 15 per cent), chemical fertilizers (10 per cent) and rubber (8—10 per cent).

6 *The Terms of Trade*

It will be recalled that the 'terms of trade' expresses the relationship existing between the prices of exports and imports, either of one country or group of countries, or of one product or group of products.[1] Hence an improvements in the terms of trade of a country, i.e. a relative rise in its export prices compared to its import prices, increases its money receipts and vice versa. Though from the point of view of Third World countries a worsening of the terms of trade usually has an adverse effect, it should be noted that such a change could reflect a favourable economic situation, since lower export prices could be due to a rapid growth in productivity. In such a situation the lower export prices need not necessarily reduce the total remuneration accruing to local factors of production.

The problem of the terms of trade of less-developed countries has attracted the attention of economists in general and even more of the officials responsible for policies in the under-developed countries. As developing countries mainly export primary products and import manufactured goods, their terms of trade have usually been treated as if they were identical with the terms of trade of primary products against manufactured goods. Even if it is obvious that these two concepts (i.e. the terms of trade of primary products and the terms of trade of developing countries) are not altogether identical, their interchangeability can be accepted as a valid working hypothesis.

The lack of relevant statistics has meant that terms of trade of developing countries before 1938 have usually been measured and discussed on the basis of the terms of trade of primary products. But from 1938 onwards the U.N. have brought out data from which a relatively valid series of terms of trade of the Third World can be constructed. The different nature of these two sets of data and the rather unusual changes which have taken place since the end of World War II make it advisable to study the two periods separately. Thus I shall discuss first the terms of trade for the period 1870 to 1938 (concentrating on the years 1876/80 to 1926/29, because the depression years of 1930/39 were exceptional) and then proceed in the following section to the period 1926/29 to 1970 and will thus link the early years with the post-war period.

In the first part I shall examine the widespread and generally

111

accepted assumption that during the earlier period the terms of trade of primary products as compared to manufactures deteriorated. In the second part I shall try to single out what were the probable causes of the deterioration of the terms of trade which undoubtedly occurred after 1954.

A.   The terms of trade 1870—1938

As I have just said, the lack of statistics on the terms of trade of the developing countries necessitates an indirect approach to the subject through a comparison of prices of primary products with those of manufactures. I shall first summarize the origins of the much repeated and widely accepted assertion that long-term price changes, between the last quarter of the nineteenth century and the eve of the second world war, resulted in a 43 per cent reduction in the price of primary products compared to those of manufactures.

What this assertion implies is that a given quantity of primary produce would in 1938 have exchanged for only 60 per cent of the quantity of manufactured goods that it would have exchanged for at the beginning of the period. From this it was concluded that the under-developed countries or territories had experienced an equivalent deterioration in their terms of trade and a reduction in their ability to import the manufactures, and above all the machinery, necessary to their economic development. These estimates were made by the statistical office of the League of Nations; they were first published in a book entitled *Industrialization and Foreign Trade* (Geneva, 1945) and were repeated later in a United Nations publication *Relative Prices of Exports and Imports of Under-developed Countries*[2] (New York, 1949). It is this latter, much-quoted study which has been mainly responsible for propagating the notion of a long-term fall in the prices of primary produce in relation to industrial goods, although it should be noted that the study concentrates mostly on the period 1938—48.

On the evidence of the generally available information about the changes in productivity in the various sectors it seems doubtful to me that such a change ever occurred. I have, therefore, decided to examine the statement critically from two separate angles: from the validity of the date selected as a terminal point, and from the price indices used. I believe that a crtical examination of the figures will disprove the theory that there was a fall in the prices of raw materials, and I shall present further evidence to show that in fact a real secular improvement occurred in the terms of trade of primary products *vis à vis* manufactures. This I shall do on two fronts. I shall begin by analysing the share of transport costs in the price of primary products, since the fall in costs during the period concerned is mainly responsible for the erroneous interpretation of the relative price changes, and I shall proceed to scrutinize the price series of primary produce and industrial goods in various countries.

I. CRITIQUE OF THE ESTIMATES PROVING A SECULAR FALL IN THE TERMS OF TRADE OF PRIMARY PRODUCTS

(a) The terminal date of calculations

Ignoring for the moment the fundamental problem of the price series itself, I shall first try to show that the date chosen as a terminal point for comparing the relative change in the price of primary products and manufactures is an irrelevant one. For my immediate purpose I am therefore assuming that the League of Nations estimate, and others similarly constructed, are correct.

We have seen that the deterioration in the terms of trade appears most obvious when the years 1870–80 are compared to 1930–38. But the 'thirties were the years of the Great Depression, and as far as prices are concerned they were totally abnormal. For proof of this it is only necessary to calculate the 'depreciation' of the prices of primary products compared to the years before the crisis. For instance, according to the League of Nations figures, the deterioration for the period 1876/80 to 1936/38 was 43 per cent and for the period 1876/80 to 1931/35 59 per cent. But if we take only the years up to 1926/29 the deterioration was no more than 20 per cent and up to 1911/13 no more than 7 per cent. Furthermore, if a change in the terminal date so reduces the degree of the so-called secular deterioration in raw material prices an even more striking change can be demonstrated by choosing a different starting date. Between 1896/1900 and 1926/29 there was actually an improvement of 3 per cent. Irrespective of the indices used this shows how extremely cautious one should be before drawing any conclusions or constructing any theories based on a comparison of series, the terminal date of which falls during the depression years of the 'thirties. By substituting the terminal date 1926/29 the deterioration is cut by half (20 per cent). We shall now see how far this deterioration corresponded to reality by examining the validity of the price indices used.

(b) The validity of the price indices

Before proceeding to a critique of the index used by the League of Nations I must mention another estimate of the value of world trade in manufactures and primary products, made by Arthur Lewis.[3] An examination of the basic data this author uses will reveal that the two estimates are almost similar (at least for the period 1870—1920). For wholesale prices between 1870—1920 the index is the same as that of the League of Nations except some differences of weights between the two series used in constructing the total index of primary products (including food). For the prices of manufactures the series are the same up to 1913; after that date, instead of using only the British export and import prices for these goods, Lewis gives an average of British and American prices. Therefore there are no great differences between the two series. Thus according to the League of Nations figures the relative deterioration in the prices of primary products for the period 1876/80—1936/38 is 43 per cent as against 31 per cent in Lewis's figures, while the deterioration for the period 1876/80—1926/29 is 20 per cent as against 13 per cent. Consequently to simplify matters I shall confine myself to an analysis of the League of Nations estimate, which is in any case much more widely known. In addition, the analysis will be limited to the period 1870—1929, so as to eliminate the abnormal effects of the depression.

The first, and a very surprising, point to be noted is that the price indices of world exports are only those for British exports: thus, if there is a deterioration in the terms of trade this concerns only one country, not the whole world. Let us now look at the indices themselves and consider how far the British figures can be used to reflect the world situation — a hypothesis that cannot be excluded *a priori.*

Beginning with prices of manufactures, we see that the index is an average of the import and export price indices constructed for Great Britain by Schlote.[4] In comparing this index with those of the other great economic powers it appears that there is a rise of 33 per cent registered for 1872—1928,[5] but taking the average of Great Britain and the United States, as Lewis does, the rise is only 26 per cent, and according to Kindleberger's index for industrial Europe,[6] we find that there is actually a fall of 13 per cent. Therefore, insofar as an index of world export prices of manufactures is required at all, the one upon which the League of Nations estimate is based is obviously badly distorted. It seems more likely that during the period 1872—1928 world industrial prices remained relatively stable than that they rose by 33 per cent as the League of Nations index indicates or fell by 13 per cent as Kindleberger would have us believe — as his figures did not take account of the U.S., for which there is a rise of about 20 per cent.

If therefore, as seems probable, there was relative stability in export prices of manufactures between 1872 and 1928 (expressed in gold values) rather than a rise of one-third, the relationship between the prices of raw materials and manufactures would turn out to be radically different from that commonly assumed.

The prices used in the League of Nations indices of primary products between 1870 and 1930 are those of Sauerbeck's index of wholesale prices of primary products in Britain,[7] corrected to allow for the fall in the value of sterling between 1921 and 1925.[8] Thus again the index is based on purely British figures. It shows a rise in prices of 10 per cent (1872—1928). When this index is compared with other indices of wholesale prices for raw materials we see that there was little difference between English and European prices (expressed in gold values), the English rising slightly more slowly. On the other hand the difference with the United States is more important since prices of raw materials there rose by about 20 per cent. It seems therefore that 10 per cent may be too low an estimate of the rise, and that an intermediate figure of between 10 and 20 per cent should be adopted. Thus in global terms for the period between 1872 and 1928 we find (again, in gold values):

(1) Relatively stable or slightly falling prices for manufactures;
(2) A rise of 10 to 20 per cent in prices of raw materials.

The conclusion is thus that the terms of trade for primary products improved by between 10 and 25 per cent instead of worsening by about 20 per cent.

Even more significant than the disputable validity of the price indices of manufactures and raw materials, is another even more important distortion responsible for the impression of deteriorating raw material prices. Judging from an analysis of the methods of calculating the various price series for raw materials it appears that these indices are nearly all based on import prices,[9] which are c.i.f.; while those for manufactures are based on import and export prices thus only 50 per cent are c.i.f. The distortion introduced by this factor is important for the three following reasons:

(1) Between the years 1870 and 1928 transport costs fell considerably;

(2) The share of transport costs is obviously more significant for raw materials where the average specific value is much lower than for manufactured goods;

(3) Finally the share of transport costs in prices of manufactures is lower not only because of the latter's higher specific value, but also because imports of manufactures made in industrial countries move on average a much shorter distance than do primary products imported into these countries.

Consequently a comparison between two price series so constructed is, in the last analysis, directly affected by the fall in transport costs, since by comparing these two series we have on the one hand the price of raw materials plus 100 per cent of transport costs, and on the other hand the price of manufactures plus only 50 per cent of such costs. And on top of this transport costs for primary products are proportionately higher than those for manufactures. By using such a biased index it is possible to exhibit a relative worsening in the price of raw materials. The bias is particularly marked for Britain because locally-produced raw materials compared to total consumption in that country were at a very low level and shrank considerably during the period.

These elements confirm my hypothesis of the improvement in the relative prices of raw materials – a hypothesis which is directly opposed to the one generally accepted for the period 1876/80–1926/29,[10] and which I now propose to substantiate with additional argument.

II. ADDITIONAL PROOFS OF THE REALITY OF A SECULAR IMPROVEMENT IN THE TERMS OF TRADE OF PRIMARY PRODUCTS

The first proof is based on an estimate of the proportionate share of transport costs in raw material prices for the period 1876/80–1926/29. The second entails a comparison of the prices of certain pairs of commodities (primary products and manufactures) in three countries for the same period. The third, which is methodologically the most important, consists in presenting some data on the terms of trade of under-developed countries, or those exporting raw materials, during the period 1870–1929. It is possible to combine the results of these calculations with some others of the terms of trade derived from indices of domestic prices of primary products compared to those of manufactures: they will be seen mainly to re-inforce those produced by our second argument.

(a) The part played by transport costs in the prices of primary products (1876/80—1926/29)
This is a field which has been very little studied; consequently the facts offered here are rather fragmentary. The problem will be approached in two ways:

(1) from the macro-economic aspect by comparing world values of the exports and imports of raw materials, and
(2) from the micro-economic aspect by comparing the relative transport costs of some primary products.

(1) A comparison of world values of primary products imports and exports
Since imports are expressed in c.i.f. prices while exports are expressed in f.o.b. prices, the difference between the world values of imports and exports gives us an approximation of the relative cost of transport and associated charges. But it is, of course, a rather crude measurement with a wide margin of error, mainly because of the incomplete nature of the statistics. Besides (and in the present context this is significant) the fall in transport costs stimulated growth in the trade in commodities which had a low specific value. As a consequence the transport charges measured as a percentage of the total value of imports tended to fall more slowly than the absolute cost of transport. However, in spite of this bias, which does not favour our thesis, it can be seen, if we look at existing statistics for the period under discussion (1876/80 to 1926/29), that the gap between the f.o.b. value of world exports of primary products and the c.i.f. value of world imports of similar goods fell from 23.1 per cent to 10.9 per cent.[11] By way of comparison we should note that the similar gap for manufactures fell from 8.3 per cent to 4.2 per cent during the same period.

These two proportions represent a relative fall in transport costs of 53 per cent, which is enough alone to explain a drop of about 12 per cent in the import prices of primary products without any fall in export prices. However, remembering that a drop in transport costs leads to a growth in the trade in goods with a low specific value, the percentages must be greater, and certainly great enough to account for a drop of more than 15 per cent at the least in the price of imports of primary products without a drop in export prices. What follows will confirm this conclusion.

(2) A comparison of the relative transport costs of some primary products

The figures in Table 35 enable us to appreciate the real fall in freight charges which occurred between 1876/80 and 1926/29. Of course freight charges are only one element in transport costs since the cost of insurance also enters into the total charge and this also fell markedly during the period. Thus we can see from the table that in 1926/29 rice costing 227.0 shillings in Burma cost 284.5 shillings in Great Britain — a difference of 57.5 shillings of which only 26.8 shillings were actual freight charges.

It will be seen from the table that a marked drop in freight charges occurred between the years 1870 and 1920. It would be pointless to try to extract a simple average from these scanty figures; however, they are sufficient to give us an idea of the size of the relative drop in transport costs. Thus, we see that in 1876/80, in transporting coal from Great Britain to Constantinople, freight charges alone amounted to 157 per cent of the cost of the coal itself — while freight charges to Hong Kong would have amounted to 300 per cent. This percentage fell to 74 in 1926/29. For wheat transported from the United States to Great Britain the percentage cost fell from 22.2 to 5.1 per cent and for rice coming from Burma to Great Britain from 84.3 to 11.8 per cent. Insurance[12] and other costs would probably have increased the percentages by about 100 per cent for 1876/80 and 1926/29.

These relative declines lend confirmation to the earlier estimate based on the macro-economic figures. It appears probable that the drop in transport costs alone is responsible for the relative 15—25 per cent fall in import prices of raw materials from 1876/80 to 1926/29. For manufactured goods with their higher specific values, freight costs played a smaller role. We can assume that the freights of manufactures would be responsible for a drop of only 5 per cent. All things considered this makes it probable that the fall in transport and allied costs which occurred between the years 1870 and 1920 masked a relative 10—20 per cent rise in the export prices of primary products compared to those of manufactured goods. This rise, combined with the changes in the underlying price indices themselves, probably led to improved relative prices of raw materials of about 20 to 40 per cent.[13]

This estimate is supported by the following brief analysis of price changes and by the analysis of the terms of trade for some specific countries which I shall make in section (c) below.

ble 35   *Relationship between freight costs and prices of selected primary products 1876/80—1926/29*

	Average 1876—80	Average 1926—29	Variation 1876/80—1926/29
HEAT (U.S. $ per bushel)			
Price in U.S.A.	1.35	1.78	+ 32%
Freight from U.S.A. to G.B.	0.30	0.09	− 70%
% relationship b:a	22.2%	5.1%	− 77%
OTTON (U.S. $ per 100 lbs.)			
Price in U.S.A.	9.3[1]	18.6	+100%
Freight from U.S.A. to G.B.	0.7[1]	0.6	− 14%
% relationship b:a	7.5%	3.2%	− 57%
OAL (G.B. shillings per long ton)			
Price in G.B.	9.7	17.1	+ 76%
Freight from G.B. to Constantinople	15.2	12.6	− 17%
% relationship b:a	156.7%	73.7%	− 53%
CE (G.B. shillings per long ton)			
Price in Burma	70.0[2]	227.0	—
Freight from Burma to G.B.	59.0	26.8	− 55%
% relationship b:a	84.3%	11.8%	− 86%
UGAR (G.B. shillings per long ton)			
Price in Java	325.0[2]	±380.0[2]	—
Freight from Java to G.B.	73.3	26.4	− 64%
% relationship b:a	22.6%	6.9%	− 69%
OTTON SEED (G.B. shillings per long ton)			
eight from Alexandria to G.B.	19.4	14.2	− 27%

855—60

rices calculated from prices in G.B., *less* freight costs plus handling, insurance and miscellaneous charges.
urces: FREIGHT (excluding *cotton*), average calculated from tables of maximum and minimum freight
arges for 1876—80, given in the weekly journal *Fairplay* of 1920, and for 1926—29 in the annual
pplements of the same journal for the years 1927—30.
OTTON, D. C. North, *The Economic Growth of the United States 1790—1860* (Englewood, 1961), p. 258;
rived from *New York Shipping and Commercial Freight Prices, Wheat and Cotton,* HISTORICAL
ATISTICS OF THE U.S. (Washington, 1960).
OAL, B. R. Mitchell and P. Deane, *Abstract of British Historical Statistics* (Cambridge, 1962).
CE and SUGAR, 1876—80 see coal; 1926—29, *International Yearbook of Agricultural Statistics* (Rome
rious issues).

(b) Comparative changes in price of some raw materials and manufactures

As we have seen, the overwhelming incidence of imported products in the samples of most wholesale price indices renders the latter useless as a measure of the changes in export prices of raw materials. This bias is increased by the wide availability of statistics relating to import prices (especially in indices stretching back to the nineteenth century), which gives them a disproportionate importance in the

Table 36   Changes in prices of some primary products and manufactures between 1876/80 and 1926/29

	Average 1876–80	Average 1926–29	Variation 1876/80– 1926/29
GREAT BRITAIN			
Coal: export f.o.b.			
(long tons, shillings)	9.7	17.1	+ 86%
Pig iron: Scottish			
(long tons, shillings)	52.5	77.8	+ 48%
FRANCE (Fr. tons)			
Coal	13.7	107.4	+684%
Wheat	292	1,548	+430%
Potatoes	75	520	+593%
Meat[4]	1,828	11,580	+533%
Cast iron	92	460	+400%
Steel rails	239	821	+244%
Cement[2]	70	252	+260%
Hand tools[3]			+407%
UNITED STATES			
Coal: anthracite (short tons)	3.38	11.10	+228%
Corn (bushels)[1]	1.35	1.67	+ 24%
Raw cotton (100 lbs)	11.7	18.6	+ 59%
Raw wool (100 lbs)	88.5	115.4	+ 30%
Steel rails (long tons)	52.6	43.0	− 18%
Nails (100 lbs)[1]	2.85	1.81	− 36%
Cotton cloth (100 yds)	79.0	125.8	+ 59%

[1] Adjusted to allow for variations of quality or type of product
[2] 1883 and 1926 respectively
[3] Average growth of wholesale prices of 14 handtools for 1879 and 1881 compared to 1926 and 1931; derived from the individual series in Fourastié's book, quoted below.
[4] Averages of beef, veal and pork
Sources: GREAT BRITAIN, B. R. Mitchell & P. Deane, Abstract of British Historical Statistics (Cambridge, 1962). FRANCE, coal, wheat, potatoes and cast iron, Annuaire statistique de la France, retrospective section; other commodities, J. Fourastié, Documents pour l'Histoire et la Theorie des prix (Paris, n.d. 1958?). U.S.A., Historical Statistics of the United States (Washington, 1960).

price structure. Indeed almost all the raw material price series available for the nineteenth century originate in statistics of foreign trade. Administrative requirements and the necessity of levying customs dues fostered greater sophistication in the statistical apparatus of foreign trade as compared to other fields of economic activity. The resulting distortion of economic records explains the non-representative character of most wholesale price indices of that era.

Because of this, in order to provide a supplementary proof of the hypothesis that no relative deterioration in raw material prices took place, I have attempted to assemble for each of three important countries (Great Britain, France and the United States) a series of primary-product prices which are not those of imports, and to compare their development with that of series for manufactured goods. The figures in Table 36 are rather few, as homogeneous series are not easy to find, but the extent to which they agree is very significant.

It can be seen that in each case the prices of manufactures have increased less than those of raw materials. One could not attempt to calculate a numerical difference on the sole basis of the commodities represented in the table, but the facts confirm those put forward earlier which reveal an improvement in primary-product prices compared to those of manufactured goods between the third quarter of the nineteenth century and 1926/29.

*(c) Data on the terms of trade of under-developed or of
primary-goods producing countries and on the terms of trade of
primary products in domestic trade (1870–1929)*
The relatively small number of examples quoted here must be stressed. The main reason for this paucity is the absence of basic statistics and the very few researchers working on the problem. Six cases of external terms of trade and three cases of terms of trade based on domestic price indices will be analysed.

For terms of trade proper the analysis will deal with three non-European primary-product exporting countries: India, Australia and Canada. Around 1900 these three countries provided about 35 per cent of the combined total exports of under-developed and primary-product exporting countries.[14] To these three cases we shall add those of Norway, Finland and Denmark. This analysis being the best means of determining the probable change in the terms of trade of the Third World, an attempt will be made whenever possible to push the inquiry back to 1870 (in some cases back to 1860). Now let us look at the facts.

For India the data is taken from Bhatia's study[15] which reveals that between 1866/75 and 1926/29 there was an improvement of 31 per cent (between 1861/65 and 1926/29 of 39 per cent) in the 'barter terms of trade'. The number and choice of the commodities used to construct the index of export prices (28 commodities) and import prices (11 commodities) gives a real value to these conclusions. For Australia the improvement in the terms of trade was no more than 7 per cent between 1870/74 and 1926/29,[16] but in this case the index of import prices used has not been clearly defined. The Canadian figures, which seem to have been calculated in a most complete way, indicate that between 1869/73 and 1926/29 there was an improvement in the terms of trade of 84 per cent.[17]

Alongside these figures we can place those of the terms of trade of some European countries specializing in the export of agricultural goods and raw materials. Thus Norway's foreign terms of trade (excluding services) improved by some 55 per cent between 1867/73 and 1930,[18] while for Finland the improvement between 1867/73 and 1909/14 was 44 per cent.[19] This probably indicates an average improvement between 1867/73 and 1926/29 of more than 50 per cent. Finally in Denmark, where the agricultural products were more sophisticated, the terms of trade improved by 39 per cent between 1875/79 and 1926/29.[20] One need hardly add that the bias attendant on the fall in transport costs also affects these figures, and in the examples quoted here would in fact exaggerate the improvement in the terms of trade, although its effect would be reduced by the fact that imports consisted mainly of manufactured articles of a high specific value.

To move on now to an analysis of some domestic price indices. For France we have the index of prices calculated by Lévy-Leboyer[21] according to which the terms of trade between agricultural and industrial prices improved by 6 per cent between 1866/75 and 1926/29 (by 17 per cent between 1856/65 and 1926/29). In Germany[22] the terms of trade of agricultural products compared to machinery and agricultural tools improved by 27 per cent and 41 per cent respectively for the same periods. In Japan, between 1878/81 and 1926/29, the improvement was about 330 per cent for prices in the agricultural sector compared to industry.[23] In this last case the range of commodities considered is relatively limited, and the agricultural market was protected to some degree against the import of cereals.

Thus these figures confirm those put forward earlier. It goes without saying that there is no question of drawing from these indications a more precise figure of the degree of the improvement of the terms of trade between primary products and manufactures, but they provide additional confirmation of the results of my own estimates suggesting a probable improvement between the years 1870 and 1926/29 of 20 to 40 per cent in the export prices of primary products relative to export prices of manufactures.

B. The terms of trade 1926–1970

We have seen that, contrary to generally accepted notions, the secular change of prices up to 1926/29 favoured primary products; and we have further concluded that there was an improvement of anything from 20 to 40 per cent in the export prices of primary products relative to the export prices of manufactures. We must now enquire to what extent this tendency has been modified in more recent times. I shall again omit the exceptional years 1930–39 from the analysis and concentrate on the years 1948–70.

Valid (U.N.) series for terms of trade of the under-developed countries exist from 1948 onwards and reveal that the terms deteriorated after 1954. Before discussing this, however, we must determine to what extent the price structure of the early 1950s differed from that of the years 1926/29. This is important because if the price structure in this period (compared to 1926/29) was characterized by a relatively high level of the prices of primary products, this would imply that the fall after 1954 could have been an adjustment.

I. CHANGES IN THE PRICES OF RAW MATERIALS AND MANUFACTURES, 1926/29–1950/54

The Bureau of General Economic Research and Policies of the United Nations[24] has calculated for some periods a price index of raw materials exported from under-developed countries.

Despite imperfections this index[25] is nevertheless of considerable value, largely because of the number of commodities included. From 1924/28 to 1950/52 the index of primary-product export prices grew by 14 per cent, while that of manufactures fell by 10 per cent, giving a comparative improvement in primary-product prices of

Table 37   *Index of export prices of primary products*
from less-developed countries (1924/28 = 100:
prices converted to constant 1934 U.S.
dollars)

	1934/38	1950/52	1959/61
Cereals	34.6	117	89
Meat	46.8	108	139
Bananas, oranges, tangerines	49.4	134	121
Sugar	36.6	105	86
Coffee, Cocoa, tea	29.1	129	102
Tobacco	47.9	96	109
Oilseeds and oils	32.2	121	103
Cotton, wool, jute, sisal	32.1	131	81
Rubber	21.8	63	50
Non-ferrous metals	41.1	123	114
Petrol, coal	41.6	117	117
TOTAL	34.8	114	95
Manufactures[1]	46.3	90	98

[1] Exports to the U.S.A.
Sources: Derived from *Studies in World Economy*, Vol. 1 (U.N., 1963).

about 27 per cent. This should be lowered to about 24 per cent to allow for the great rise in primary-product prices caused by the Korean War in 1950/52.

This estimate must now be compared with others. An index of primary-product prices calculated by the GATT[26] shows an even more marked relative growth: about 50 per cent from 1926/29 to 1949/51, expressed in constant U.S. dollars. (It should be remarked that GATT also used the export prices of the U.S. to calculate prices of manufactures.) Kindleberger's index for this period is of little significance since in 1952 the economy of most European countries was still restricted by post-war reconstruction, and this was reflected in the price structure. On the other hand the great rise in prices occurring in most of these countries did exert considerable influence.[27] These factors explain the 11 per cent deterioration shown in this index. Lewis's index, however, shows an improvement of 14 per cent between 1928 and 1950, and changes in the domestic price index of the U.S. also show a relative improvement of about 10 per cent for primary products compared to manufactures. From another index of export prices calculated by the statistical office of the United Nations,[28] based on a weighted average of national indices of countries representing more than 85 per cent of world trade, we find a relative improvement of 21 per cent between 1926/29 and 1950/52 and of 24 per cent between

1926/29 and 1950/54. Examination of some individual prices of both primary and industrial products suggests a similar change. Consequently it is likely that the U.N. estimate of a 25 per cent improvement in export prices of Third World primary products is realistic though perhaps slightly overestimated. The range was probably somewhere between 15 and 25 per cent.

Of course, this applies specifically to the period between 1926/29–1950. Compared to the years 1936/38 the improvement in prices of primary products would turn out to be still greater, since in the years between 1926/29 and 1936/38 the prices of primary products deteriorated more markedly by comparison with those of manufactures. Indeed, the primary product price index calculated by the U.N. indicates a rise in the price of raw materials of 228 per cent between 1934/38 and 1950/52, while for manufactures this rise is only 94 per cent. This represents a relative improvement in primary-product prices of 69 per cent. But if we direct our attention to the more significant change between 1924/28 and 1950/52 we also note that the price level in 1950/52 (even excluding 1951) shows a very pronounced improvement in primary-product prices, i.e. as suggested above, of about 15 to 25 per cent.

In order to arrive at a more balanced judgement on the changes after 1950 we have to try to put the 1950/52 levels into a comparative perspective. With this in mind we must consider the changes which occurred between 1926 and 1950 in a wider context. In an earlier passage we estimated that primary-product prices between 1870 and 1926/29 had improved by anything from 20 to 40 per cent, or by an average rate of 0.3 to 0.6 per cent per annum. Between 1926/29 and 1950/52 the improvement accelerated to a noticeably higher rate of 0.6 to 0.9 per cent per annum. Thus if the changes occurring before 1926 were to be considered 'normal' it would follow that the level of raw material prices of the year 1950 was relatively high. It is obvious that such a manner of determining the 'normal' level of prices is arbitrary, but a truly objective definition of a 'normal' price in this field is virtually impossible. Yet to neglect such a definition altogether raises difficulties, such as implicitly assuming that the 1950 levels was 'normal'. An acceptable solution, therefore, might be to regard the changes occurring between 1870/1926 as 'normal', and from this to conclude that the level of primary-product prices was relatively high in 1950 by comparison with those of industrial products – about 5 to 10 per cent above the level to be deduced from an extrapolation of the long-term trend. Such an assumption throws a very different light on the fall which occurred from then onwards, allowing it to be seen, at least partially, as an adjustment of prices. The word 'partially' is used advisedly since, as we shall see in the following pages, the fall actually went far beyond the limits of such an adjustment.

II. CHANGES IN TERMS OF TRADE, 1948–1970
(a) The figures

Thanks to improved statistical material we have enough data for this period to measure the changes in the terms of trade for countries or groups of countries as well as for groups of commodities. The availability of this double series also allows us to confirm that the working hypothesis, in which the two series are regarded as equivalent, is valid for practical purposes – at least till the early '60s.

As far as changes in the terms of trade of developing countries are concerned, the years 1948–70 can be divided into three distinct periods. The first is from 1948 to 1955, and is characterized, apart from annual fluctuations such as the 1951 rise due to the Korean War, by relative stability both in developed and under-developed countries. The second period (1954/55 to 1962/63) is marked by a considerable deterioration of the terms of trade of the under-developed countries – about 11 per cent between 1950/55 and 1962/63. During the same period the terms of trade of the developed countries improved by almost 10 per cent. Although these two contrary movements are connected to a large degree, the links are not entirely reciprocal, since while commodities originating in the developed countries represented more than 70 per cent of total imports of Third World countries, the products from the Third World provided no more than 19 per cent of total imports in developed countries. The third period, beginning in 1962/63 and going on till at least 1970 (and even until the beginning of 1973), was marked by relative stability in the movement of the terms of trade both in the third and the developed world. However, whereas in the Third World the trend was stabilized near the lowest level since the end of the war, for the developed countries stability occurred at the top of the curve during the same period. Moreover, the deterioration in Third World terms of trade since 1962 has been halted mainly by the growing part which manufactures began to occupy in their exports. Thus, if one were to look only at the terms of trade in primary products it would appear that since 1962 the decline has been gently slowing down, but that there has been no actual stabilization. From 1952/54 to 1960/62 this deterioration was 15 per cent, while from 1960/62 to 1968/70 it was no more than 3 per cent.

Naturally when we turn to individual countries we find that there are great divergences from the average figure quoted above, because on one hand export prices of various raw materials have changed in different ways (not to speak of the actual size of the swings in

Table 38 *Changes in the terms of trade* (1963 = 100)

	LESS-DEVELOPED COUNTRIES			DEVELOPED COUNTRIES	Terms of trade of primary against manufactured products[1]
	Export prices	Import prices	Terms of trade	Terms of trade	
1938	34	43	80	99	—
1948	109	113	95	95	—
1950	102	91	112	91	128
1951	128	107	119	88	128
1952	117	109	106	91	116
1953	109	103	105	94	114
1954	111	99	112	92	119
1955	111	101	110	92	115
1956	110	102	107	93	111
1957	110	105	104	92	111
1958	105	101	104	96	105
1959	103	98	106	97	104
1960	103	99	104	98	101
1961	100	99	102	99	98
1962	97	100	98	100	97
1963	100	100	100	100	100
1964	103	102	101	100	101
1965	102	103	99	100	98
1966	104	103	101	100	97
1967	103	103	100	101	95
1968	103	102	101	101	96
1969	106	105	101	101	96
1970	109	109	100	102	94

[1] Trade between developed and developing areas
Sources: Various issues of *Statistical Yearbook* and *Monthly Bulletin of Statistics* (U.N.); for recent data *Monthly Bulletin* of April 1973.

prices), while on the other, some countries possess a highly specialized foreign trade, with the result that swings in either direction tend to be more extreme.

Returning to the average for the Third World, we may assume that a marked fall in the terms of trade was a phenomenon limited mainly to the period 1952–62, and it was accompanied – as already stated – by a recognizable improvement in the terms for the developed countries, which in turn led to an even more marked comparative worsening of the terms of trade between the two worlds. The divergence was about 14 per cent from 1950/54 to 1961/63; and the deterioration was even worse for the terms of trade of raw materials compared to manufactures (exchanged between under-developed and developed countries), reaching 19 per cent between these dates.

Since the price level for raw materials in 1950/54 was quite high (from 5 to 10 per cent higher than the extrapolated curve of the long-term trend) we must assume that perhaps one-third or one-half of the drop was in fact an adjustment, as defined earlier in this chapter. Consequently we may conclude that during this period there was a real fall of about 10 per cent in prices of primary products compared to manufactures, which led, given the structure of foreign trade, to a similar real drop in the terms of trade of the under-developed countries. This fall may be thought to be rather exceptional, given the earlier changes and the economic level of the period, thus justifying the interest taken in the problem by the United Nations Conference on Trade and Development (UNCTAD), which was held in Geneva in 1964 but had been convoked in 1961.

For the less-developed countries themselves the consequences of the adverse trade balances were especially serious because amongst manufactures it was capital equipment that suffered the greatest rise in prices.[29] The worsening in the terms of trade between primary products and capital equipment was 38 per cent[30] between 1954 and 1962 in the exchanges between developed and under-developed countries. Such a deterioration obviously posed formidable problems for most under-developed countries for whom, as we have seen, foreign trade forms a very important part of their national product.

On the basis of this worsening of the terms of trade calculations can be made showing statistically that the loss of resources which ensued formed a very important fraction of the financial aid granted to the Third World. Taking the extreme case (i.e. accepting that relative price levels in 1954 were 'normal' and that the prices of primary products compared to capital equipment worsened by 38 per cent) in 1962 there was a loss of resources by the under-developed countries of about 11 billion dollars, or about 130 per cent of the total financial aid received by them in the same year. (According to existing data — see Chapter 10 — the amount of aid in 1962 can be put at about 8.5 billion dollars.) Of course, such an estimate distorts reality. But even if we assume a more realistic figure of 12 per cent as the degree of deterioration in terms of trade, we still arrive at an estimated loss of resources in 1962 of around 3.5 billion dollars, or about 40 per cent of the total aid (generously defined) given to under-developed countries during this year. For 1970 the loss could be estimated at 5 billion dollars, or about 35 per cent of aid. It is obvious that this situation had a very strong impact on the development possibilities of the Third World, and fully deserves the interest which has been displayed in it. In the following pages the causes of this deterioration in the terms of trade will be examined briefly.

(b) A brief review of the possible causes for the worsening terms of trade

Within the framework of the present analysis I do not intend to study the causes of the deterioration in depth, but merely to present a straightforward critical examination of the principal factors which have been advanced in explanation of it.[31]

The several theses may be summarized in the following six propositions:

1. The demand for raw materials compared to that for manufactures is relatively inelastic.
2. Technological progress has reduced the input coefficients of raw materials in manufacturing industry.
3. The import of raw materials into the developed countries has been reduced by restrictive measures.
4. Synthetics have been developed and are put to ever-increasing use.
5. The allocation of the gains accruing from a rise in productivity have differed in their effects on primary products and manufactures. In manufactures the effect was rising prices and higher remuneration of factors of production; in raw materials the effect was to lower prices and to bring about a standstill or a reduction in remuneration of factors of production.
6. The supply of raw materials greatly increased.

It is obvious that a combination of some of these factors is possible, and it has been suggested that this was the case. Before passing to the separate examination of each explanation, I should point out that most theories have been based on the hypothesis which postulates a secular deterioration in the relative prices of primary products. But, as we saw earlier, there was, on the contrary, an improvement in these prices up till 1950/54. By eliminating the hypothesis of a deterioration we should be able to scale down some of the explanations, i.e. numbers 1, 2 and 3 and (at least partly) number 5. Indeed, a relative inelasticity of demand for raw materials, a continuing reduction in the input coefficients of raw materials and restrictions on imports have existed since the beginning of the industrial revolution and have not up till now (or had not at least until 1950/54) caused a relative worsening of the prices of raw materials. Moreover, we cannot exclude the possibility that the same factors might have prevented a greater improvement in the relative price of primary products than the one that actually took place. On the other hand there are some important industrial products, especially semi-finished ones, whose share in finished products has

Table 39   *Changes in the export prices of primary products
(for all non-communist countries) 1958 = 100*

	1950/54[1]	1961/65	Variation 1950/54– 1961/65
Food products	105	98	− 7%
Coffee, tea, cocoa	111	76	−32%
Cereals	115	102	−11%
Non-food agricultural products	118	103	− 9%
Fats	111	97	−13%
Textiles	137	108	−20%
Wool	147	116	−21%
Minerals	90	93	+ 3%
Metals	99	102	+ 3%
Fuels	88	91	+ 3%
GENERAL INDEX	106	98[2]	− 8%
Natural rubber	107	98	− 8%

[1] Excluding 1951
[2] The following are the changes in the index for recent years

1963	100	1966	104	1969	104
1964	103	1967	101	1970	108
1965	103	1968	100	1971	115

Sources: Excluding rubber, derived from various issues of the *Monthly Bulletin
of Statistics* (U.N.). For recent data see the *Bulletin* for March 1973. Rubber:
author's estimates based on export prices of rubber from the following countries:
Malaya, Thailand, Ceylon and Nigeria.

decreased while their price has increased. This is especially true of
iron and steel. Finally it should also be remembered that the
elasticity of demand for cereals is less than that for coffee, tea or
cocoa, although the prices of the second group fell much more
heavily than those of the first group (see Table 39). Similarly there
are industrial products for which the demand is very inelastic, but
whose prices have nevertheless risen.

To facilitate a critical examination of point number 4 I have
worked out in Table 39 the variations in the export prices of
different groups of raw materials between 1950/54[32] and 1961/65.
The figures suggest that the introduction of synthetics did not by
itself constitute a sufficiently valid explanation of some of the price
falls. Primary products such as fibres, textiles, metallic metals and
rubber which were directly threatened by these products have
decreased less quickly than, or in a manner not fundamentally
different from, other products such as coffee, tea and cocoa for
which a synthetic substitute does not exist. The fact remains that

Table 40 *Changes in the share of synthetics in world output of textile fibres and rubber* (1000 tons)

	1938	1948	1958	1970
TEXTILE FIBRES				
Total natural[1] and man-made fibres	9,300	10,300	14,900	22,200
Cellulose synthetic fibres[2]	880	1,150	2,270	3,440
Non-cellulose synthetic fibres[3]	–	34	420	4,930
Total man-made fibres	880	1,190	2,690	8,370
Synthetics as % of total	9%	11%	18%	38%
RUBBER[4]				
Total natural and synthetic	931	2,150	3,520	8,800
Synthetic	6	600	1,550	5,900
Synthetics as % of total	0.6%	28%	43%	67%

[1] Cotton, wool (washed), flax and silk
[2] Rayon, fibranne
[3] Nylon, orlon, perlon, etc.
[4] Excluding China
Sources: Author's estimates derived from *Statistical Yearbook* and *Monthly Bulletin of Statistics* (U.N.); *Production Yearbook* and *Monthly Bulletin of Agricultural Economics and Statistics* (F.A.O.) and *Textile Organon*. (For natural fibres the figures are five-year averages centring on the chosen year, except for 1970 when the average is for three years.)

this factor must have had some effect since the expansion of synthetics has been very great.

Table 40 above provides evidence for some such effects in the case of textile fibres and rubber. It should be remarked here that because they are lighter and more durable, a given quantity of man-made fibres corresponds to a greater quantity of natural fibres, so as long as we base our percentages on weights we are apt to under-estimate the real share of man-made fibres. In addition to man-made fibres and synthetic rubber we must also consider synthetic detergents which compete with fats, as well as plastic materials[33] whose characteristics enable them to some extent to replace leather, wood and metals. As the share of these products before the war was extremely low and as today they form a significant, not to say the larger, fraction of output, it is obvious that the prices of the raw materials for which they are substitutes were bound to be affected. But this is not an adequate explanation by itself since, as we have seen, a deterioration in price had also occurred for most of the products for which there are no substitutes.

There remain two other explanations to analyse, numbers 5 and 6, i.e. the difference which exists between the under-developed and the developed countries in the allocation of the gains from increasing productivity and the great increase in the supply of primary products.

The difference in allocation of productivity gains can be only a partial explanation because, as we have already noticed, a similar structure had also existed in the past without lowering prices; and secondly because it is hardly likely that the difference between the increase of productivity in tropical agriculture and that of manufacturing industry in developed countries between 1954 and 1962 would have corresponded to the deterioration in the terms of trade which had taken place, i.e. 19 per cent. But these conclusions must once more be carefully scrutinized in relation to prevailing commercial policies. The developed countries have sought in the past, and seek now, to keep down raw material prices: such policies would have more chance of success if resistance and impediments on the part of primary producers were not sufficient to prevent the gains from productivity being translated into lower prices. The resistance was lacking mostly because of the small degree of trade-union pressure and the absence of well-organized combinations of sellers. This thesis is the one put forward by Prebisch in particular and is implicit in the creation of UNCTAD (United Nations Conference on Trade and Development). We must also call to mind the figures compiled here for the chapter on foreign trade, from which it emerges that in 1970 Third World exports destined for the developed countries formed 11 per cent of their G.D.P. while developed countries' exports destined for the Third World formed only 2 per cent of their G.N.P. We should note moreover that pressure of this nature on the part of the developed countries ought not to be considered purposely contrived, but merely as the logical consequences of a market economy and a liberal system of international trade. What also supports the thesis connecting the worsening of the terms of trade with the different allocation of gains in productivity accruing to developed and under-developed countries is the differences in price changes of commodities with similar functions but different origins. The prices of such commodities produced in the Third World compared to these of commodities produced in the developed countries clearly differed. Thus the price of beet sugar rose or remained stable while the price of cane sugar fell. There were the same changes to be observed in the price of fats — a rise in butter, a fall in oilseeds — and fruits — a greater increase in the fruits of the temperature zone and a slighter increase for tropical fruits. These changes are based on computations of price variations between 1952/54 and 1961/63 based on F.A.O. data made for 21 commodities or groups of commodities. At the more general level the indices of export prices, calculated separately by the U.N. for the developed and under-developed nations, show a similar trend. The general index of raw materials and sub-groups has changed more favourably for the developed than for the under-developed countries.[34] Of course the support policies for agricultural prices in the developed countries are usually the cause of these differences, but the very existence of such support policies confirms the validity of the hypothesis of a differentiation in the way the gains from productivity have been distributed. It should be noted, however, that the composition of the exports of these groups of commodities is very far from being identical in the developed and under-developed countries.

To the extent that political independence in a large number of colonial territories has coincided with the fall in prices we may be justified in enquiring how far independence increased the pressure of the purchasers of primary products. Given the new political structure, the dangers (social as well as political) of a fall in the remuneration of factors of production have no longer concerned the buying countries, while this was certainly not so under the colonial regimes. This may seem a paradoxical hypothesis but it is one most worthy of consideration.

We come now to the last point, that of increases in supply. We can see that in fact the output of primary products in the under-developed countries grew enormously. Where minerals and fuels are concerned, we saw in the chapter on the extractive industries that output rose from an index number of 12 in 1936/38 (100 = 1963) to one of 108 in 1963/65, i.e. an increase of 800 per cent. For agricultural export crops the average increase in output between 1934/38 and 1963/65 can be estimated to be about 106 per cent.[35] As the domestic consumption of these commodities in the less-developed countries is in most cases very low, we can, roughly speaking, take the volume of their domestic production to represent their supply on the international market. On this basis and judging from the size of the increased supply, it appears more than likely that there occurred an excess of supply over demand, and that this is a valid explanation of the fall in prices.

The foregoing critical examination of the explanatory factors, although extremely brief, does allow us to suggest a variety of tentative answers. As so often happens in the social sciences, an explanation by one single factor is too simplistic. Reality can more often be seen in the conjunction of several causes, and this is certainly the case here. We may conclude that the relative worsening of primary-product prices which occurred after 1954 resulted from a combination of the following factors, in order of decreasing importance: a great increase in the supply of primary-products from the less-developed countries; a difference between the less-developed and the developed countries in the manner in which the gains from increased productivity accrued; the perfection and high output of a wide range of synthetic commodities.

Three other factors listed here also in order of decreasing importance had a much more limited influence: the relative inelasticity of demand for raw materials compared to manufactures; the reduction of the input coefficient of raw materials in manufacturing industry due to technological progress; measures restricting the import of primary products into the developed countries.

Research on the problems of the terms of trade done since the first edition of the present study appeared shows proof on the one hand of the reality of the secular improvement of the terms of trade of primary products up till 1950/54 and, on the other hand, highlights a factor capable of explaining, at least in part, the break in the trend after that date. The factor, which so far as I know has not yet been taken into account as an explanation of the phenomenon, is the profound change which has recently occurred in the rate in the growth of productivity in agriculture as compared to industry. In fact, up to 1940 in the U.S. and the 'fifties in Europe, productivity (both of labour and of other factors) increased much more rapidly in industry than it did in agriculture; while since then the opposite has been true.[36] Such a radical change is obviously capable of causing a deterioration, even if only a partial one, in the terms of trade of agricultural commodities in the temperate regions as compared to manufactures. But as we do not have any valid figures for the changes in the productivity of export crops of countries of the Third World it is difficult to be sure whether this factor also occurred in their case. We have seen that for food crops productivity stagnated. But it is possible, even probable, that the trend in productivity was different for export crops because the prevailing systems of cultivation facilitated the swifter and more general introduction of important innovations in agricultural equipment, in selection of plants, and fertilizers, pesticides and herbicides.

As there are no figures for productivity in these sectors a large question mark hangs over the causes of the new trend – a trend which could be most harmful to the Third World if it should turn out not to be due mainly to this last cause.

7   *The Level of Education*

INTRODUCTION

In this short chapter, which is to some extent outside the main subject of our enquiry, I shall attempt to diagnose briefly the changes in a field which is not strictly speaking economic but which nevertheless interacts with the economy in an important way.

If the 'take off' in the modern developed countries was able to get under way without being handicapped by the low level of literacy of the population, it was because conditions at the beginning of the nineteenth century were so totally different. Industrial technique was largely improvised and based on simple empirical grounds. Today conditions are totally different: science plays an overwhelming part in technology, and thus in economic and industrial life. For this reason the level of literacy has a much greater impact now than it did in the early nineteenth century,[1] and this is why of late, particularly in the last two decades, so much emphasis has rightly been placed on education in developing countries.

This chapter is an attempt to measure how far these efforts have been successful. The first part of the chapter deals briefly with long-term changes in the level of literacy and primary schooling; in the second part more recent changes in secondary and higher education are discussed. The delay in compiling educational statistics has meant that we cannot in all cases include, as we have done in other chapters, figures for very recent years.

A. The level of literacy and primary schooling

As statistics for the period before 1950 are so few and unreliable, I have sought to measure short- as well as long-term changes through differences in the level of illiteracy registered for the various age groups. Thus in Table 41, besides the level of illiteracy in the population over 15 years of age I have computed, on the basis of the last census, the level of illiteracy for some older age groups. This provides a fairly valid estimate of the situation in earlier years.

Before looking at the changes I shall comment briefly on the differences in the levels of 1960. Leaving aside the differences, sometimes quite large ones, existing between countries, we should note the superior position of the Latin American countries, in which the level of illiteracy is half that in the Afro-Asian and Middle Eastern countries. We should also note that in this respect the Middle

East does not occupy the intermediate position between Latin America and Asia which it does in certain other fields.

In spite of the weight of population increase reflected in the enormous rise in the number of children of elementary school age,[2] great progress in education has been made in most of the Third World. A comparison of the percentages of illiteracy for the age

Table 41 *Changes in the rate of illiteracy*

	% of illiteracy amongst over-15s*		% of illiteracy by age group in 1960 census				
	1950	1960	10—14	20—24	35—44	45—54	55—6
AFRICA							
Madagascar	66.5[6]	—	—	—	—	—	—
Morocco	—	86.2	67.2	85.0	87.4	87.8	88.9
Nigeria	88.5[5]	—	—	—	—	—	—
Senegal	—	94.4[9]	88.6[12]	93.0	95.3	95.6	97.1
Tunisia	—	84.2[7]	73.4	85.0	87.5	89.2	91.5
AMERICA							
Argentina	13.3[2]	8.6	5.2[13]	—	7.1[13]	—	15.7[1]
Brazil	50.6	—	—	—	—	—	—
Chile	19.8[5]	16.4	9.7	11.1	16.6	20.0	25.9
Cuba	22.1[6]	16.2	—	—	—	—	—
Mexico	43.2	34.6	28.4	28.0	33.3[10]	38.0[10]	44.9[1]
Peru	—	39.4[9]	26.3[14]	29.4	42.3	47.3	52.3
Venezuela	47.8	34.2	22.9[12]	25.1	38.9	46.1	53.5
ASIA							
Ceylon	37.0[1]	32.3[6]	—	—	—	—	—
India	80.7[4]	72.2[9]	57.7	66.4	74.6	78.2[11]	—
Pakistan	81.1[4]	81.2[9]	72.3	76.9	—	—	—
Indonesia	—	57.1[9]	27.9	42.5	62.6	73.4	80.1
Philippines	40.0[3]	28.1[9]	27.1	15.4	33.4	40.2	52.0
Thailand	48.0[2]	32.3[9]	14.3	16.0	39.6	56.7	68.8
MIDDLE EAST							
Egypt	80.1[2]	80.5	59.6	77.3	80.8	84.7	86.3
Iraq	—	85.5[8]	67.4	78.0	89.0	90.6	93.6
Iran	—	87.2[7]	71.7	84.1	88.5	91.4	92.5
Turkey	68.1	61.9	44.8	49.1	63.7	73.3	83.0

*Except Peru +17 years; Madagascar, Senegal, Argentina +14 years; Tunisia +10 years; Nigeria +7 years; Mexico (1950) +6 years.
[1]1946 [2]1947 [3]1948 [4]1951 [5]1952 [6]1953 [7]1956 [8]1957 [9]1961
[10]30—39, 40—49 and 50—59 years respectively
[11]45—59 years [12]15 –19 years
[13]14—29, 30—39 and more than 50 years respectively
[14]17—19 years
Sources: Derived from figures collected from *Demographic Yearbook* (U.N.), for 1955, 1963 and 1964, and *Statistical Yearbook* (UNESCO), for 1964 (Paris, 1966).

groups 10 to 14 years and 20 to 24 years, shows a great improvement. Thus for India the percentage fell from 66.4 to 57.7 per cent; the fall for other Asian countries is less obvious, but is nevertheless substantial. The Philippines, where we can see a marked increase, are somewhat of an exception. However illiteracy in this country is lower than in other Asian countries. A great drop in the percentage of illiterates can also be seen in the African and the Middle Eastern countries, particularly in Egypt where the level of illiteracy for the 20 to 24 year-olds is 77.3 per cent and for the 10 to 14 year-olds is 59.6 per cent. Progress in Latin America has been more moderate, and this can be explained by the relatively high absolute level of literacy.

Over the longer term it can be shown by comparing the levels of the age groups over 35 years of age that educational progress in earlier periods was much slower than it is at present. One should remember, of course, that since there is a correlation between the level of education and standard of life there is usually a higher mortality among illiterates. This results in an under-estimation of the level of illiteracy among age groups above 45 years, and reduces the apparent extent of real progress. Allowing for this factor the changes in recent years (say from 1948 to 1960) are significant compared to the earlier period (say from 1910 to 1948). The years 1948—60 witnessed great progress with the pace quickening between 1969—70, as we shall see.

For the whole non-communist, under-developed world the estimated level of illiteracy amongst the population of 15 years and over fell over the long term as follows:[3]

1900	±80 per cent
1930	±76 per cent
1950	±74 per cent
1960	65 per cent
1970	56 per cent

These average levels, of course, conceal profound differences between countries and even between the wider regions. In 1970 the level of illiteracy was highest in Africa with 76 per cent (86 per cent in 1950), followed by Asia with 50 per cent (78 per cent in 1950) and by Latin America with 24 per cent (42 per cent in 1950).

Progress will appear even more rapid when numbers of pupils enrolled in primary education are considered. Even though too much importance should not be attached to these figures, they reflect, nonetheless, real changes. In 1950 there were slightly fewer than 65 million pupils enrolled in primary schools in the non-communist under-developed countries; by 1960 this figure had risen to 119 millions, and by 1970 to 202 millions. According to my calculations and estimates for the same region the number of pupils was about 7 million in 1900, 11 million 1910 and 37 million about 1937/38. At the regional level the change was marked by an equalizing trend in the rate of school attendance (i.e. the proportion of children attending school). It was in Africa where the rate of school attendance was the lowest that the numbers of pupils and the rate of school attendance grew the fastest; in Latin America which had the highest starting level, progress was the slowest. Around 1970 the rate of attendance at the elementary level for the whole Third World was about 57 per cent (31 per cent in 1950 and 45 per cent in 1960); for Latin America the figures were 78 per cent (46 per cent in 1950); for Asia 56 per cent (32 per cent in 1950) and for Africa 43 per cent (18 per cent in 1950). This progress is amazingly rapid, much more than in the developed countries at any stage in their development. During the nineteenth century in Europe the annual rate of growth in the number of pupils at the elementary level was about 1.8 per cent.[4] The annual rate of growth in school attendance can thus be estimated to be 1 per cent, or less than one-third of that of developing countries at the present day.

It is a harder matter and a somewhat arbitrary exercise to try to make comparisons between the enrolment ratios since in this respect we can observe great differences which had nothing to do with the corresponding stages of economic development. Thus in the mid-nineteenth century Germany, Switzerland and most of the Scandinavian countries had rates of school attendance well above that of England, which was economically further developed.[5]

The differences become progressively less visible with the approach of the twentieth century because, with the widespread introduction in Europe of compulsory elementary schooling around 1880, school enrolment ratios tended rapidly to approach 95—98 per cent.[6] It can be estimated that this rate of 95—98 per cent had been reached in almost every European industrialized country in about 1910. The level of school enrolment in the rest of the under-developed world in 1970, i.e. 57 per cent, is the same which Europe (excluding Russia) achieved in about 1860. At that time the percentage of the labour force employed in agriculture was about 55—60 per cent as against a little below 70 per cent for the under-developed countries today, and the proportion of the population employed in manufacturing industry was about 18—20 per cent as against 10 per cent for the under-developed countries now.

Such an extremely swift progress in elementary schooling created problems by its very speed: in particular it encouraged a rural exodus, as we shall see in the next chapter. The pace of progress and the present level of education does not mean that all problems of the adult working population in the primary or even secondary sectors have been solved by this means. Given that tertiary employment, especially in the public services, absorbs a high proportion of the educated, it follows, that, in spite of educational levels of about 60 per cent, levels of illiteracy of about 60–80 per cent (excluding Latin America) will be likely to be found amongst those employed in industry and especially agriculture for a long time to come. This rate is high enough to obstruct the diffusion of innovations into those sectors. Thus any effort aimed at adult education should clearly receive top priority.

Such an effort to concentrate on adult education seems to have been attempted in China, at least in some periods. But it is difficult to distinguish at all clearly how far it was successful, since, as in the field of primary education in general, we possess no figures for any period more recent than 1958 when we know that some 90 million children attended primary schools. This would form a school enrolment ratio of about 60 per cent (compared with 43 per cent in the non-communist under-developed countries). It appears probable that the ratio has not noticeably increased and that the campaign for increased literacy undertaken in the popular communes during the Great Leap Forward obviously did not succeed and has not been pursued with the same enthusiasm since then.[7] Although it is rash to hazard figures, it is probable that the level of illiteracy in the adult population of China (about 1970) lies somewhere between a minimum of 25 per cent and a maximum of 45 per cent. This is definitely lower than the level for non-communist Asia which for the same period is 50 per cent, although the disequilibrium between the urban and rural proportions is probably less marked in China.

Thus, there is no doubt that improvement is taking place in the field of primary education and it deserves to be recorded because, as I remarked earlier, it reflects a great educational effort. However, it has to be pointed out that the diagnosis made here deals solely with the quantitative side of education. There are obviously qualitative problems which are impossible to analyse within the framework of the present study. These arise as much from over-crowded classes, the over-expansion of school population and the shortage of qualified teachers as from the content of what is taught. The curriculum is often badly adapted to local conditions because it is closely copied from that of the former colonial powers and was intended for pupils with a different mentality and standard of living. The last point would not of course apply to China.

This problem together with the one related to the inefficacy of the school system, which is becoming increasingly serious, formed the major themes at UNESCO's recent international conference on education.[8] In fact it is not only that the content of primary education using text books from former metropolitan countries is so often badly adapted to local needs, but also that its effect is limited. A large number of pupils never finish their course of study. The drop-out rate is considerable and rises, for example in Brazil and Algeria, to as much as 60 per cent, with a consequent increase in the cost per pupil completing his education.

B. Secondary and higher education

Progress in literacy and primary education has been followed by even more rapid progress in education at the secondary and higher level. Details about the changes in the total number of students in these two educational levels will be found in Table 42.

In educational establishments up to secondary level there were 43 million students in 1970, i.e. nearly six times more than in 1950. To put it in another way the number was not far short of that in the western developed countries (55 million), while in 1950 there had been only one-third as many. The Third World will surpass the western countries in absolute numbers of students by 1975. But in terms of attendance rates the gap is still an important one; in 1970 the rate is about 26 per cent in the Third World and about 75 per cent in the developed countries.

As is the case with other indicators, regional differences are considerable, as also are differences between countries. Ranking is about the same as for the economic factors. The attendance rate is highest in Latin America (about 37 per cent in 1970), followed by Asia (about 26 per cent) and lowest in Africa (about 17 per cent). In general, the levels of attendance achieved by the Third World in 1970 are much higher than those in the industrialized countries at the time when they had attained a similar stage of development. Thus a secondary education attendance rate of about 26 per cent was only achieved by the developed countries in the decades between 1930 and 1950, i.e. at the moment when their *per capita* standard of living was about six to eight times as high as that in the currently less-developed countries. This shows how pressing is the problem facing the under-developed countries regarding the need for modern technology.

Table 42   *Changes in numbers of students at secondary and higher level of education* (in thousands)

	1950	1960	1970
SECOND LEVEL[1]			
Less-developed countries[5]	7600	18200	42500
Africa	480	1660	4420
Asia	5410	12190	27250
Latin America	1710	3890	10720
China	1310	8520[4]	–
Developed countries[3]	30500	45700	70700
World[5]	38000	63900	113200
THIRD LEVEL[2]			
Less-developed countries[5]	940	2100	5600
Africa	40	140	350
Asia	620	1390	3740
Latin America	280	570	1520
China	139	900	–
Developed countries[3]	5380	9090	20440
World[5]	6300	11200	26100

[1] General, vocational and teacher training
[2] Universities and other institutions of higher education
[3] Including communist countries
[4] 1958
[5] Excluding China (mainland), North Korea and North Vietnam
Sources: Derived from UNESCO *Statistical Yearbook 1972* (Paris, 1973).

As it was in relation to primary education, the relative nature of the figures and the problem of the content of the education has also to be considered. The relative nature of the figures emerges mainly from the fact that the number of pupils actually completing their secondary studies is very low, well below that of the average rates in the developed countries. The problem of the educational content is similar to that found in primary education. But, in addition, as we shall see in Chapter 9, there is the problem in urban areas of high unemployment amongst young people with secondary education.

Expansion has been even more rapid in education at the third, mainly university, level. From about 900,000 in 1950 (350,000 in 1937), student numbers in the non-communist under-developed countries rose to 2.1 millions in 1960 and the figure stands at 5.6 millions in 1970. To this must be added the 200,000 students who are following university courses in the developed countries.[9] The regional differences are, as in other fields, considerable (see Table 42).

In spite of such a very rapid expansion the gap between the

enrolment ratios in the Third World and the developed countries still remains a large one: a ratio of about 1 to 6 in 1970. But here also even more than for other types of education, the rates achieved in 1970 were, relatively speaking far higher. In fact, an enrolment ratio of 4 per cent, which was that of the Third World in 1970, had not been achieved in most European countries until after the second world war. It had of course been reached much earlier in the U.S. (about 1920). Valid international comparisons of this kind are, however, rather difficult to make for a number of reasons.

In many countries and disciplines such a rapid expansion of higher education produced a serious disequilibrium between supply and demand, encouraging qualified students either to emigrate, or at least not to return to their own countries if they had received their education abroad. This is the notorious 'brain drain' which has been such a controversial topic in recent years.

If the problem of students not completing their courses is less serious for higher education than for the lower levels, that of the orientation of the studies themselves has proved to be a continuing one. In fact the total number of students in technical and scientific disciplines is quite small. There are no world statistics available, but from computations I have made myself based on 101 under-developed countries whose students form more than 95 per cent of the total, the distribution as a percentage of the total in 1966—68 was as follows.[10]

Literature, education, fine arts	40.3
Law, social sciences	22.2
Exact and natural sciences	6.0
Engineering	15.3
Medicine	9.8
Agriculture	4.5

Comparisons between regions are not very useful in this field, since local needs are so different. However scientific disciplines absorb about 45 per cent of students in the western European countries, about 65 per cent in the East European countries, while we can see from the list above that the figure in the under-developed countries is only 36 per cent. But there is a further problem of adjusting supply and demand which, even in the developed countries, is proving hard to solve. Not the least part of the problem is that it creates yet another vicious circle in the Third World. Few scientists are produced since the demand for them is limited, while the setting up of enterprises needing highly qualified personnel is handicapped by the shortage of specialists.

So far as China is concerned such data as is available from 1950 to 1960 will be found in Table 42. During this period, and in quantitative terms, progress was clearly faster than in the remainder of Asia. But we know that the cultural revolution (beginning in the autumn of 1965 and intensified in 1966) brought the whole problem of secondary and higher education into question and even led to an almost complete closure of educational institutions at these levels. It was only in 1967 that such education was gradually re-started.[11] On the basis of admittedly exiguous information it appears that student numbers in 1970 were fewer than in 1960. Furthermore the kind of education was very different to what was formerly given, or is given now in the West, or even in the Soviet Union. This fact, combined with the shortage of information, makes further enquiry into such questions very uncertain.

8   *Urbanization*

Urbanization in its early manifestations is more often treated as a factor in the progress of civilization than as an outcome of economic development which made it possible. But historians, looking at the ebb and flow of urban population from the early Dark Ages onwards, saw that it provided a useful way to measure the rise and fall of prosperity in western Europe. With the coming of the industrial revolution the issue grew in size and kind: in size because in a large economically integrated unit[1] urban population for the first time could exceed 10 to 15 per cent of total population to reach at first 30 per cent and then 50 per cent within a historically short period; in kind too, because the links between urban population on one hand and industrialization and economic development on the other were becoming closer and more direct.

It is true that there is not always perfect correlation between the level of economic development and the degree of urbanization. Many diverse factors, geographical and social as well as political and historical, play their part in the pace and form taken by the concentration of population in an urban setting.[2] Thus, by choosing, say, pairs of countries with a similar general structure within the confines of Europe we can see at least three cases in which the more urbanized country is the less economically developed.[3] But after about 1930 a new phenomenon which might be termed 'urbanization without industrialization' began to appear in the Third World. This phenomenon very rapidly acquired an inflationary character and in the early 'sixties began to present most serious problems of urban unemployment and under-employment. A discussion of these particular problems will, however, be deferred until Chapter 9.

In the first section of this chapter I shall examine the question of urban development in the narrow sense of the term; in the second section I shall consider the question of whether the towns of the Third World are really, as they are sometimes described, 'cities that came too soon'.[4] The causes of the rapid acceleration in the process of urbanization will then be reviewed in the third section. The analysis of the many problems raised by the different types of urban centres in the various under-developed countries and the manner of their formation will be omitted. It is difficult to give a short account of the research done in this field because of the enormous number of such studies. By 1966 at least 300 scholars had devoted themselves to the problem of urbanization in Africa alone,[5] and Verhaegen gives no less than 2,544 references in his bibliographical study relating to Africa published in 1961.[6] All the three sections will be confined to the non-communist under-developed world for the simple reason that the problems raised by the growth of towns in communist countries are so totally different. However, I shall as before, take a very brief look at the changes which have taken place in China (section D below). The consequences of all these changes will be discussed in the next chapter which is devoted to the problems of employment.

The basic material upon which this chapter is based (with the exception of section D) comes from a study I recently completed at the request of the International Labour Office.[7] Readers with a special interest in these particular problems may find there a more detailed discussion of the issues and many more references than I have had room for here.

A. Changes in urbanization

Thanks to recent studies by the Department of Economic and Social Affairs of the United Nations, we have at our disposal a fairly exhaustive statistical analysis of changes in urban population in the different countries and regions of the world.[8] But as the figures do not go farther back than 1920 it is impossible to make use of them for a comparison between the pace of urban growth in under-developed countries and developed countries at similar stages of development. For this reason I have had to compute some figures for Europe covering the period 1850–1920 by adopting the same criteria to define urban population as those used in the United Nations survey.[9]

Two indicators are used in Table 43 to measure the pace of urbanization in different regions. The first is simply the annual average rate of growth of the urban population. However, this indicator (which is widely used) operates under a shortcoming here because to a great extent it reflects the differences in the pace of growth in total population. The second indicator shows the average rates of growth in the level of urbanization, i.e. change in the percentage of urban population as compared to total population.

Between 1920 and 1960 urban population in under-developed countries grew at an average rate of 4.0 per cent per annum, i.e. at a rate which was twice as high as that of the developed countries in a

Table 43   *Average annual rate of growth of urban population and rate of urbanization (percentage)*

	1850—1920	1920—1960	1960—2000
GROWTH OF URBAN POPULATION			
Non-communist, less developed countries	—	4.0	4.1
Africa	—	4.3	4.6
America	—	4.4	4.2
Asia	—	3.8	4.0
Developed countries[1]	2.5	1.9	1.7
GROWTH OF RATE OF URBANIZATION[2]			
Non-communist, less developed countries	—	2.3	1.6
Africa	—	2.6	1.9
America	—	2.1	1.2
Asia	—	2.2	1.6
Developed countries[1]	1.5	1.1	0.8

[1] Including East European countries
[2] Rate of urbanization = percentage of the total population living in agglomerations of 20,000 inhabitants or more
Sources: After 1920 derived from *Growth of the World's Urban and Rural Population, 1920—2000* (U.N., 1969). Before 1920, author's figures (see text).

similar period (even when the exceptional pace registered in this field by the U.S.S.R. is included). The divergence is even more noticeable if we look at variations which occurred in the rates of urbanization. Urban population in the Third World countries grew in succeeding decades by the following annual rates:

1920—1930	2.9 per cent
1930—1940	3.4 per cent
1940—1950	4.1 per cent
1950—1960	5.1 per cent
1960—1970	4.1 per cent[10]

The concentration of population in towns, like most phenomena which have an upper limit, is a logistic curve. Consequently to be significant all comparisons must relate to similar stages of development. This has been attempted in Table 44.

Before passing to a short commentary on the figures in this table, two points must be made. The first concerns changes between 1960 and 1970. The figures for 1970 are projections made by the U.N.

department of Economic and Social Affairs. These assume a marked slowing down in the pace of migration to towns in the less-developed countries. Although we must of course await the results of censuses taken around 1970 for definitive figures, it nevertheless transpires, from such partial data as we have, that such a slowing down is most unlikely to have occurred. The alternative figures which I put forward in to Table 44 have been computed on the basis of changes which will probably occur in the 34 countries forming 53 per cent of the total population in the under-developed world.

The second point concerns changes in the urbanization of under-developed countries before 1920. The few figures at our disposal suggest that the pace of urbanization before 1920 was markedly slower than between that date and 1930.

Table 44 *Comparative changes in rates of urbanization 1850–2000*

	Rates of urbanization[1] % age		Average annual growth of rate of urbanization % age	
	Europe	Less developed countries[3]	Europe	Less developed countries[3]
1850	15.0	—	—	—
1880	22.0	—	1.2	—
1900	31.0	—	1.7	—
1920	34.7	6.7	0.6	—
1930	37.2	7.8	0.7	1.6
1940	39.5	9.7	0.6	2.2
1950	40.7	12.9	0.3	2.9
1960	44.2	16.7	0.8	2.6
1970[2]	47.1	19.7 (21.0)	0.6	1.6 (2.2)
1980[2]	49.5	23.2	0.5	1.6
2000[2]	55.0	31.7	0.5	0.8

[1] Percentages of the total population living in agglomerations of 20,000 or more inhabitants
[2] United Nations predictions. The figures in brackets are the author's estimates for 1970.
[3] Non-communist
Sources: See Table 43, and text.

When in about the years 1860–70 Europe had reached a level of urban concentration of 15 per cent the rate was increasing by 1.2 per cent per annum. In the under-developed countries at the same stage, in about 1950, the increase was at the rate of 2.6 per cent. The divergence was even greater in the earlier stages. Thus in Europe, not counting England and Wales, urbanization rose from 11 per cent to 16 per cent between 1850 and 1880, which is an increase of 1.3 per cent per annum, while at the same stage in the under-developed countries the rate was 2.8 per cent. It should be said here that there is a tendency to exaggerate the effect emigration had on relieving demographic pressure in Europe. Between 1850 and 1880 the net balance of emigration from Europe can be estimated at no more than 6 per cent of the total increase in population; and, if the United Kingdom is excluded, the percentage falls to 4 per cent. This means that Europe's population, excluding the United Kingdom, would in 1880 have been only one to two per cent higher had the possibility of emigrating not existed.

We can, thus, conclude that the pace of urban concentration in the under-developed countries was in reality very rapid and not at all commensurate with that of the European countries at the time when they had reached a similar stage in their economic development.

B. Urbanization and levels of economic development

The rapidity of urbanization in the Third World — one is tempted with reason to describe it as 'urban inflation' — poses an important question. Was it, or was it not, the consequence of the speeding up of economic growth? The two phenomena had in the past been closely connected; and some developed countries, notably Russia, had experienced an even higher pace of urbanization than have the under-developed countries precisely because of the very rapid transformation of their economies. We must repeat the reservations already made about correlating levels of development and urbanization: but, nonetheless the conclusion demonstrated in many studies, both geographical and historical, is that such a correlation does exist, if the comparison is restricted to economies of one particular type.

We now have to see whether the movement of population into towns which has recently taken place in the Third World can be considered as conforming to a traditional pattern or whether it should be treated as a genuinely inflationary process producing a state of 'hyper-urbanization'.[11] Table 45 shows comparative changes in urbanization rates and proportions of the labour force employed in manufacturing industry both for Europe (excluding England) from 1850 to 1930 and for the under-developed countries from 1920 to 1970. The percentage of the population employed in manufacturing is considered to be the least objectionable of the straightforward indicators of the level of industrialization, when making comparisons on the historical and international plane.

In continental Europe the level of urban concentration remained lower than that of employment in manufacturing industry until about 1890, i.e. the moment when the percentage of persons employed in manufacturing had reached 18 per cent. Although the level of urbanization did not exceed the level of manufacturing

Table 45 *Comparison between the levels of urbanization and percentages of the active population employed in manufacturing industry*[1]

		Percentage of urban population (A)	Percentage of active population in manufacturing industry (B)	Relationship of A to B
EUROPE[2]	(excl. England)			
	1850	11	16	− 30
	1880	16	18	− 10
	1900	24	20	+ 20
	1920	29	21	+ 40
	1930	32	22	+ 45
LESS DEVELOPED NON-COMMUNIST COUNTRIES				
	1920	6.7	8.5	− 20
	1930	7.8	8.5	− 10
	1940	9.7	8.0	+ 20
	1950	12.9	7.5	+ 70
	1960	16.7	9.0	+ 85
	1970[3]	19.7	10.0	+100
	1970[4]	21.0	10.0	+110
AFRICA	1960	13.4	7.0	+ 90
AMERICA	1960	32.8	14.5	+125
ASIA	1960	13.7	9.0	+ 50

[1] Brought up to the nearest unit for rates of urban population and percentages of active European population; to the nearest half-unit for percentages of active population in the less-developed countries; and to the nearest five units for the differences.
[2] Excluding U.S.S.R.
[3] U.N. projection
[4] My own estimates
Sources: Urban population rates, see Table 43; active population, author's estimates.

employment until then, from that time onwards the gap between the two widened progressively until at the present moment it is nearly 100 per cent. In the less-developed countries this stage (i.e. equal level of urbanization and of manufacturing employment) was reached between 1930 and 1940, at a time when the percentage of workers in manufacturing industry was less than 9 per cent. Thus the gap between the two levels widened to 100 per cent in less than 30 years whereas in Europe a similar change had been spread over more than 80 years. The degree of urbanization in under-developed countries was the same in 1960 as it had been in Europe in 1880—85 when the latter's percentage of working population engaged in manufacturing was twice that of the less-developed countries.

Some part of the gap arises from the differing structure of foreign trade in the two regions. Whereas, about 1890, Europe had (as it still does) a favourable trade balance in the exchange of manufactures, under-developed countries have, for the whole period under consideration, had a large deficit in this field. Commercial activity associated with the 'exchange' of such a large quantity of manufactures and raw materials obviously requires additional urban working population, but the addition would be fewer than that needed to produce the imported manufactures locally. To enable comparisons to be made, therefore, the percentage of the labour force engaged in manufacturing in the under-developed countries would have to be increased by a certain proportion. Exactly what the proportion should be is very difficult to determine, but it may be assumed to be roughly 20 per cent. This adjustment would raise the level of the labour force engaged in manufacturing in 1970 to 12 per cent of total population. Thus, even allowing for such an adjustment, the gap between the position of the under-developed countries in 1970 and Europe's position at the moment when it was at a similar stage of urban concentration would still remain substantial.

The gap is no less evident if we use output per capita as a yardstick.[1][2] Here is the comparison expressed in this way:

	Level of urbanization	Period	National product per capita (1970 US $ and prices)
Under-developed non-communist countries	21	1970	340
Continental Europe	21	1890	650

The gap in the level of income per capita at approximately similar stages of urbanization is about 90 per cent, which is very much more than any margin of error which can be attributed to the data.[1][3] The comparisons could be refined even more, but the conclusions would be no different because insofar as the Third World is concerned the situation is one of genuine 'hyper-urbanization'.

An analysis of the causes of such a situation will be made in section C. But first of all we must take note of the very important regional differences in urbanization levels, which were evident as

Table 46 *Levels of urbanization in non-communist less-developed countries (percentages of total population in agglomerations of 20,000 or more inhabitants)*

	Africa	America	Asia	TOTAL
1920	4.8	14.4	5.6	6.7
1930	5.9	16.8	6.6	7.8
1940	7.2	19.3	8.6	9.7
1950	9.7	25.1	11.6	12.9
1960	13.4	32.8	14.5	16.7
1970[1]	16.0	37.8	17.1	19.7
1980[1]	20.0	43.1	20.6	24.2
2000[1]	28.3	53.6	28.1	32.6

[1]Projections
Sources: Derived from *Growth of the World's Urban and Rural Population, 1920–2000* (U.N., 1969).

early as 1920. Regional data can be found in Table 46 and data for individual countries in the synoptic table in the appendix.

C. Causes of urban inflation

It will be recalled that this chapter is mainly based on a study which I undertook at the request of the International Labour Office. What follows is a summary of the second chapter in that study.

The search for causes of urban inflation can be narrowed down to an investigation of the exodus from the countryside, because, even though natural population growth in cities had an important role to play, immigration has had an even greater impact. Thus we can estimate that between 1950 and 1970 migrations from rural areas have been responsible for 45 to 55 per cent of the increase in urban population in the non-communist, under-developed countries. The influence of migrations has had even greater significance on the size of the working population since from 55 to 65 per cent of the growth in the number of urban workers resulted from this cause.

Classical theories about migrations have always underlined the significance of the so-called 'push-pull' factors; and amongst the 'push' factors over-population in agricultural areas takes pride of place. If this factor is one of the most plausible explanations for internal or overseas migration in industrial countries, it is obvious that in view of high demographic pressure in the under-developed world, it would play an infinitely greater part there. International and regional differences would lend additional weight to this factor.

Which regions would be most likely to be subject to over-population cannot be revealed by simple measurements based on agricultural area per farmer. Nevertheless it is a reasonable presumption that the two phenomena are correlated even though the many other variables prevent us from isolating the correlation.

If over-population of agricultural land has pride of place amongst the 'push' factors, the higher level of urban incomes forms an essential element in the 'pull' factors.[14] An analysis of the three main methods of measuring the gap (and its changes) between incomes in town and country (national accounting, wages and household budgets) shows indeed how important it has been. The average difference between wages of agricultural and unskilled industrial labourers is roughly 80 to 150 per cent. If average agricultural wages are compared with average industrial wages the difference is between 100 and 200 per cent. But if we take incomes, the difference is only about 60 to 120 per cent. Here it should be pointed out that these figures designate not the extreme limits of the statistical spread on these three differences (and least of all the upper limit) but merely the approximate range of the average difference.

It is difficult to be sure how the gap between rural and urban incomes changed over a period of time. Most studies, without always advancing soundly based arguments,[15] conclude that the divergence increased. So far as I have been able to test this hypothesis, there is a distinct probability, although no absolute certainty, that it is correct.

The sizeable gap between urban and rural incomes is peculiar to the under-developed countries, since it is much smaller, and even in some cases non-existent, in the modern industrialized countries after their 'take off' period. Without going into the reasons for this here, it is clear that the dualistic structure of most under-developed economies is the most important cause. The general adoption of minimum wage legislation appears also to have contributed to this situation.

The maladjustment of education to real economic needs, both in a quantitative and a qualitative sense, is an almost universal problem but is accentuated in the Third World by three factors: the advanced state of contemporary technology; widespread illiteracy; and a legacy of an educational system modelled too closely on that of the erstwhile metropolitan power. Rural emigration is hastened by this educational maladjustment, as is confirmed by many studies. René Dumont's conclusion is typical: 'The number of young people who are prepared to go back to the land after more than three or four years in the classroom is infinitesimal'.[16] The following figures give, for one part of the Ivory Coast, the percentage of persons intending to emigrate, according to their educational level.[17]

	Men	Women
Illiterates	8	11
Those who can read and write	42	55
Those with school-leaving certificates	61	75

And it is more than a declaration of intent, because over 60 per cent of young people between the ages of 15 and 29 who had graduated from school had already left the area while those who remained considered their stay to be no more than a temporary one. The connexion between educational level and propensity to emigrate, especially to towns, emerges from most studies into the causes of migration in the Third World, although it is a characteristic which is not, of course, peculiar to under-developed countries alone.[18] The significance of this factor is also obvious when we recall from the previous chapter how immensely rapid expansion of education in the Third World has been.

Among other factors favouring a rapid movement of population into towns the following must be singled out: the impact of colonialism, as well as the opposite process; the inherent attractions of town life; and the existence in rural communities of social constraints of one sort or another. The latter certainly motivates a substantial number of migrants, although it ought not to be thought of as peculiar to the Third World alone, and therefore as a significant cause of its urban inflation. However, it cannot be totally ignored, particularly as the special character of many traditional rural societies in the Third World is often put forward (wrongly in my opinion) as a contrast to contemporary society in the West. It would be better if the comparison was drawn between traditional societies everywhere. But this point of view certainly does not mean that some social constraints, such as tribalism, do not favour rural emigration. The existence of tribalism makes migration between rural communities harder. It indirectly encourages migration into cities which are of course 'de-tribalized' communities *par excellence*.

The impact of colonialism on the process of urbanization is a complex one, because it is the result of phenomena working in opposite directions. As has been remarked above, until the 1950s increasing imports of manufactures — by causing handicrafts in the Third World countries to shrink — helped to put a brake on the growth of urban centres. In many countries this state of affairs was re-inforced by administrative action taken by colonial authorities to limit immigration into cities. On the other hand the creation of colonial administrations and the development of export crops were factors which led not only to the creation of new urban centres,[19] but also to the growth of older towns. Furthermore the imposition by many colonial governments of certain duties and taxes tended to favour migration. Again, in some countries, for instance in the Maghreb, the policy of colonial settlement led to the indigenous population being replaced by Europeans and this favoured a drift from the countryside. In general it appears that until 1920 the working of contrary forces more or less counter-balanced each other because the level of urbanization could not be considered excessive by the standards of the Third World as a whole. But the compensating effects did not, of course, operate at the same level in individual countries.

The breakup of colonialism, on the other hand, seems quite unequivocally to have stimulated the movement of population into towns which was the result of five main causes:

1. The breakup of colonialism was accompanied almost everywhere by an excessive administrative expansion
2. Policies of industrialization, especially those based on import substitution, caused industrial employment to increase more rapidly than hitherto.
3. In nearly all countries in which colonial powers had instituted administrative measures to limit emigration into selected urban areas, such measures were abolished or made more flexible after independence.
4. The balkanization of some colonial empires, or parts of empires, encouraged urban growth by creating new political and administrative capitals. It should be noted in this connexion that in the case of former capitals whose geographical range of influence was reduced this gave rise to unemployment.
5. In some cases political troubles caused refugee movements which enormously increased the population of some cities.

This brings us to the last factor which has been termed 'the inherent attraction of town life'. The importance of this factor has often been commented on, and rightly so. From the Greek city state to today's megalopolis via the medieval city the life of the town has attracted people in all walks of life, each man or woman finding in it some satisfaction that country life could not provide at all or could provide only partially. But what makes the modern situation so different, in the West as well as in the Third World, is that prodigious advances in communications have enabled the existence of urban facilities and satisfactions to be more widely known and therefore to be much more attractive. Aspirations towards what is thought to be a 'better' life must often play their part in the decision to move to a city, whether or not such an aspiration can be fulfilled. By abandoning rural society for that of the town, peasants hope to leave an undeveloped world, often confused with an inferior 'civilization' and to join an advanced world equally wrongly associated with a superior civilization.

The combined effect all these factors have on population movements is heavily influenced one way or another by such considerations as the existence of channels of migration, geographical distribution of urban nuclei, types of agriculture, etc.

We have finally to return to the natural growth of urban population. This was very rapid in the Third World because of two sets of factors. To begin with there were the factors which explain general population growth in the Third World, i.e. a large reduction in mortality due to the use of medical techniques without a parallel reduction in the birth rate. To these general factors we may add another: contrary to what happened in western countries, a move to a town meant in most Third World countries an increase in the expectation of life. In the West during the nineteenth century, and even in some cases during the early decades of the present century, a move to the city meant a considerable reduction in the expectation of life. The difference in the death rates by ages between urban and rural societies was so pronounced that one could almost say that city life itself became a brake on urban expansion. Throughout the nineteenth century (and before) mortality was higher in urban areas, this was due to a variety of reasons (amongst which living and working conditions were the most important). Differences between countries make it difficult to lay down any average figure for differences in mortality, but it must lie somewhere approximately within a spread of 20 to 40 per cent.[20] After all, was not the city considered a couple of hundred years ago to be the 'graveyard of the countryman'?[21] The high deathrate affected even small children, and its prevalence in city life was one of the factors that delayed a general fall in mortality.[22] In fact a higher urban mortality is still to some extent present in some western countries, although the differences between town and country at the present time are very slight. In underdeveloped countries, on the other hand, because modern medicine is more efficacious in an urban setting, urban mortality is noticeably lower than rural mortality.

Thus, as we have seen, there are many important factors which help to explain the growth of town population in the Third World. It has not been possible within the scope of the present brief survey to enquire into the causes and the pace of urbanization in individual countries since this would obviously have taken us into too great detail. However, regional evolution and projections were shown in Table 46 and recent levels of urban population for all countries for which figures are available will be found in the synoptic table (see appendix). The following section provides a very rapid sketch of urbanization in China.

D. Urbanization in China

The first point to notice is that at the beginning of the century China was far more rural than the rest of the Third World, most probably because it had never been directly colonized. Thus, in 1900 it possessed no more than eleven cities of more than 100,000 inhabitants with a total population of about 6 million people altogether. On the other hand, India, another relatively rural country with only 70 per cent of China's population, had eighteen cities of more than 100,000 inhabitants, totalling 5 million people. The population living an all agglomerations of 20,000 inhabitants and over formed 5 per cent of total Chinese population in 1920, rising to 6 per cent in 1930 and to 9 per cent in 1950; this latter figure compares with one of 12 per cent for India and one of 13 per cent for the whole of the non-communist under-developed world.

Two phases can be distinguished in the period between 1949 and 1970. The first, which came to an end with the Great Leap Forward, was marked by rapid growth. By1960 population in towns of 20,000 inhabitants or more is estimated to have been 13 per cent of the total, compared with 14 per cent for India and 17 per cent for the non-communist Third World. Between 1949 and 1961 the urban population of China rose at an average rate of 5.5 per cent per annum,[23] i.e. at a pace not so very different from that of the rest of the Third World. After 1961—62 it became more and more apparent that a new policy was being put into effect which, to begin with, i.e. during the first years years after the Great Leap Forward when agricultural production fell, took the form of returning many townspeople to the villages. From that time on the accent was on the need to re-distribute population in favour of the countryside and to establish industrial production in a large number of rural centres. Because of this policy and the measures taken to promote it, helped by the small difference (not more than 9—10 per cent) between urban and rural incomes, it is probable that there was actually a reduction in the share of urban population. In absolute terms the number of people living in cities in 1970 was most probably near what it had been in 1960, or even slightly less. Therefore, in view of the growth in total population it is likely that the rate of urbanization (defined as agglomerations of 20,000 inhabitants or more), which for 1970 can roughly be estimated at about 10—12 per cent, actually fell;[24] the comparable rate for India was 16 to 17 per cent, and for the whole of the under-developed, non-communist world was 20 to 22 per cent. Likewise it is possible to say that while the non-communist, under-developed world was becoming a town-dwelling society without industrialization, China was making strenuous efforts to achieve industrialization without urbanization.

9 *The Labour Force &*
Employment

INTRODUCTION

This chapter will be limited to the non-communist less-developed countries, firstly because of the lack of valid statistics for China and other Asian communist countries, and secondly because the problems of employment and unemployment in these countries are so very different from those of other countries. I shall divide the chapter into two sections, one dealing with the labour force as a whole and the other with the questions raised by unemployment and under-employment. But before I begin to analyse the figures, I should point out how relative and arbitrary all notions of employment and unemployment are when applied to societies of the Third World. The relative notions familiar to most readers are based on conditions which prevail in industrialized societies and differ in many respects from those in under-developed countries. I shall have to return to this point in greater detail at the beginning of section B.

A. The labour force

Without going into greater detail, we should note that the generally accepted definition of 'labour force', or active population, refers to those persons who are either gainfully employed or else unemployed but seeking work, and it does not include students, housewives, those living on their own means, or retired people. The inclusion of the armed forces varies from country to country, but in the majority of cases and for the purposes of international statistics they are included. One of the main causes of lack of uniformity, however, is the inclusion or exclusion of some women in the agricultural labour force in consideration of which the exact criteria to be used are a matter of nice distinction.

I. PAST CHANGES AND FUTURE PROJECTIONS OF TOTAL LABOUR FORCE

The increase in the size of the labour force in the under-developed countries has been less than that of total population mainly because the base of the age pyramid is getting larger as a result of the population explosion. From 1900 to 1950 the size of the economically active population in the non-communist, under-developed countries grew at an average rate of 0.8 per cent per annum. From 1950 to 1970 the rate rose to 1.7 per cent (Africa 1.6 per cent; Latin America 2.5 per cent; Asia 1.7 per cent). These are extremely high rates. By way of comparison the rate by which the European labour force rose during the nineteenth century was only 0.7 per cent per annum and the rate of growth during the second half of the eighteenth century was even lower. Because of these extremely high rates the Third World labour force multiplied 2.5 times between 1900 and 1970 rising from some 270 millions to some 660 millions. In the decades to come growth is likely to be even faster. Thus, according to recent I.L.O. projections[1] the labour force will probably increase at an annual rate of 2.4 per cent between 1970 and 1985, resulting in that period in a 43 per cent enlargement of the labour force in the under-developed countries. Growth as between wider regions is likely to be more uniform than it was in the past: 2.3 per cent in Africa, 2.4 per cent in Asia and 2.6 per cent in Latin America.

This great expansion of the labour force cannot be modified by any of the contingent measures for population control since employable persons who will enter the labour market between 1970 and 1985 were already born in 1970. Thus there are certain to be great problems ahead, although of course it is possible that our estimate of the exact scope of the problem is subject to a margin of error, more especially to mistakes in projecting death rates for adults and children and 'activity rates' (i.e. the percentage of active population to total population) for different groups. But the margin cannot be very large, and the annual rate of growth of the labour force between 1970 and 1985 will almost certainly be within the range of 2.1–2.7 per cent, equivalent to a global increase of between 37 and 50 per cent in fifteen years. In terms of jobs required, however, this growth presents enormous problems. Some 130 to 170 million new jobs will have to be created between 1970 and 1985 in order to absorb the increase in the labour force alone, without making any inroads into the existing numbers of the unemployed or under-employed. We shall have to return to this problem at a later stage.

II. THE STRUCTURE OF THE LABOUR FORCE BY BRANCH OF ACTIVITY

Details of changes in the structure of the labour force by branch of activity in the Third World (i.e., as always throughout the chapter, in the non-communist Third World) will be found in Table 47. The reader's attention is drawn to the inevitable margins of error, mostly arising from gaps in basic statistics,[2] and it must also be pointed out that the figures for 1970 are only provisional since the results of censuses made in 1970–71 are not yet available for a certain number of countries.

Table 47 *Changes in the structure of the active population of the less-developed countries between 1900 and 1970, according to type of employment*

	1900	1920	1930	1950	1960	1970
Percentages:						
Agriculture	77.9	77.6	76.6	73.3	70.7	66.0
Extractive industries		0.4	0.4	0.6	0.6	
Manufacturing industries	9.8	8.5	8.5	7.6	8.9	13.0
Construction		1.0	1.1	1.8	2.0	
Trade, banking		5.4	5.4	5.8	5.9	
Transport, communications	12.3	1.6	1.8	2.0	2.2	21.0
Services		5.5	6.1	8.9	9.6	
TOTAL	100.0	100.0	100.0	100.0	100.0	100.0
Absolute figures (millions):						
Agriculture	213.0	238.0	249.0	304.0	366.0	435.0
Extractive industries		1.1	1.3	2.5	3.2	
Manufacturing industries	26.5	26.0	27.7	31.5	46.0	85.0
Construction		2.9	3.6	7.2	10.6	
Trade, banking		16.4	17.6	24.2	30.8	
Transport, communications	33.5	4.9	6.0	8.3	11.4	140.0
Services		16.9	19.9	37.0	49.9	
TOTAL	273.0	306.0	325.0	415.0	518.0	660.0

Sources: P. Bairoch, *La structure de la population active du Tiers-Monde, 1900–1970*; but the absolute figures have been revised so as to make them correspond with the revised population figures (Chap. 1).
Note: The small extent to which the figures have been rounded up does not imply any corresponding margin of error.

(a) The structure by branch of activity around 1960–70

Before examining the main changes in the structure of the Third World's labour force by branch of activity and discussing the problem of how to absorb surplus agricultural labour, we shall analyse very briefly the situation as it has been in recent years.[3] As might be expected it reflects the low level of economic development in 1970. The labour force engaged in agriculture is slightly less than two thirds of the total: in the developed countries a comparable proportion was so occupied at the beginning of the nineteenth century, i.e. a century and a half earlier. But for more than a century the Third World has been in an active economic relationship with the already industrialized regions, with the result that the economies of the various less-developed countries have been heavily affected and distorted. The distortion has been passed on to the structure of employment and its main manifestation has been what is described as a hypertrophy of the tertiary sector of employment. It is present to a greater or lesser extent in all countries, but that it is present in the Third World as a whole is most evident. Thus, although in 1960 Third World economy, measured by the percentage of the labour force employed in agriculture, was at the same level as that of the industrialized countries of western Europe and North America around 1810, the Third World possessed the same proportion of persons employed in trade and banking as had been reached by the industrialized countries around 1890. In transport and services the corresponding period is that of 1840–50. On the other hand the proportion of the labour force engaged in the manufacturing and extractive industries is lower than it was in the advanced countries in about the year 1800. But the percentage employed in the construction industries corresponds fairly closely to the level of development reached.

The high level of tertiary employment can be explained by the excessive development of commercial activity and public services in most of the countries concerned and by the impossibility of absorbing in the secondary sector all the surplus labour from agriculture. The small proportion in manufacturing already noted results from a combination of two factors. Firstly, the less-developed countries are large net importers of manufactured goods: secondly, these countries possess factories employing mid-twentieth century techniques in which productivity is high while at the same time having a low per capita consumption, equivalent to early or mid-nineteenth century levels of consumption in the West. Where the extractive industries are concerned the low level is also explained by the advanced technology of mining enterprises mostly due to the use of modern equipment developed in the course of the last war.

It is obvious that the situation in the various countries and in the larger regions differs markedly, the best example of the difference is provided by the comparative figures of Latin America and the remainder of the Third World.[4] Around 1970 about 40 per cent of the labour force in Latin America was engaged in agriculture as against 70 per cent in Asia and 75 per cent in Africa. Tertiary hypertrophy was very advanced in Latin America: in 1970 more than 35 per cent of the labour force was employed in this sector – the same proportion as for Europe (excluding the U.S.S.R.) in about 1955. For figures relating to individual countries, the synoptic table on page 244 should be consulted.

(b) Changes between 1900 and 1970

A few words first about the changes which took place prior to 1900. The almost total absence of censuses in this period (with the exception of India and certain Latin American countries) permits only very crude extrapolations to be made, based on 1900 figures and the known facts of economic development. Thus we can postulate that in the mid-nineteenth century and the preceding decades the relative importance of the primary sector should have been about the same as it was in 1900, whereas the secondary sector, not yet much affected by the import of industrial products, should have occupied a slightly higher percentage of the labour force to the detriment of the tertiary sector.

Turning to the outstanding points of development between 1900 and 1970, we find a slight fall in the relative position of agriculture in spite of the fact that population growth led to a great increase in the absolute numbers of the agricultural labour force. Between 1900 and 1970 the labour force in agriculture more than doubled. This fact has the most weighty economic consequences, since with so little agricultural land available it meant that the area of cultivated land per agricultural worker fell by almost half. This largely explains the problems encountered in the Third World in attempting to increase agricultural productivity (see Chapter 2). We should note, however, that the reduction of the relative level of the agricultural labour force accelerated after 1950, even though because of population inflation the increase in absolute numbers of rural labourers was even higher. There was a greater rise in these twenty years than during the preceding fifty years.

Where the secondary sector is concerned we can discern a different trend in the extractive and manufacturing industries. In extractive industry employment grew in both absolute and relative terms. The change can be explained by the growing part the Third World played in world production in this sector (see Chapter 3). It will not, however, escape notice that even in 1960 this sector of employment remained relatively unimportant: 0.6 per cent of the total labour force. This explains in large part the few linkage effects which the increased exports of mineral products, which formed more than 40 per cent of total Third World exports, had on the total economy. It should also be noted that a large proportion of the labour employed in the extractive industry was engaged in activities connected with the domestic market — sand and gravel, building stone, etc. This proportion was certainly more than 50 per cent of all employment in the extractive industries. The border-line case of a sector with a low employment rate, but a high value in world exports is oil. According to my estimates, about 0.02 per cent of the total labour force of the Third World is thus employed, but it produces more than 33 per cent of the total value of exports around 1970.

The relative importance of manufactures shrank between 1900 and 1950. Without taking into account the possible distortions arising from the different criteria of censuses,[5] the fall largely reflects the disappearance of the large number of craft workshops condemned by imports of manufactures from the developed countries whose productivity was very much higher. Such growth in employment as there has been since 1950 reflects the great increase in the domestic output of the Third World in this sector (see Chapter 4). But the low relative share of manufacturing industry (probably slightly above 10 per cent in 1970) underlines the difficulties encountered by this sector in the past, which will continue to be encountered in the future in absorbing a substantial portion of the surplus rural labour force. The difficulty of absorption, moreover, helps to explain the rapid growth in the labour force in the tertiary sector. Between 1900 and 1970 absolute numbers have almost quadrupled. This brings us to a consideration of the problems of the surplus population of the countryside.

(c) The problem of the absorption of the surplus rural labour force
In considering the changes that have taken place between 1950 and 1960, and on the basis of demographic trends we can estimate that the rural labour force between these two dates has grown by about 81 million persons. But during the same period manufacturing industry has provided no more than 14 million extra jobs, while the labour force in this sector has itself, through natural increase, grown by some 7 million persons. Even by assuming, quite arbitrarily, that a quarter of the natural increase in the industrial labour force has moved on into the tertiary sector, the conclusion emerges that the growth of employment in manufacturing has not provided jobs for more than 10 per cent of the surplus rural labour force. Moreover, even this level, modest as it is, is high when compared to the change which occurred in the same field between 1920 and 1950. During those thirty years the growth of employment in manufacturing

industry had been on such a small scale that it had not even been capable of absorbing the natural increase in the labour force already at work in the sector. In fact the growth in employment had corresponded to only about one-half of the natural increase of the working population. This was bound to contribute largely to the hypertrophy of the tertiary sector of employment, though a certain amount of labour was absorbed by more rapid growth in employment in mining and particularly in construction. Computations of the same kind made for the period 1960–70 (although the figures are more provisional) allow us to conclude that, during this decade, the new jobs in manufacturing industry had absorbed about 10 to 12 per cent of the surplus labour force of the countryside.

I have made similar computations for the European countries during the first twenty years for which valid censuses of the labour force are available (usually 1840/50 to 1860/70). These reveal that the rate of absorption was from 40 to 100 per cent, with the average lying around 50 per cent. For the whole of early industrialized Europe[6] between 1880 and 1900 this rate was about 80 per cent. But in 1880 no more than 46 per cent of the labour force in this part of the world was employed in agriculture. On the basis of the above figures we can estimate that in the advanced countries the rate of absorption since the earliest phases of industrialization must have been about 30–40 per cent. The difference between rates such as these and those being achieved at the present time by the Third World is not, however, the result of faster expansion in manufacturing industry in the developed countries (on the contrary the growth of industrial production in under-developed countries is, as we saw in Chapter 4, higher at present than it was in the developed countries during the nineteenth century), but is due essentially to differences in population growth. Moreover, a theoretical calculation for the Third World between 1950 and 1960 based on the hypothesis of a population increase of 0.6 per cent per annum, in economic conditions like 1950 and postulating increases in output and productivity of the same order as occurred between 1949/51 and 1959/61, would result in a hypothetical rate of absorption of 70 per cent. By reducing the rate of growth of industrial output by 1.7 (i.e. the gap between the real growth of population: 2.3 per cent – and the one assumed here – 0.6 per cent) we still come to an absorption rate of more than 30 per cent.

The gradual improvement in the rate with which the surplus rural population of the Third World was being absorbed between 1950 and 1970 compared to the years 1920–50 should not, however, let us assume that this trend will necessarily continue in the future. On the contrary it seems to me that, in the medium term (10–15 years) we may find that the rate, already a limited one, will decline. Three factors will combine to cause this trend. First of all there is the certainty that, whatever success is achieved by the campaigns for birth control, there will still be an increase in the labour force due to the existing age structure of the poplation (see section I of this chapter). Then there is the strong probability that the rate of increase in industrial production, largely due to import substitution will slow down: indeed the limits to what is possible are already close to being achieved. Finally, there is the probability that productivity in manufacturing industry will rise faster than it has done in the past.[7]

These changes explain why, since the beginning of the 1960s the problems of unemployment, but more particularly of urban unemployment, have reached such overwhelming proportions. These problems themselves will now be examined.

B. Unemployment and under-employment

Before considering the various points in this connexion we must remind the reader that concepts of unemployment and under-employment as they have been formulated in the West cannot be applied to such very different societies except in a very crude and approximate way. In many parts of the Third World the extended bonds of kinship and the importance of alternative activities greatly ameliorate the social and economic plight of an unemployed person without taking account of the income a large part of the urban population receives from activities outside the law. On the other hand of course, since there is generally no unemployment benefit the economic plight of urban unemployed labour is worse. A further, and important, reservation is that in many, one might almost say all, traditional societies in the Third World the lack of a regular job is not necessarily felt to be a disadvantage. As Jacques Berque has rightly pointed out 'it is the intrusion of Western values that has led to a situation in which the traditional leisureliness of a peasantry becomes the joblessness of underdevelopment.'[8] It does not do, of course, to idealize the life style of the traditional society, where normal conditions for the majority were punctuated by periodic harvest failures which were as often as not followed by famine and death, and only a minority was always able to live in plenty. But it is also true that in many cases the process of colonialism caused a fall in the standard of life of a large fraction of the population, who were either dispossessed of their land or forced into cultivating plantation crops.

colonialism caused a fall in the standard of life of a large fraction of the population, who were either dispossessed of their land or forced into cultivating plantation crops.

Moreover, the notion of unemployment as we understand it today is relatively new even in the West. The very use of the word 'unemployment' in English is comparatively recent, appearing in a text for the first time in 1888.[9] In French the word for an unemployed person (*chômeur*) in the sense we use it today was first recorded slightly earlier in 1876.[10] The verb *chômer* actually comes from the low Latin *caumare* deriving from the Greek *kauma* =- burning heat. Thus *chômer* originally meant 'to rest during the heat of the day'.

As for the concept of under-employment, the criteria by which it is determined are totally subjective and strongly conditioned by historical situations peculiar to modern western society. While in most countries it is true that a certain amount of under-employment exists, it should be remembered that the criteria generally used to determine under-employment, and more especially the average norm of work which a labourer can perform, are those appropriate to a particular society at a particular stage of development. Indeed, leaving aside the changed attitudes introduced by the Reformation, it should be remembered that the industrial revolution was responsible, amongst other things, for a substantial increase in the number of hours worked during the year in both town and country.[11] In the countryside the introduction of modern methods of agriculture brought about an intensification of labour, the disappearance of the fallow, the diffusion of new crops and the integration of livestock rearing and agriculture; all these factors united to increase considerably not only productivity but also the average load of labour. The factory established in the towns had replaced the craftsman's workshop and had thereby enormously added to the number of hours worked, not to mention also lowering of the age at which the individual commenced work and increasing the pace at which he worked. During the nineteenth century, particularly the first half of the century, a working day of 14–16 hours became customary and, Sundays apart, the number of days taken off for holidays was reduced to ten or even fewer. This added up to about 300 working days per annum, or put in another way, about 4,600 hours per annum compared to less than 2,800 which had been usual in the same societies a century or two earlier.

Gradually, through a reduction in the number of hours worked per day and by introducing the annual vacation, which had replaced the many saints' and holy days of pre-industrial Europe, the advanced countries returned to an annual number of working hours approaching or even below that which had been customary before the industrial revolution. But, in assessing the level of under-employment which exists in the under-developed societies today, there is a tendency to regard the reduced number of hours now worked in the advanced countries as a situation without precedent, arising solely from higher productivity made possible by modern technology.

Another consideration which is generally overlooked is the limitations imposed by climate. Without accepting a narrow geographical determinism, there is no doubt that the tropical or semi-tropical climates of the larger part of the Third World make prolonged sessions of work less acceptable than they are in the temperate regions where most of the advanced countries are situated. This applies especially to certain seasons of the year.

There are in addition many other problems that arise from the lack of statistics or any other way of evaluating the extent of un- and under-employment, as well as from the fact that such estimates as do exist cannot be used to make comparisons. This last point, and more particularly the existence of differences between urban and rural conditions, makes it essential to examine the two sectors separately, as has been done by Turnham in his recent excellent study.[1][2]

I. RURAL UNEMPLOYMENT AND UNDER-EMPLOYMENT

Unemployment in the countryside is relatively low in the Third World, as it is in most societies. The lack of rural employment is usually reflected to a greater or lesser degree by a state of under-employment, rather than by actual overt unemployment in the modern sense of the term. If we leave out of account some isolated cases in which, often because of the way they are measured, unemployment rates are between 8 and 12 per cent, estimates for the majority of the less-developed countries mostly put rural unemployment between 3 and 5 per cent of the labour force,[13] with the average for the Third World as a whole probably lying between 3.5 and 4.5 per cent. It is pointless to make a comparison with the developed countries since figures for the eighteenth and nineteenth centuries are much too unreliable to enable us to postulate any rates which are even relatively accurate. The most one can say is that the rates should have been about the same as, or slightly below, those of the Third World at the present time.

Under-employment in the rural areas is clearly much more extensive. But in trying to find out just how extensive it is we come up against some difficulties which have not yet been satisfactorily resolved. Without returning to the basic issue of concepts we can say that there are three main ways in which the problem could be approached. The first is by trying to calculate the number of hours worked. The second approach is by determining the rural labour surplus. In this approach labour would be treated as a factor of production and an estimate of the normal labour requirements for a given agricultural output would be made. This estimate would then be set against the available labour force. There is a third approach which is, however, hardly ever used; to determine what is a 'normal' agricultural income and to compare it with actual income received.

We will not review the meagre results obtained from these three methods of investigation. Here I shall merely try to fix a possible order of magnitude for existing rural under-employment. On the basis of a rather conservative estimate a figure of 20 to 30 per cent may be put forward for the Third World as a whole,[14] although some writers, notably Ardant, put the figure as high as 50 per cent.[15] Here again, even more than for unemployment, any comparison with conditions in advanced countries at the time of their 'take off' is quite out of the question, and it should also be remembered that this chapter is restricted to the non-communist world.

II. URBAN UNEMPLOYMENT AND UNDER-EMPLOYMENT[16]

The great speed with which the process of urbanization has proceeded in the Third World was described in the preceding chapter. The most important result has been the very great deterioration of the possibilities for employment in most urban centres.[17] The number of additional workers who came onto the labour market as a consequence of migrations to towns between 1950 and 1970 can be estimated as some 60 to 70 millions. This figure is the same as, or slightly higher than, the total number of urban jobs known to exist in the year 1950.

The doubling of the urban working population occurring between 1950 and 1970 has created an employment situation so unfavourable that it was bound to be reflected by the under-employment in the tertiary and other sectors of the labour force, and by an unemployment rate which climbed in most countries to an unacceptably high level. I have been able to assemble some figures for the 34 less-developed countries for different dates mostly between 1964 and 1968 although they are unfortunately both incomplete and not strictly comparable. Urban unemployment in four of these countries was 20 per cent and over; in eight countries it was 15 to 20 per cent; in eight more it was 10 to 15 per cent; and in the remaining fourteen it was almost invariably above 5 per cent. These rates would probably be enhanced if the statistics were more uniform. Thus in nine cases the urban rates are those for the capital cities, whereas it seems to be a general rule that unemployment rates in capital cities are lower than they are in other urban centres.[18] Due to the scarcity of available statistics, it is difficult to determine the exact changes in the urban unemployment rates in recent years. What is almost certain is that between 1950 and 1970 the rates definitely increased, since the situation at the beginning of the period was, generally speaking, much better. The period when conditions deteriorated most was probably between 1950 and 1960/65. It should be noted, nevertheless, that beyond a certain point a deterioration of the labour market will be reflected more by an increase in under-employment than by rising unemployment rates.

It is possible to try to fix a rough order of magnitude for the absolute number of urban unemployed in the under-developed countries. Assuming an average urban unemployment rate of 12 per cent for 1970 and of 11 and 10 per cent respectively for 1960 and 1950 and an activity rate in urban areas of about 50 per cent, we find the following changes in the number of urban unemployed:

1950	6–8 millions
1960	11–13 millions
1970	20–24 millions[19]

It is more than likely that the real changes were more dramatic than these figures suggest. The actual range could lie between the lowest figure for 1950 and the highest figure for 1970. It should also be pointed out that, taking a somewhat wider definition of an urban area i.e. one based on the various national definitions, the unemployment figures quoted above would be even greater: from 20 to 32 per cent (according to whether we postulate the unemployment rates of the smaller towns representing either 70 or 100 per cent of the unemployment rates prevailing in the larger towns). If we include these urban areas the estimated number of urban unemployed in 1970 goes up to between 25 and 32 millions. (It should be recalled again that the chapter is limited to the non-communist Third World.)

The situation is aggravated by the fact that unemployment bears particularly heavily on young people. Indeed, on the basis of figures which are very significant although admittedly not complete, it appears that unemployment in the 15 to 24 age group is twice the average, which is itself, of course, affected by the massive inclusion of the youthful unemployed. Out of seventeen countries for which Turnham[20] has assembled such figures, three have unemployed rates amongst young people near to or above 40 per cent; five have rates of 20 to 29 per cent; another five have rates from 10 to 19 per cent; and only two countries have rates less than 8 per cent.

Another serious feature is that the urban unemployed person in the Third World is nearly always one who has had an average education, i.e. a young person who has completed six to eleven years of schooling. The highest unemployment rates are to be found in this catagory. Next comes the group who has had only a primary education, or one to five years of schooling; then comes the illiterate group and only lastly the group whose education has continued beyond the secondary level.

Before passing on to discuss urban under-employment it should be emphasized that the magnitude of the problem is unique to the Third World countries. Leaving aside the modern period when urban employment in industrialized countries is, of course, very low, it should be noted that even at the end of the nineteenth century — the earliest period for which we possess relevant figures — the situation of employment in western towns was always much better. In round figures urban rates of unemployment in Great Britain were about 6—7 per cent; in Germany 4—5 per cent; in France 5—6 per cent; and in the United States probably 3—4 per cent.

Without in any way attempting to idealize the deplorable conditions which prevailed amongst the labouring classes of the towns during the 'take off' period in western societies, it appears likely, in the light of the figures presented above and corroborated by other information of a non-quantitative kind, that the average degree of 'unemployment' was much lower than that which now prevails in the cities of the Third World. However, unemployment rates probably fluctuated more in the course of the nineteenth century than they do in the Third World at the present time. One might almost say that urban unemployment during the 'take off' of the western world was cyclical rather than structural.

In considering the problem of urban under-employment we must first of all recall how arbitrary it is to apply such a concept to under-developed societies. But, even ignoring this, it is clear that the definition and criteria which have to be accepted before we can estimate levels of under-employment are almost as varied as the estimates themselves. This is why all the facts have to be treated with such extreme reserve and why we have to be particularly on our guard when it comes to drawing international comparisons from the very few figures we are going to provide.

The available estimates reveal very high rates of urban under-development in Latin America, ranging from 20 per cent for Panama to 28 per cent for Chile, with one exception, Argentina, where the rate is probably only 17 per cent.[21] Estimates of urban under-employment for other areas are even fewer, but in general the rates are lower. On the global level there is one good general indicator of the degree of urban under-employment.[22] This is the hypertrophy of the tertiary sector which I have already mentioned, and which is such a feature of the vast majority of under-developed countries. It is rather unwise to attempt to attach any order of magnitude to urban under-employment in the Third World as a whole, but in very broad terms one might say that the possible range lies between 10 and 25 per cent.

*   *   *

Thus the labour situation is very grim and the outlook for the future is even grimmer. We may assume that in 1970 genuine total unemployment, i.e. unemployment in the narrow sense of the word, together with under-employment, expressed as involuntary in-activity, probably affected some 20 to 30 per cent of the labour force, i.e. between 130 and 200 million persons in the non-communist Third World. But between 1970 and 1985 the labour force is likely to increase by another 270—290 million souls. Therefore, if we wish to reduce real unemployment to a tolerable level (say 10 per cent) no less than 350—400 million *new* jobs will have to be created in the Third World within the next fifteen years. This means a number similar to that which was created during the previous 80 to 120 years.

The staggering immensity of the problem cries out for some original solutions and in this respect, at least, it is well to note that, mainly due to the efforts of the International Labour Office,[23] there are some signs of an awakening of the world's conscience to the terrible implications for the economic future of the under-developed world.

Macro-Economic Data

INTRODUCTION

I had originally itended to devote more space to this chapter than I have finally done, but after scrutinizing the statistics in greater detail I have decided to shorten my study. Indeed it has seemed to me that because the estimates for some countries are uncertain and for many others entirely lacking, any lengthy treatment of the subject must be largely arbitrary. The chapter will consist of three parts:

A. Capital formation and imports of capital equipment
B. Financial aid
C. Growth and level of national product or national income

A. Capital formation and imports of capital equipment

The two following topics will be briefly considered under the headings: changes in the rate of capital formation; and capital equipment as a share of imports.

I. CHANGES IN THE RATE OF CAPITAL FORMATION

Rates of capital formation should, theoretically speaking, provide us with an indicator of the effort made by various countries to achieve economic growth, but unfortunately several factors combine to reduce the value of this indicator. First of all there is a considerable margin of error, especially where agricultural investment is concerned. Knowing the difficulties of trying to compile measurements of this kind for the developed countries, one has to be even more cautious when it comes to the under-developed countries. Furthermore, although the capital formation rate gives us some indication of the relative size of the collective effort, the extent to which the effort has been successful must also be measured and here the gaps are even more obvious. Again, speaking theoretically, the capital-output ratio should give us a yardstick of this success, but it turns out to be difficult to detect to what degree the differences between the countries are due directly to the different margins of error. We calculated some years ago the capital-output ratio for twenty-seven under-developed countries during the period 1954—60. The range lay between 2.6 and 10.0 with an average of 4.4 for nineteen of the countries where the margin of error was least. For these reasons great caution must be exercised when considering the data relating to capital formation rates for the three different periods beginning with 1950, which have been computed in Table 48. (Data prior to 1950 is lacking for almost every country.)

Making due allowance for these warnings, the following points can be deduced from the table. So far as changes are concerned we can see a divergence between the Latin-American countries and the rest of the Third World. The capital formation rate of the Latin-American countries rises from 1950 to 1960 and tends to fall from 1960 to 1970. The changes for the other under-developed countries are slightly more favourable, for in them the number of cases of a rise have exceeded the number of cases of a fall. But, again generally speaking, the change between 1950 and 1960 appears to have been more favourable than the one between 1960 and 1970.

Because of the reservations made above, I shall not attempt to draw any conclusions as to the actual rates of capital formation. In order to put the problem of the modern Third World in its historical perspective I shall simply note that the advanced countries were able to 'take off' with much lower capital formation rates than the under-developed developed countries of today, since their rates ranged from 5 to 10 per cent. Since population growth was very low these investment levels were sufficient to generate economic growth. On the other hand, the capital formation rates in the developed countries are, at the present moment, generally higher than in the under-developed countries, as – with a few exceptions – they exceed 20 per cent. The higher rate of capital formation combined with the lower population growth help to explain the widening gap between per capita incomes in the developed countries and in the Third World countries. This gap will be discussed in section C (IV) below.

Before passing on to the next section we shall deal very briefly with capital formation in China. On the basis of Eckstein's computations made to fit Chinese statistics into the framework of western accounting, it appears that fixed capital formation formed 10.3 per cent of the Gross Domestic Product in 1952 and about 13 per cent in 1957.[1] In the period of the Great Leap Forward rates were higher, as is evident from Hollister's estimates.[2] These show gross fixed capital as a percentage of Gross National Product to be 12.4 per cent for 1952 (5.5 per cent for 1950); 15.9 per cent for 1957; 23.9 per cent for 1958; and 25.7 per cent for 1959. Pre-1958 rates are similar to those of other under-developed countries. Thus it would seem, assuming the faster growth achieved (see below), that

Table 48 *Changes in rates of capital formation
1950–1968/70* (rates of gross fixed capital
formation as percentages of GDP in current
prices)

	1950	*1959–1961*	*1968–1970*
AFRICA			
Ghana	–	20	11
Kenya	–	17	19
Morocco	19[2]	10	14
Nigeria	6	12	15[4]
Sudan	–	12	12[4]
Tunisia	–	18[3]	22
Zaïre	21	15	26
Zambia	–	21	25
AMERICA			
Argentina	20	21	19
Brazil	15	17	16
Chile	9	16	15
Colombia	14	18	19
Ecuador	9	14	15
Guatemala	10	10	14
Mexico	12	15	19
Peru	15	18	12
Venezuela	26	20	24
ASIA			
Ceylon	9	15	18
India	8	14	15[4]
Pakistan	–	12	13[4]
Indonesia[5]	–	10	11
Philippines	11	13	19
Taiwan	11[1]	16	22
Thailand	12[2]	14	24
MIDDLE EAST			
Egypt	–	16	12
Iran	–	16	20
Syria	–	15	15
Turkey	10	15	19

[1] 1951   [2] 1952   [3] 1960/61   [4] 1967/69
[5] Including increase in stocks
Sources: Derived from the following U.N. publications (various years):
*Economic Survey of Latin America, Etude sur la situation économique
de l'Asie et de l'Extrême-Orient,* and *Monthly Bulletin of Statistics;* also
National Accounts of Less-developed Countries, 1950–1966 and *Latest
Information on National Accounts of Less-developed Countries*
(Development Centre of O.E.C.D., Paris, various years).

the efficiency of investment was greater in China. Eckstein himself comes to this conclusion, especially when comparing Chinese and Indian figures. But the data is too uncertain for us to be able to extract any valid conclusions in this connexion.

II. CAPITAL EQUIPMENT AS A SHARE OF IMPORTS

A good measure of the level of development a country has achieved is its degree of dependence on the outside world for its capital equipment, although, as is always the case with individual indicators, it does not provide by itself a wholly balanced picture. The results of calculations made to estimate the share of imports in the domestic consumption of capital equipment can be seen in Table 49. To express it in another way, I have put the total represented by capital equipment (including transport equipment, but not private cars) as it emerges from estimates of the structure of fixed capital equipment, against the total represented by imports of the same products. To reduce the effects of annual fluctuations and the delays between the date when equipment was imported and when it was put into service, the percentage has been calculated on a three-year average. The omission from our calculations of exports of capital equipment can be justified by the negligible value of this item in the foreign trade of the Third World countries. Thus in 1970 for all under-developed countries together, imports of machinery amounted to a total value of more than 19 billion dollars, while exports formed no more than one billion (of which more than 500 million dollars were destined for other under-developed countries).

The number of countries included in Table 49 is limited because complete data for most under-developed countries is lacking. In interpreting the percentages quoted in the table we have to allow for the fact that the unit value of capital equipment – as seen in estimates of capital formation – is higher than appears in import statistics, since it includes various supplementary costs (profit margins, transport, handling and erecting costs, etc.). The difference means that import rates should really be increased by a certain percentage, but to determine exactly what this should be is not easy, although one can safely say it would exceed 10 per cent.

The figures in Table 49 show the overwhelming part imported equipment plays in the capital formation of the Third World, especially if we exclude certain countries such as Burma, Tunisia, the Philippines and Uganda whose low rates should be ascribed to a statistical bias rather than to a more advanced level of development.

Table 49   *Share of imports in the gross capital
formation of machinery and transport
equipment*

COUNTRY	1954–1956	1961–1963	1968–1970
Argentina	—	58[3]	21
Burma	57	47	—
Ceylon	122	66	64[7]
Chile	—	—	40
Egypt	—	61	42[7]
El Salvador	—	64	70[7]
Ghana	103[1]	96	101
Honduras	85	86	105[7]
India	—	35	26[7]
Jamaica	—	62	39
Korea S.	—	65[6]	82
Malaysia	—	110[5]	—
Mexico	—	55	44[7]
Morocco	—	82[2]	88
Nigeria	84	94	71[8]
Panama	—	66	65
Philippines	69	53	92
Sudan	—	104[4]	61[7]
Syria	—	—	68
Tunisia	—	50	68[9]
Turkey	—	64	39
Uganda	—	67	—

[1]1955–57 [2]1960–61 [3]1960–62 [4]1962 [5]1962–63
[6]1962–64 [7]1967–69 [8]1966–68 [9]1966–67
Sources: Author's estimates (see text for method of calculation).

Statistical bias is also responsible for any rates that are higher than
100 per cent. If allowance is made for this factor and for the
divergences in unit costs, it appears that about 90 per cent of capital
equipment used in the Third World is at present imported.

The limited number of dates in the series does not permit a
meaningful trend to emerge. Likewise the lack of statistical uniformity makes any conclusion based on the differences between one
country and another too uncertain to be useful. The average rate
quoted above (90 per cent) provides the only comparison with the
developed countries of any real value. As far as the modern period is
concerned, we can see that nearly all essential capital equipment in
the developed countries is of local origin. For example, in France
imports form only 2 per cent of equipment in use and exports 2.4
per cent. Even if we look at the figures for some developed countries
which are relatively less industrialized we can see that the deficit in
the foreign exports of capital equipment when compared to domestic

consumption of these goods is still a small one. In Italy imports form 26.7 per cent and exports 25.1 per cent; while in Denmark imports represent 55.0 per cent and exports 44.9 per cent (both these examples are for the same period, i.e. 1961–63).

As far as the 'take off' period of the developed countries is concerned I have made an estimate for France[3] which suggests that between 1825 and 1875 imports formed less than 2 per cent of total consumption of capital equipment. English export statistics (England was the principal source of exports of capital equipment at that period) suggest that the French situation was typical of all other European countries. Even in Japan the percentage between 1914 and 1936 was no more than 15 per cent.

The gap thus revealed between the situation in the Third World countries and the developed countries makes it possible first to delineate the different paths of development taken by these two groups of economies, and secondly to lay bare the implications for economic growth inherent in foreign dependence. The manufacture of equipment played a major part in the 'take off' of the western countries in diffusing among them the effects of industrialization. I shall not elaborate here on why there was such differences; I shall merely point out that the causes can be sought in the development of technology and the reduction of transport costs.[4]

B. Financial aid

In this section we shall concentrate mainly on changes that have taken place, although there will be a brief account of how aid was and is distributed geographically.

I. GENERAL CHANGES

The more or less arbitrary way in which financial aid is defined obviously makes it hard to determine its precise volume. Without going into technicalities, however, it can be said that, apart from grants (in cash and in kind) narrowly defined, financial aid consists for the most part of a net flow of loans of more than a year's duration (approximately 30 per cent of total aid); investment and loans from the private sector (approximately 27 per cent); and guaranteed export credits (approximately 12 per cent). Thus, exclusion of the three last categories, reduces the amount of the aid given to the under-developed countries by about 70 per cent, leaving only about 30 per cent to be represented by grants and grant-like contributions. It should also be pointed out that whereas repayments of capital made by recipient countries are deducted from the amounts of net aid this is not true of the interest charges on loans.

Thus we can see that the concept of 'aid' includes a collection of elements which it is very difficult to consider objectively as 'real' aid, at least in their total amount. The determination of the size of 'real' aid as opposed to what should more properly be called 'flow of financial resources to less-developed countries,' is an extremely delicate and to some extent arbitrary matter. Tibor Mende's recently published study[5] explores the intricacies of the question in a very suggestive manner. According to him, the 'rump' that can genuinely be called aid is no more than about 22—25 per cent of the flow of financial resources to less-developed countries. This conclusion seems to me quite realistic and the figure should therefore be borne in mind throughout the discussion that follows.

The estimates of the size of the flow of financial resources to the under-developed countries come from two principal agencies. The first is the United Nations and the International Monetary Fund and the second is the O.E.C.D. Material for both is based on question-naires addressed to donor countries and on estimates complementing these. Slightly different methods are used to construct the estimates themselves and this leads to divergences between the two sets of figures, the O.E.C.D. total being about one billion dollars higher than the U.N. one. It seems likely that if the definition of foreign aid adopted by both institutions is adhered to, the O.E.C.D. estimate appears to be the more accurate of the two because it does not leave out of account transactions within certain monetary unions. It is this estimate, therefore, that I have mainly used in constructing Table 50. From this table it is possible to trace the development of foreign aid since its beginnings in the 'fifties. Owing to the fact that a large part of the Third World prior to 1950 was still subject to a colonial regime, the notion of 'aid' is not applicable to that period, especially as the data relating to financial transfers in that period is not available.

Before going on to analyse the figures in the table it should be pointed out that they include foreign aid given to some European countries which O.E.C.D. considers to be under-developed (Greece, Spain, Turkey and Yugoslavia) and which are not included in the definition usually accepted here. The sum received by these countries has on average been 6—7 per cent of the total given in the table.

The annual total of the flow of financial resources rose from approximately 4.5 billion dollars at the beginning of the 'fifties to about 16.6 billion dollars for 1969/71, i.e. an average increase of

Table 50   *Net flow of financial resources to non-communist less-developed countries*[1] (yearly averages; billions of U.S. dollars and percentages)

	From public sector[3]	From private sector	TOTAL	Breakdown of total per origin in percentage		
				Western countries		Eastern countries
				Direct	Multilateral agencies	
1950–55	1.9	2.6	4.5	97	2	1
1956–59	3.8	3.0	6.8	93	5	2
1960–62	5.7	2.7	8.4	93	4	4
1963–65	6.8	3.2	10.1	89	8	3
1966–68	7.6	4.3	11.9	89	8	3
1969–71[2]	9.3	7.3	16.6	91	7	1.7

[1] Including European less-developed countries (see text).
[2] Excluding grants made by private voluntary agencies, which amount yearly to some 0.8 billion for this period; no comparable data available for previous periods.
[3] Including multilateral agencies and communist countries.
Sources: Derived from various issues of *Development Assistance* of the O.E.C.D. and *Flow of Financial Resources and Liberalization of Terms and Conditions of Assistance* (UNCTAD, Geneva, 1971, roneo-ed).

about 6.5 per cent per annum. This rise comes mainly from the public sector. Although the latter's starting figure was very low, it increased from less than 2 to over 9 billion dollars during the same period, i.e. by 8.5 per cent per annum. Furthermore it should be noted that the main part of the rise occurred during the decade 1950–60. Since then the growth of aid from the public sector has considerably slowed down and the main part of the growth in total aid has come from the private sector, a fact to which we shall return later. Public aid should not be lumped together with grants, since the latter provided only a fraction of aid, a fraction, moreover, which has shown a marked tendency to fall. Thus, for public aid from countries of the D.A.C.[6] 'bilateral grants and contributions assimilated to grants' fell from 77 per cent in 1960/62 to 48 per cent in 1969/71. And it is once more necessary to insist on the relative nature of some grants (see in this connexion T. Mende's book referred to above).

The figures quoted above and in Table 50 are in current dollars. In constant dollars actual performance appears more limited. The problem here consists in the choice of deflator. O.E.C.D. calculated its deflator for the period 1960–70[7] on the basis of the structure of aid and corresponding price indices which resulted in a price increase of only 19 per cent (or 1.7 per cent per annum). This is a much lower rate than the rise of domestic prices within the developed countries (about 3.5 per cent per annum), but it is higher than the rise of import prices into the developing countries which increased by 1 per cent per annum in the same period. However the validity of price indices for foreign trade is questionable. If we apply the deflator used to calculate the Gross Domestic Product of the developed countries, the volume of total aid appears to increase between 1959/61 and 1966/70 at an average annual rate of 2.3 per cent which is much lower than the rate of growth of the volume of Gross Domestic Product in the developed countries.

Moreover the relative size of the aid as a percentage of the Gross National Product (at market prices) of the developed countries who are also members of the D.A.C. was only 0.76 per cent for the years 1969/71 as against 0.88 per cent for the years 1960/62. This means that the objective (one per cent of Gross Domestic Product) adopted by the second U.N. Conference on Trade and Development (U.N.C.T.A.D.) in New Delhi in 1968 has not been achieved, and, as will be pointed out in the next chapter this objective in itself was a very modest one.

The percentage obviously varies from country to country; the highest percentage contributed by any great power is from France where it is almost twice the average. Contributions from the other large countries are around the average figure.[8] Even without going into the question of what is the real cost of the aid to the donor states, the level of aid is extremely low, especially if it is remembered that a large part of the aid returns to the donors either in the form of orders or of salaries for the specialists and the administrative and technical personnel. These factors, if taken into account, would depress the real level of aid even further.

The rapid growth during recent years of aid from the private sector will be noted in Table 50. This growth is due very largely to the rise in export credits which have mounted from 0.5 billion dollars in 1960 to 2 billion dollars in 1970. As a consequence private investment has grown more slowly.

The proportion formed by aid in comparison with the Gross Domestic Product of the under-developed countries must now be examined. We have estimated[9] the G.D.P. of the non-communist developing world at market prices to be 390 billion dollars for 1969/71. This means that total aid has amounted to 4.0 per cent of the G.D.P. (and grants amount to about 1 per cent). Thus, although aid does not appear much when compared to the resources of the donor states, it forms a significant fraction of the domestic product of the under-developed countries, given the wide gap between average levels of income. It is true that aid seems puny when set against the enormous needs created by the population explosion, since with a capital-output ratio of 4.5 (which seems the most likely figure) existing aid would only be sufficient to absorb one-third of the current population growth of 2.7 per cent even if it were devoted wholly to investment.

Here, of course, we are faced with the vast and insoluble problem of determining how efficacious aid is. In some respects however, the problem is misconceived, since it would be arbitraty to try to isolate expenditures made within the total of the money flowing from foreign aid. Thus the fact that aid has been used to purchase consumption goods or for sumptuary expenses certainly does not imply, *a priori*, that the aid has been of no use, since it is easy to imagine a hypothetical case in which such transactions could release for profitable investment other resources which would have had to be used for expenditures cf this kind if the aid had not been available. It is also possible to envisage the reverse case. In actual fact the problem of determining the efficacity of foreign aid is indissoluble from that of determining the efficacity of the allocation of total national income and public expenditure. It cannot, therefore, be discussed within the framework of this study, since a complete analysis of conditions in each country would be needed and this, for most of the countries in question, is impossible because, as we know, the necessary statistics simply do not exist.

Before passing on to a brief discussion of the geographical distribution of aid a few words must be said about the foreign public debt of the developing countries. The debts mainly arise from past financial aid and are of truly heroic proportions. For the whole of the non-communist, developing world the foreign debt (public debt or debts guaranteed by the state, not yet amortized and repayable in one year or more) grew rapidly by 15 per cent per annum between 1955 and 1962 and by 12 per cent between 1962 and 1970.[10] From less than 10 billion dollars at the end of 1955 these debts have mounted to about 60 billion by the end of 1970. As debts continue to rise much faster than exports from these countries, the servicing of these debts which, in 1955, formed 4 per cent of export receipts, formed 10 per cent by 1970. Thus the reverse of the medal is negative since the servicing of foreign debt amounted to over 5 billion dollars by 1970.[11]

II GEOGRAPHICAL DISTRIBUTION OF FINANCIAL AID

An approximate picture of the geographical distribution of aid provided to the developing countries by the West can be seen from the statistics of the net flow received from the public sector of the D.A.C. countries. Figures below relate to the annual average for 1969/71. We can see that the distribution of resources to the different countries, expressed in dollars per capita, is very unequal, but the average for all undeveloped countries is $4.4.

For the three big non-communist countries of Asia the per capita figures are $1.7 for India, $3.5 for Pakistan and $3.9 for Indonesia. The figures are much higher for South Korea ($10.6), and South Vietnam ($25.8); and lower for the Philippines ($2.2), Thailand ($2.6) and Sri Lanka ($4.2).

In Africa rates for Botswana ($24.2), Congo (Brazzaville) ($22.8), and Tunisia ($24.6) are amongst the highest. The rates for Tanzania ($4.2), Nigeria ($1.8), and Ethiopia ($1.9) are amongst the lowest. Figures for some other important countries are: Ivory Coast ($11.2), Algeria ($8.7), Morocco ($7.0) and Zambia ($5.0).

In the Middle East the two extremes are represented by Israel ($22.3) and Jordan ($26.6) on the one hand, and by Libya and Saudi Arabia, where repayments are greater than receipts, on the other. Other figures are Turkey ($6.7), Iraq ($0.9), Syria ($2.9) and Iran ($1.3).

In Latin America the range between highest and lowest is narrower. The highest figures are Panama (16.1), Dominical Republic ($12.0) and Guyana ($24.4). The lowest are for Mexico ($2.9), Brazil ($2.8) and Argentina ($2.8).

As a general rule we may formulate the following 'law.' The size of public aid received per capita is a function of:

(a) the size and population of the country. The more populated a country is the smaller in general will be the level of per capita aid. This situation seems to result from the fact that in practice there is a floor and a ceiling to the total amount of aid. The floor favours little countries and the ceiling is unfavourable to the very big countries: and

(b) the political complexion of the government. In this case the law works in a more complicated way. Minimal amounts are obviously directed towards the countries totally opposed to the donor states; nevertheless some countries very closely connected with donor countries can also be found near the minimum level. Maximum amounts are received either by the 'friendly' countries whose political or military stability is thought to be precarious, or by countries who are more or less neutral and to whom aid is directed in an attempt to prevent them from going over to the opposite camp.

C. Growth and level of per capita product or national income

We shall now examine the economic growth of the less-developed countries as expressed in changes in their Gross Domestic Product. In spite of some obvious imperfections in these estimates, it still remains true that the growth rate of G.D.P. per capita at constant prices provides the least objectionable of all individual indicators capable of reflecting general economic expansion.[12]

The present analysis will be limited to the developing countries as a whole and to the larger geographical regions. Where individual countries are concerned figures giving the annual rate of growth of G.D.P. between 1960 and 1970 at constant market prices will be given in the synoptic table on page 244. The 1970 level of the per capita aggregate expressed in dollars will also be given. We shall examine such figures for mainland China as are available in order to compare them with those for non-communist Asia. The sections will end with a description of changes in levels of per capita G.D.P. between 1900 and 1970.

I. RATE OF GROWTH OF GROSS PRODUCT IN NON-COMMUNIST LESS-DEVELOPED COUNTRIES

The U.N. statistical offices calculate indices of G.D.P. for the larger groups of non-communist, developing countries, the exclusion of the communist countries being explained on the one hand by the different methods of calculating the aggregates and, on the other hand, by the lack of recent figures for China. The series goes back to 1950. I have completed the figures with estimates made by L. J. Zimmerman.[13] I have calculated weighted averages for Asia and the under-developed countries as a whole since such computations were not made in the Zimmerman series. It should be noted that the total for the less-developed countries is, in this instance, formed by the sum of the Latin American countries plus Asia; the Middle Eastern and African countries being left out. The omission does not distort the results to any great extent, for the countries left out form only 20 per cent of the total and their average lies close to the average of the whole.

We should note, however, that the two series are not strictly comparable since Zimmerman's series is based on national income and the U.N.'s on G.D.P. Moreover the figures relating to the period 1900–54 are obviously subject to a larger margin of error than the more recent U.N. ones. Nevertheless, as the point at issue is solely the rates of growth, the two series are, for this purpose, reasonably comparable. It goes without saying that the margins of error in Zimmerman's series are larger since the figures available for the early period are less reliable. This is also true for the developed countries in the same period, although the amount of information and statistical estimates available for these countries are immeasurably greater and more precise than for most of the Third World countries. But this does not mean that the U.N. series does not also contain any margin of error. The latter arises not so much from the method of calculation, as from errors in the basic figures used.[14] Furthermore, as we shall see below, there is the problem of the accuracy of the computations. For all these reasons too much importance should not be attached to the fact that the rates of growth I have calculated are given with one figure after the decimal point. The results of these calculations are given in Table 51.

The rates of growth at constant prices in the table show that the growth fell into two quite distinct periods. The first stretches from the beginning of the century until the end of the second world war and is marked by a regular rate of growth in the under-developed countries of about 2 per cent. But, as at the same time population growth was accelerating, it resulted in a continuous fall in the per

Table 51   *Annual rates of change in the Gross Domestic Product per capita* (at constant prices)

	All non-communist less-developed countries		LATIN AMERICA		ASIA excluding communist countries	
	Total	Per capita	Total	Per capita	Total	Per capita
1900–1913[1]	2.1	1.2	2.1	0.3	2.2	1.5
1913–1929[1]	1.9	0.9	2.8	1.0	1.3	0.8
1929–1952/54[1]	2.2	0.6	3.5	1.4	1.1	−0.3
1950–1960	4.8	2.4	5.4	2.5	4.1	2.0
1960–1970	5.1	2.4	5.5	2.5	4.8	2.1

[1] These are National Income series; African and Middle Eastern countries are excluded (see text).

Sources: 1900–1959 derived from L. J. Zimmerman, 'The distribution of world income 1860–1960' in *Essays on Unbalanced Growth* ('s Gravehage, 1962); 1950–1970 derived from *Statistical Yearbook* for 1970 and 1971 (U.N.); *World Bank and I.D.A. Annual Report 1972* (Washington, 1972) and *Development Assistance 1972* (O.E.C.D., 1972).

capita rates of growth: 1.2 per cent from 1900 to 1913; 0.9 per cent from 1913 to 1929; and 0.6 per cent from 1929 to 1952/54. The latter rate would be a little lower if the years 1945/48 were taken as a terminal point instead of 1952/54. Growth during this period was definitely higher in the Latin-American countries than in the Asian countries except for the years 1900–13.

During the second period there was a very great increase in the pace of growth beginning approximately at the end of the war. Global rates were nearly 5 per cent per annum and per capita rates about 2.4 per cent per annum. Here, we obviously encounter the problem of how truthfully this change in the growth curve reflects reality. Thus, in the period 1955–70 and for the non-communist less-developed countries taken as a whole, there was, according to the U.N. figures, an annual increase of 2.4 per cent in the G.D.P. per capita at constant prices. But, I have already been able to show from my own calculations made in Chapter 2 that agricultural productivity remained stable in the developing countries between 1953/57 and 1968/72, and that this probably led to a stagnation in the per capita income of the rural population which, as we have seen, forms about 70 per cent of total population. In such conditions the increase in the real income of the remainder of the population (especially that part engaged in industry) would have had to be very large indeed, even allowing for the fact that the average income of the non-agricultural section of the population is higher than it is for the agricultural population.

We saw in the chapters devoted to the manufacturing and extractive industries that both these sectors experienced a substantial expansion – 4.1 per cent per capita for manufacturing, and more for extractive industry (the latter however of minor importance). If we assume that growth in the services sector was as rapid as in industry and that average income in industry and services together was five times that in agriculture, this would account for the global rates of growth exhibited in the U.N. figures. But this assumed gap between the agricultural and non-agricultural income is clearly too great; so it seems probable that growth rates of per capita G.D.P. in the under-developed countries have been slightly over-estimated. This over-estimation does not originate in the computations made by the U.N. statistical office but in over-estimates of growth made in a large part of the under-developed world. The existence of this over-estimate is confirmed by Kuznets' recent study,[15] in which he makes certain computations and estimates intended to remove some of the statistical biases appearing in the U.N. calculations of growth in per capita output for the period 1954–58 to 1964–68. So far as the developing countries are concerned Kuznets concludes that the annual growth rate in the volume of per capita output was only 1.06 per cent instead of 2.21 per cent. On the other hand, he concludes that for the developed countries the growth rate was under-estimated: the figure should be over 4.0 per cent rather than 3.38 per cent.

If we look at the difference in the (uncorrected) rates of growth in the larger regions we can observe that (as happened earlier in the century) growth was slightly faster in Latin America than in Asia. In Africa, where before 1960 the figures are too fragmentary to be used individually, growth between 1960 and 1970 was even more sluggish than in Asia, with the annual growth rate of the volume of output per capita being 2.0 per cent.

On the other hand the inequalities of growth as between individual countries and social groups must be underlined. Regarding the inequalities between countries it should be sufficient to refer to the synoptic table at the end of the book. The inequalities between social classes is a much more serious problem. Although it is not possible to form a judgement from statistics alone, it seems very likely that in most cases only a few classes relatively favoured to begin with profited from economic growth, thus making the distribution of income even more unequal. The data on agricultural productivity which I have assembled is an indication of changes of this kind. But we must await the collection of more reliable and more abundant statistics on income distribution before we can make positive and explicit statements about it.[16]

II. COMPARISONS WITH DEVELOPED COUNTRIES

Let us now look briefly at the relationship between growth rates of G.D.P. in the advanced and in the less advanced countries. It may be accepted that in the first phases of industrialization (roughly during the nineteenth century) growth rates were between 1.5 and 2.5 per cent per annum for total gross product and between 0.5 and 1.5 per cent for per capita gross product, with the average for the latter standing at about 1 per cent. These rates apply to the great majority of the advanced countries which began to industrialize during the second half of the eighteenth century or the first half of the nineteenth. The growth rates of countries such as Italy, Japan and the U.S.S.R., which began to industrialize later, must now be considered. It has already been pointed out in the chapter on manufactures that in these countries, and in the countries with non-planned economies, growth in recent years was more rapid when compared to that of the older industrialized countries, but that in earlier periods the difference was so slight as to be almost non-existent, except in the case of the U.S.S.R. Here, however, the question of different economic regimes and systems of national accounting is relevant. From fragmentary figures collected in order to compute levels of industrial development I have derived the same conclusions for growth over longer term. So far as the growth of national product (in per capita terms) is concerned, changes in different countries were very similar. Thus the annual growth rate of national income per capita between 1880 and 1960 was 1.7 per cent for Italy and 2.1 per cent for Japan.[17]

Contrary to what is generally believed, growth rates in the developed countries have been higher in the last twenty years than they were in the nineteenth century. Thus from 1950 to 1970 the growth rate per annum of G.D.P. has risen to 4.5 per cent (i.e. about 3.5 per cent per capita). Consequently it seems that between 1900 and 1950 the growth rate of total domestic product of the less-developed countries was similar to that of the advanced countries during their own 'take off'. But the greater population growth in the Third World countries means the per capita rates have been less, approximately one-third less, than those of the advanced countries. The rates achieved since 1950 insofar as they reflect reality, are actually higher than the rates for the 'take off' period of the developed countries. This comparison, however, is not really valid since it is one between medium-term rates of growth in developing countries and very long-term rates in the developed ones. On the other hand, in view of the acceleration of more recent growth in the developed countries, actual rates of increase of domestic output per capita in the Third World are not so high as the present rates in the western developed countries.[18] Consequently the gap between development levels in these two groups of countries is constantly widening, as we shall see below.

Before going on to consider what changes have occurred in China a global figure should be calculated for the level of G.D.P. at market prices. According to my own estimates this amounts in 1970 to 390 billions (in current dollars) for the non-communist under-developed countries and to 2090 billions for the non-communist developed countries.

III. MAINLAND CHINA

It must first of all be recalled that the concept the communist countries employ to determine their gross product, which they call material product, differs quite noticeably from the one used in the West. The essential difference is that, contrary to what happens in the West, national accounting in the Eastern countries does not take into account activities which do not contribute directly to the material production. This excludes public administration, national defence, personal and professional services and similar activities. It should be noticed, however, that distribution in the wider sense of the term — restaurants for instance — enters into the calculations, insofar as it contributes to the distribution of material goods.

Methodological differences of this sort, quite apart from any possibility of voluntary over-estimation, present obvious difficulties for international comparisons. When considering growth rates, we have to ask ourselves whether the bias would tend to raise or to lower the expansion rate. It would appear that the tendency would be to raise the estimated rates since the components of domestic product which are omitted would be expected to have a slower rate of growth than the whole. Nevertheless as it forms only a small part of the whole (± 16 per cent), its impact on the final figure is a limited one. Even assuming a rate of growth for this part of the total of less than 50 per cent of that of material product, the rate of growth of the total would only be reduced by 8 per cent.

There is also the recurring problem of the reliability of the official estimates. As a scientific approach to this problem is obviously difficult, I shall give here, as I have on each occasion when Chinese figures have been discussed, two sets of figures, one being the official set, and the other that compiled by western experts. But both the official and the unofficial comprehensive estimates of material output growth (and one explains the other) for all practical purposes stop at 1960, i.e. at the end of the Great Leap Forward.

I shall divide the changes between 1950—70 into two periods — 1950—57 and 1957—70. Official statistics for the period 1950—57 reveal an annual rate of growth of net material production at constant prices of 12 per cent. Western estimates reduce this rate to about 7 per cent.[19] Assuming, therefore, a rate of population growth of 2.0 per cent, this gives us an increase in income per capita of respectively 10 per cent according to official estimates and about 5 per cent according to western estimates.

The second period (1957—70) reveals a situation which in statistical terms is very hard to evaluate. We must remember that

1958 saw the beginning of the notorious Great Leap Forward, which was followed in 1960 by a period of adjustment that seems in 1961 and 1962 to have been marked if not by a recession then at least by a status quo in total output or a set-back in per capita output. From 1963 onwards progress again seems to have got under way. To judge from the evidence in miscellaneous sources, growth began to increase from 1964–65 onwards. According to official estimates the net material product at constant prices increased by 34 per cent in 1958 and 22 per cent in 1959. At that date all comprehensive statistics stop, and from then until 1973 only vague indications have been published in the form of a growth rate in certain sectors compared to that of the preceding year, but generally without any reference figures. From this incomplete data for the period 1960–70 and from the more complete data available for 1958 and 1959, we can conclude with our usual reservations that the Chinese authorities assume for the whole period 1957–70 an annual rate of growth of the total volume of material production of about 6–7 per cent.

There are obviously very few western estimates for the period in which we are interested and most of those stop in 1959. They give a rate of growth for 1958 and 1959 which is less than half of the official estimates.[20] On the basis of western estimates of industrial and agricultural growth (reference should be made to the relevant chapters for the sources of these estimates) it is possible to arrive at an average rate of growth of the total volume of Chinese output for the period 1957–70 of 4–5 per cent per annum. This rate, 4–5 per cent, is obviously no more than an indication, since, as was pointed out above, most western estimates terminate in 1960. In fact we shall have to wait until the Chinese government sees fit to publish sufficiently detailed statistics for one recent year before we can resume our attempt at estimates more accurate than the ones cited here.

If the rates quoted here for the whole of the period 1950–70 are now compared to the corresponding rates for the non-communist Third World countries (see Table 51) it appears, as the figures for agriculture and industry foreshadowed, that growth in China has been faster, even if we take only the western estimates. For the whole period 1950–70 per capita output in China increased at the rate of about 6–7 per cent (according to official estimates) or about 3–4 per cent (according to western estimates). The corresponding rate (not corrected for possible over-estimation) for the non-communist under-developed countries of Asia is about 2 per cent, and about 2.4 per cent for the whole of the under-developed world. If the western estimates are taken, rates as high as those of China can be found and are even surpassed in some non-communist under-developed countries (for example in Taiwan, 6.3 per cent between 1955 and 1968; in Thailand, 5.3 per cent between 1958 and 1965; in South Korea, 6.2 per cent between 1960 and 1969; in Puerto Rico, 6.4 per cent between 1960 and 1967; in Zambia, 8.8 per cent between 1964 and 1967). But the exceptional nature of the growth of Chinese national product resides in the *combination* of the three following facts:

1. the growth took place over a fairly long period;
2. it took place in a country with an enormous population;
3. it took place in a country receiving very little foreign aid.[21]

IV. CHANGES IN PER CAPITA INCOME AND PRODUCT

Table 52 brings together the results of our calculations about the changes in the level of per capita income between 1900 and 1970 expressed in constant dollars of 1970. There are two distinct series. The first, which runs from 1900 to 1952—54 concerns per capita national income and is based on Zimmerman's figures,[22] from which are made estimates concerning the under-developed countries of Latin America, South East Asia and the Far East. On the basis of the two latter regions I have calculated a weighted average for non-communist Asia, excluding the Middle East. In order to calculate the level of per capita national income for the whole of the under-developed world I have assumed that the countries for whom Zimmerman did not make any estimates (Africa and the Middle East) had, taken together, a per capita income similar to that of Asia, as was the case in 1958.

Insofar as the developed countries are concerned, I have been forced to recast the individual figures for the various countries in order to make the composition of the whole similar to the definition adopted for the non-communist advanced countries which has been used in the second series and throughout this study.

The second series from 1958 to 1970 is based on the calculations of the statistical offices of the U.N. which have been supplemented for 1970 by my own estimates on the basis of the figures of each country. In both cases the results have been recalculated in terms of 1970 dollars by using the implicit price deflator resulting from the calculations of United States' gross product at constant prices.

It must be pointed out that the figures for 1900 to 1952/54 are not strictly comparable with those for the more recent period especially where the under-developed countries are concerned. It is also likely that the series covering Latin America over-estimates the real development: a likelihood revealed when the figures are put beside those for 1960.

As the modern tendency is to formulate the evidence of national accounts in terms of per capita gross product, I have shown in Table 53 figures for the medium-term changes of this aggregate in the larger regions and including China.

Table 52 *Long-term changes in national income per capita* (in U.S. dollars of 1970)

	Less Developed Countries[1]			Developed Countries[1]		
	Total	Latin America	Asia	Total	United States	Europe
1900[2]	110	230	90	640	1360	500
1913[2]	120	240	110	775	1580	595
1929[2]	130	280	115	930	1840	660
1952/54[2]	150	390	110	1360	2850	840
1960	170	380	130	1780	3350	1270
1970	210	500	150	2610	4270	2050

[1] Excluding Communist countries
[2] Not strictly comparable with recent data (see text).
Sources: 1900–1952/54 derived from L. J. Zimmerman, *The Distribution of World Income 1860–1960*; 1960–1970 derived from *Yearbook of National Accounts Statistics 1971* (U.N., 1973).

The figures for China included in this table have been calculated in the following way: the base figure for 1953 is based on two estimates – Eckstein's,[23] who concludes after a detailed study of Chinese national income, that G.N.P. per capita expressed in American prices for 1952 was between $80 and $120, and, if the median of the spread is taken, $100 and W. W. Hollister's,[24] who gives $145 in American prices for 1955, i.e. a figure which is 45 per cent higher than Eckstein's for 1952. Allowing for probable changes between 1952 and 1955, the average of the two estimates gives us a figure for per capita national product expressed in American prices for 1953 of about $120. But, as with other countries, the figures do not allow any correction for differences in purchasing power.[25] I have therefore reduced China's figure to about $70 for 1953 or about $110 in 1970 dollars. This is the western estimate; official ones give a figure 10 to 15 per cent higher, i.e. about $80 or $120 in 1970 dollars. I have applied annual growth rates given in the preceding section to these 1953 figures and reference must be made to that section for reservations expressed about the rates, especially those from 1960 to 1970.

Attention must also be drawn to the fact that, as already pointed out, the figures given in the table are expressed in dollars based on money conversions determined by national rates of exchange. But as we know, current exchange rates do not always represent the real relationship between local prices and those operating in the United States. Some research has been done to try to provide a statistical estimate of the differences,[26] especially by Gilbert and Kravis. But as yet these estimates have not yielded results which can be considered entirely satisfactory or which cover the whole period and all the countries in which we are interested. According to estimates made by Delahaut and Kirschen,[27] the gap between the prices in under-developed countries and those in the United States was about 80 per cent in 1957. If this is so, we should have to increase the level of income of the less-developed countries by about 80 per cent to allow for the different structure of prices. It should be noticed nevertheless that the gap of 80 per cent applies specifically to the relationship of the under-developed countries and the U.S. But as the price structure in the other developed countries differs from that of the U.S., the rate of correction should be about 65–70 per cent if the average level of the under-developed countries is compared to the advanced countries taken together. Some such implicit allowances for the differences must be made if the gap separating the average levels of income in the Third World and the advanced world is to be assumed. As can be seen from Tables 52 and 53, because of the slower rates of growth taking place in the non-communist under-developed countries, the gap which exists between them and the advanced nations is increasing steadily and rapidly.

Thus the divergence between per capita income or product, which was about 1:6 in 1900 (and 1:5 in 1860), rises to 1:7 in 1929, 1:8.5 in 1953 and 1:13 in 1970. In my opinion the divergence for 1980 will be larger still, since I believe that the next few years will bring a slowing down of the growth rate of per capita national product due to the combined effects of population growth (which in turn will lead to a slower pace of agricultural productivity growth or, as this has already occurred, to an absolute decline) and a reduction in industrial expansion. But projections in this field are always extremely hazardous.[28]

If we now make an allowance for the differences in the price structures, the gap between the level of the Third World and the non-communist advanced world which was, as we saw, about 1:13 in 1970 becomes 1:8. The gap is admittedly smaller, but nonetheless

Table 53 *Gross Domestic Product per capita* (in constant
1970 U.S. dollars)

	1900	1953	1960	1970
Non-communist less-developed countries				
TOTAL	105	155	180	230
Africa	–	–	130	160
Latin America	220	350	420	540
Asia	90	105	120	145
Middle East	–	–	330	470
China (mainland)				
Official estimates	–	±120	±300[1]	±350
Western estimates	–	±110	±170[2]	±160
Non-communist developed countries				
TOTAL	705	1455	1965	2900
United States	1495	3200	3690	4730
Europe	550	875	1375	2260

[1] ±175 for 1957   [2] ±130 for 1957
Sources: 1900, author's estimates based on Table 52. 1953–70 (except China, see
text), derived from *Yearbook of National Accounts Statistics 1971* (U.N., 1973)
and previous issues of those publications.

substantial. Under a relatively optimistic hypothesis, which assumes
that the non-communist under-developed countries would experience
a future rate of growth similar to that achieved between 1950 and
1970, these countries will need about 90 years to reach even the
present level of the developed non-communist countries, allowing for
this difference in price structure, and 110 years if the allowance is
not made.

But the gap which separates the average level in non-communist
Asia from that in China is more important in its implications. While
in 1953 China's level of per capita output was about the same or
even slightly less than that of the other Asian countries, by about
1955, thanks to a faster growth achieved since then, it had surpassed
non-communist Asia's. By 1960 it was higher by some 40 per cent, if
we use western estimates, and by 150 per cent if we use government
figures. The gap is a little smaller in 1970 (about 45 per cent and 140
per cent respectively), but it should be remembered that 1960 was
the peak year of the Great Leap Forward and that the figures for
1970 are much more unreliable. All extrapolations of this trend are
hazardous where changes in recent years are concerned.[29] I shall not
pursue the economic and political implications opened up by these
changes, since I shall discuss them in the next and concluding chapter
of this study.

II   *General Conclusions*

In the last chapter we were able to sketch out a global diagnosis of
economic change in the Third World, and to lay bare the bones of
the problem – the painfully slow progress of economic growth since
1900, which remains, despite a slight improvement since 1950,
insufficient to prevent the gap between per capita incomes in the
Third World and the developed countries from widening still farther.
The sectoral analysis contained in the preceding chapters has helped
to explain the causes underlying the sluggish economic growth and to
fill in the details of the global diagnosis. But the component parts of
the problem are many and complex and it is an illusion to suppose
that the balance sheet could be either brief or straightforward. We
have seen, for instance, that the great expansion of the extractive
industries, which on a superficial analysis might appear to be a good
thing, has in fact had more unfavourable effects than favourable
ones. On the other hand an analysis of the terms of trade enabled us
to revise the unfavourable verdict on the secular changes in the terms
of trade of raw materials that has for so long been generally
accepted.

There is also the problem of regional differences, since (as was
pointed out in the introduction) this study cannot claim to analyse
economic change in all the 170-odd territories that go to make up
the Third World. Nonetheless an attempt has been made to provide
some account of the more obvious variations.

The question mark raised by the presence of China, an undeveloped country with some 800 million inhabitants that has opted for a
path to development different from that of the rest of the Third
World, has also been brought into the open, irrespective of the
economic and political undertones which such a discussion must
introduce.

For all these reasons the conclusions which now follow will be
treated in three separate sections. The first will give a sectoral
diagnosis of economic change in the non-communist Third World,
with reference, where necessary, to larger regions. The second will be
devoted to a comparison of China with the other under-developed
countries, but more particularly of China as against non-communist
Asia. Lastly, the main outlines of a plan will be sketched out which
might go some way towards solving the crucial problems of
under-development.

194

A. Sectorial diagnosis of non-communist Third World

We shall begin with the population question. Chapter 1 presented the quantitative elements of the problem, which revealed two important factors in the under-development equation. The first relates to the magnitude of population growth. While we keep as a reference for the past an annual rate of 2.2 per cent, this has today already risen to 2.6—2.7 per cent. The second factor concerns projections for the future. We must prepare ourselves for the rate to reach 2.8 per cent during the next ten or fifteen years, whatever the effort to be expended on the various birth control campaigns, and whatever the results to be achieved thereby. This population explosion — no other expression will do — bears no resemblance to the slow increase experienced in western societies before and during their 'take off', and is one of the major explanations of the unfavourable trend in the production of food, revealed by the index of agricultural productivity. The implications of this most unfavourable diagnosis are all the more significant when one remembers that the main reason why agriculture is so essential is that more than three-fifths of the Third World's labour force and nearly three-quarters of the labour force in Asia and Africa works on the land. We shall return to this aspect of the problem later.

The number of persons engaged in producing food in the Third World has doubled during the last half-century as a direct result of the population explosion. This fact, combined with the small amount of agricultural land available, has caused the old law of diminishing returns to reappear in a most disagreeable form. According to my calculations, agricultural productivity in the Afro-Asian countries has fallen by some 20 per cent between 1922—26 and 1968—72. The greater availability of land in most Latin-American countries has helped, at least partially, to prevent a similar deterioration in that part of the world. It is, in fact, possible to establish a correlation between the availability of land and the level of productivity. Similarly a correlation exists between low agricultural productivity and the presence of plantation agriculture, the explanation probably being that the plantations have occupied the better lands. But perhaps more significant is that this correlation indicates that plantation agriculture has relatively few positive effects on food production technology.

If we look at the actual level of agricultural productivity we can see the difference between the Latin-American and the Afro-Asian countries is in a ratio of about 2 to 1, while the countries of the Middle East occupy a position between the two. The productivity of agriculture devoted to growing food in most of the African and Asian countries is below the point at which we have estimated they would be safe from risk of famine.

Even the relatively high level of agricultural productivity which has permitted Latin-American countries to enjoy a more advanced industrial development cannot be considered wholly satisfactory, except perhaps in Argentina. Between 1913 and 1970 the situation has at least been relatively static. But even if the position is not as dramatic as it is in Asia, it is still a fact that rapid progress in the industrial field cannot be expected without an increase in agricultural productivity. We shall have to return later to this aspect of the problem.

Thanks to similar computations, made for an earlier study, it has been possible to compare the actual levels of agricultural productivity achieved by the less advanced countries with those of the more advanced countries at the time of their 'take off'. This has produced the following conclusions. The average level of agricultural productivity in the African and Asian countries, which form four-fifths of the Third World population, is about 50 per cent below what was achieved by the developed countries at the start of the industrial revolution. Actual productivity achieved by the less-developed countries is about the same as it was in the European countries before their agricultural revolution. As was pointed out in *Révolution industrielle et sous-développement*, the western countries had undergone what Marc Bloch called the 'agricultural revolution' before embarking on the accelerating process of industrialization traditionally known as the industrial revolution. The earlier 'revolution' had made it possible for agriculture to increase its productivity by 40 per cent within a period of about forty to sixty years, and thus to transfer to expanding industry part of its labour force, purchasing power and savings. But most of today's developing countries wish, either consciously or unconsciously, to skip this stage even though other structural pre-conditions for development have made the 'take off' much harder now than it was in the nineteenth century when most European countries and the United States were trying to emulate England's example. Failure to understand these historical differences is all the more serious because increasing agricultural productivity is so particularly difficult. Agricultural productivity depends much more on structural factors than does industrial productivity. For instance, even if land ownership and political factors are left out of consideration, an increase in the area under cultivation per agricultural labourer is an essential condition for rising productivity. But, faced with a population explosion on today's scale, it is impossible for even the most favourable hypothesis to assume anything other than a *slight* increase in total area under cultivation, and a status quo as regards area per labourer.

Recently much has been heard of the 'green revolution' and the possibilities of growing new varieties of cereals, especially high-yielding rice, selected to match the climate and soil chemistry of the Third World. As so often happens, early optimism has now been succeeded by exaggerated pessimism. The favourable results to be expected were perhaps over-estimated, and what was probably no more than a normal rise in output due to favourable weather conditions was interpreted as a revolution. The new seed has, it is true, increased yields and productivity on farms where it has been sown, but a wider use of the seed, the experts tell us, would mean a more intensive application of fertilizers and pesticides, which would reduce the pace at which the new seed could be introduced. Another handicap is that the new varieties of cereals (particularly rice) are not always acceptable to the people they are intended to feed. In addition more irrigation is required. Thus, the real problem is not so much the actual *discovery* of new ways to increase output and hence productivity, as of better and faster ways of *introducing* the new techniques, given existing ecology, soil chemistry and social habits. Even then, there are dangers in concentrating on a limited number of seed varieties in countries which are ill-equipped to fight plant diseases.

We know that in nineteenth-century Europe new agricultural methods spread only a few miles a year. Modern methods of communication could certainly help to speed the spread, but we should not forget that country people today are still largely illiterate. In these circumstances the main problem is not so much to discover innovations as to propagate information about them. It is therefore much too early to pass a balanced judgement on what has so far taken place. A verdict cannot probably be delivered before 1980 and meanwhile there remains the possibility of a serious famine in the Third World which, by 1980, will have to find food for nearly one-third more mouths than in 1970. We cannot as yet speak of a revolution, and can only nourish a fervent hope that we shall live to see the fear of famine recede and to witness a worthwhile increase in agricultural productivity in the near future.

An improvement in agricultural productivity is likewise absolutely essential for the prospects of industrial development. For, if our study of manufacturing industry has revealed unmistakable signs of substantial gains in this sector, particularly since the end of the last war, it has also shown us that agriculture has a part to play in the growth of industry, notably through its effect on the purchasing power of the agricultural population. If the expansion of manufacturing industry has been possible up to now without a noticeable enlargement of the domestic market, it is due to the fact that domestic production has mainly been substituting for imports. As the limits of import substitution are approached we may expect a reduction of industrial expansion, unless agricultural productivity increases. Besides a comparison of development in manufacturing industry has revealed that the level reached by the Afro-Asian countries in 1970 is very low, close to that of the western countries in the early years of their industrialization (1770–90, say, in England, or 1800–10 in France). Latin America's level, on the other hand, is higher – nearer to that of France in 1880–90; and in the case of Argentina and Chile nearer to what France had achieved by 1900–10. In this field, as in agriculture, the Middle East occupies an intermediate place between Latin America and Asia, although nearer the latter. We may compare the level it has reached with that of France in 1840–50 or England in 1800–10.

The part played by the extractive industries in the industrialization and general development of the Third World is a complex one. As has been pointed out before, this sector underwent, particularly after 1948, a very considerable expansion (an annual rate of growth between 1948 and 1970 of more than 9 per cent), but in fact the expansion, which was helped by the fall in transport costs, had a negative rather than a positive effect. Intended mostly to serve consumption in the manufacturing industries of the advanced economies, the output from extractive enterprises so far has hardly encouraged any extension of economic activity within their own lands. Accompanied usually by the use of foreign capital equipment and export of profits, the present rapid growth of extractive industries could mean that future development is mortgaged, since there is a very real danger that by the time the economies of which they form part have reached a stage in their development when they could compete with the developed countries in the transformation of raw materials, their mineral resources will have been exhausted – or at least much reduced in economic value through having had much of their potential skimmed off.

This brings us to a discussion of foreign trade, since, contrary to the experience of the western countries in the first phases of their 'take off', foreign trade is very important to the developing economies. For instance, total exports form at the present time about 15 per cent of G.N.P. of the non-communist, under-developed countries, and for some of them the rate exceeds 30 per cent. The structure of foreign trade simultaneously reflects their low stage of development (a heavy reliance on raw material exports and manufactured imports) and their acute dependence upon markets in the advanced countries of the West. This is revealed by the fact that around 1970 exports from Third World countries to the developed countries represented 11 per cent of the Third World's G.N.P., while exports from developed countries to the Third World represented only 2 per cent of the G.N.P. of the developed countries — a proportion which is continuing to decrease.

Because of the relative preponderance of foreign trade the terms of trade form one of the major factors in a global diagnosis. For this reason economists and politicians in the under-developed countries have concentrated (and maybe over-concentrated) on this problem. A critical analysis of the indices of export prices used in the past to estimate the terms of trade has enabled us to conclude that the generally accepted view that there was a secular deterioration in the terms of trade of raw materials as compared to manufactures is erroneous. The great fall in transport costs, occurring between the third quarter of the nineteenth century and the 1920s, masked an improvement in the relative prices of raw materials, and hence of the terms of trade of the under-developed countries, of between 20 and 40 per cent. We must remember, however, that in the short term (between 1954 and 1962) there was a deterioration of the terms of trade which went far beyond a mere re-adjustment of the relatively high prices of raw materials during the early 1950s.

This particular deterioration, which incidentally did not continue beyond 1962, obviously led — given its magnitude (14 per cent approximately) — to a reduced inflow of resources that partially offset international aid received during the period. On the basis of a rough calculation of the relationship between prices of raw materials and capital goods, one can see that the deterioration in the terms of trade caused a loss of resources about equivalent to total aid received, defining 'aid' in broad terms, but well above real total aid.

Before we leave the sectoral diagnosis which reveals negative effects predominating, and go on to a comparison between China and the non-communist Third World, the positive aspect of educational progress should not be left out of our balance sheet. Although the present state of progress is not sufficient to provide for the requirements of modern technology, there has been considerable advance, in spite of a population growth resulting in even greater proportionate rises in the population of school age. This conclusion applies, of course, to education in the quantitative sense; there are many other problems associated with the quality of education. In this context it should be emphasized that the irrelevance of educational content and the rapid increase of school enrolment, combined with the gap between rural and urban wages, contribute to the drift from the countryside to the towns. Allowing only for what happened between 1950 and 1970, the migration balance sheet in the non-communist, under-developed countries shows a surplus of 100–120 million people in favour of the cities. The gathering speed of this rural exodus together with the rapid natural growth of city populations has produced a veritable urban inflation. Urban population rose from some 47 million persons in 1920 to 120 million in 1950 and to 370 million in 1970.

This rapid growth of urban population has not been paralleled with development in productive employment; has created a serious problem of under-employment which is one of the causes of the hypertrophy of the tertiary sector of employment; and has led to soaring levels of unemployment. The unemployment rate has reached 10–20 per cent in many Third World cities, and is particularly evident among young people with an average level of scholastic achievement. Thus unemployment in the cities has added to the traditional under-employment of rural society to enhance enormously the need for productive employment. To reduce real, i.e. full, under-employment (unemployment properly defined plus under-employment expressed as total inactivity) from the 1970 level of 20–30 per cent to a figure of 10 per cent by 1985, it will be necessary to create 350–400 million new jobs in the under-developed world, i.e. more than were created during the entire century previous to 1970.

B. China compared to the rest of developing countries

We now turn to the second set of conclusions which concern the comparison between China and the non-communist Third World. The diagnosis for the non-communist, under-developed world is a generally negative one. The early effects of industrialization are more than offset by stagnation, if not regression, in the agricultural sector. The Third World has started badly and the chances of a sudden acceleration into economic development in the near future are slim. China, by contrast, appears to have achieved such a successful 'take-off'. We are, of course, faced with the difficulty of assessing the statistical information contained in two separate series of economic indicators. The first, coming from official sources, presents development in an extremely favourable light, whereas the second series, prepared by western experts, throws considerable doubt on these figures. But a successful Chinese 'take-off' is obvious even if we base our diagnosis on the lower western estimates, and the success appears even more noticeable when compared with the performance of the non-communist, under-developed world.

China appears to have recognized the priority that should, in our opinion, be awarded to agriculture, and it seems as if her efforts in this direction have borne fruit, not perhaps as abundantly as the jubilant announcements of the Great Leap Forward would have us believe, but very considerably nevertheless. According to western estimates of agricultural output, productivity has increased by about 30 per cent in this sector between 1953–57 and 1968–72. If this fact has important political implications for the present and the future, it also has positive implications on the purely economic plane in that it demonstrates effectively that agricultural development is not impossible within the framework of the conditions prevailing in the less-developed countries of Asia, i.e. great population growth coupled with a limited quantity of land on which fertility is mediocre and where climatic conditions are mostly unfavourable. It is theoretically conceivable that agricultural development in such circumstances would be impossible and the regression in agricultural productivity suffered by countries in Africa and Asia suggests on practical grounds that it has been so. Nevertheless we must remember that China, by comparison with the other larger Asian countries, has slightly more agricultural land available and that she was not subject to a colonial regime in the same direct way as India was. That a colonial regime could have had positive effects, such as the creation of a considerable educational, medical and transport infrastructure (India possessed 59,000 km of railway network in 1920 as against China's 10,800 km) while at the same time have had such a depressing influence on the cultivation of food crops was, amongst other reasons, due to the large plantation economy. But China through the growth of productivity in her agriculture has progressed beyond the point at which nationwide famines are likely and has consequently been able to industrialize faster than the rest of Asia.

The combined effect of rapid growth in both sectors has meant that since 1955 China has had a higher level of per capita income than the rest of Asia, whereas in 1950 she had about the same or even less. By 1970 per capita income was as much as 50 per cent higher even by western estimates. If official figures are taken, growth would appear to have been even faster and the divergence still greater. We must not forget, however, that the main part of the process of catching up and overtaking was achieved during the decade 1950–60. Because of bad harvests and the disorganization of industrial production after the Great Leap Forward and disturbances to output caused by the cultural revolution, Chinese economic growth slowed down considerably in the decade 1960–70. Even so, it remained slightly faster than that of the rest of Asia taken as a whole, even though not faster than that of some countries taken individually. If the next decade resembles 1960–70 rather than 1950–60 the difference will, however, no longer be so marked.

China's success and the, at least partial, failure of the non-communist Third World pose the question as to what are the causes underlying the difference. Unfortunately there are no clear cut answers to this question, since if, to simplify the matter, we take the two great Asian powers, China and India, we have to admit that before 1949, while their levels of economic development were fairly similar, their structural conditions were much less so. In addition to differences in agriculture which have already been taken into consideration (availability of land and the existence of a plantation economy), we also have to admit that the absence of a direct and long-established colonial regime in China must have influenced the industrial sector: English manufactures had penetrated the country sufficiently to cause the handicrafts of India other than those engaged in 'art' products largely to disappear, whereas they continued to exist in China and played their part in the process of industrialization. But the fact that India received more financial aid than China must also be recorded.

Structural differences like these, as well as others equally influential in the realms of religion and the social framework, prevent one from concluding that the extent of China's economic success should be attributed to the prevailing political regime. But I think we may safely say that the Chinese way is very likely to be at the root of such economic success as this country has achieved, although it is by no means certain it would work equally well if applied to other societies. The effects of sheer size are also left out of consideration. China forms an economic unit with a larger population than that of 164 countries taken together out of the total of 170 which makes up the Third World.

The Chinese example, on the other hand, lends additional confirmation, if that were needed, to our thesis that agriculture is of prime importance for economic growth. In my book *Révolution industrielle et sous-développement* I had already arrived at this conclusion on historical grounds. It was possible to assemble evidence of the major part played by the increase in agricultural productivity in the genesis of the industrial revolution in the western countries. The diagnosis of the economic growth of the non-communist Third World in modern times has shown that agriculture has played, and still plays, a crucial role in industrial conditions. The relative success of China provides, therefore, this additional proof.

C. Options for future actions

This brings us to the last part of our summing up in which we shall make certain recommendations suggested by the foregoing diagnosis. Obviously these will be generalized options since the great number and variety of individual cases require strategies taking full account of local factors. The only distinction which it is possible to make here is between conditions in Latin America and in the rest of the Third World.

The first and most important recommendation relates to the priority which agriculture demands, a priority already stressed. If the existence of an agricultural surplus in the West and the low cost of transport means the Third World is now less dependent upon agricultural output than the advanced countries were in the early nineteenth century, it is nonetheless absurd to expect any industrial development without some prior growth in a sector which provides the livelihood of ±70 per cent of Third World population (and hence of consumers), particularly in Africa and Asia.

Appropriate ways of encouraging agricultural productivity locally need not be spelt out here, since they belong more to the competence of agronomists than to that of economists. But, as René Dumont points out, it is possible technically speaking to raise productivity. As for general recommendations, given the observable differences between agricultural productivity in Afro-Asian and Latin-American countries, it is clear that the problems of the latter are sociological and political rather than technological, since without agrarian reform a rise in productivity could have but a minor influence on development because the mass of the agricultural population would not be in a position to share in any of the benefits.

The effects of population growth on the agricultural sector are such as to block progress and even, as we have seen, to cause productivity to fall. This is in itself sufficient justification for a birth-control policy, if indeed any justification were necessary when we call to mind actual rates of population increase in the Third World (2.6–2.7 per cent per annum). With the exception of China, where population growth appears to be slightly lower — less than 2.0 per cent — and the territories with a high rate of European immigration (where the problem is different in any case) we cannot quote the example of a single large country which has up to now succeeded in 'taking off' into economic development with a population growth rate of more than 1.1 per cent. This is why, while giving priority to food-producing agriculture, it is *at all costs* essential to try to restrict long-term population growth. There is little hope, as we have seen, of any slowing down of population growth in the short term, because of the actual age structure. But if we desire to reduce future growth, and this is an imperative rather than a wish, then fertility must soon be substantially reduced. In this connexion it is most regrettable that the various United Nations agencies occupied with the problems of economic development should devote so little effort to this end. Because most under-developed countries do not possess large enough scientific and medical infrastructures of their own, it would be desirable to create an international agency which could concentrate on the following activities:

1. Stimulating scientific research into techniques of birth control by improving the co-ordination and diffusion of work already in progress; by subsidizing such; and possibly, by establishing an international research centre as has been done for cancer research.
2. Building up a corps of specialists who could undertake local birth-control campaigns and study the psychological aspects of the problems with the object of using propaganda techniques that take local attitudes and customs into consideration.

Let us now pass on to the industrial sector and examine the extractive and manufacturing industries separately. So far as the latter is concerned my view is that it would be desirable to hold back on the hasty construction of extremely modern industries, however justified this might be on psychological grounds. Such a policy would be likely to prejudice the more general progress of development because of its high cost and because it would not stimulate local activities since nearly all the machinery and, later on, spare parts would have to be imported. Policy-makers should not be afraid to set up tariff barriers to protect local industries, even if this would at the outset keep in operation factories with a low productivity manufacturing articles of a quality clearly inferior to those of the developed countries. At a later stage tariff barriers should be flexible enough to stimulate some sectors of industry by allowing enterprises whose performance was marginal, to disappear eventually. In addition, and I shall come back to this point later on, it seems essential for the state to play a leading rôle in industrial investment. It is unrealistic to expect a class of capitalist entrepreneurs to emerge as they did in the West during the eighteenth and nineteenth centuries. Such a class was able to play its part at that time because a combination of circumstances existed then which no longer exists now. Amongst the favourable conditions were an elementary technology; small units of production; a large body of skilled craftsmen; greater intensity of capital per worker in agriculture than in industry; a total absence of social legislation; no international or even inter-regional competition; and high rates of profit in industry. If state intervention is now accepted, then the choice of types of enterprises and sectors to be encouraged is easier if based on a logical plan. Without discussing which of the various types of investment are desirable I shall emphasize that in considering the broad choices the essential criterion should be the extent of the induced effects on local production.

Although I consider that the success of industrialization in the Third World is primarily dependent on domestic demand, it is nonetheless true that foreign trade can make a certain contribution. Given a low level of domestic wages, some industries in under-developed countries could produce at competitive prices, and, consequently, could find export markets. This is particularly so in industries such as textile manufacture which employ a large amount of unskilled labour. Lowering tariff or other barriers in the developed countries would help the Third World to export larger quantities of such products. But, while encouraging trade with the developed countries, it is also essential for trade between Third World countries themselves to be intensified, particularly since the domestic market in most of these countries is too small to provide outlets for a wide range of manufactures. Consequently a programme of integration, which in some cases has already been initiated, would be needed. The latter policy holds perhaps the greater promise for industrialization since dependence on exports to advanced countries invites the risk of introducing a new division of labour which would confine the industries of the Third World to sectors characterized by moderate growth rates.

As has already been stressed, extractive industry faces the difficult question of expendable resources. Just because these resources are non-renewable it might well be unwise to encourage too great an expansion, particularly since the locally-induced effects are generally very small. Detailed studies would have to be made into the implications of all the choices available, and the long-term advantages and disadvantages of exploiting national resources must be carefully weighed in the balance. In most cases it would probably be more prudent to hold back development of mining until the national economy was in a position to use its own raw materials.[1] It must also be remembered that the political conditions of today, which have fragmented the old colonial empires, have created the possibility that the interests of small countries possessing great mineral wealth might conflict with the interests of the larger region of which they form a part.

The main trends of industrial history demonstrate the need for a wide choice between modes of development or economic regimes likely to favour growth in the unpropitious conditions of the Third World today. It does not seem possible that a liberal regime, such as the free market economy which was the setting for the western industrial revolution, could nowadays be capable of giving less-developed countries similar opportunities for advance. It must be recalled that growth in a market economy, even if we take no account of the social problems caused by the early phases of industrialization, was painfully slow and was spread over a period of about a century, or a century and a half. As readers have been reminded earlier in this study, the total Gross National Product of the modern developed countries during the nineteenth century only grew at a rate of about 2 per cent per annum, which is a far slower rate than that of the population increase in the Third World today.

To solve these difficult problems some system of planning will be required though this need not necessarily be totally centralized planning. Such a system is, in any case, wishful thinking where under-developed countries are concerned, since it pre-supposes an administrative, statistical and technological infrastructure that simply does not exist. Similarly, it would be foolish in the early phases to attempt to modify the system of private trading or to change existing systems of land-holding and types of cultivation too quickly and too radically. But the fundamental choices should be subject to a national plan and the state should, in addition to the traditional fields of centralized powers, intervene extensively in the following ways:

1. by stimulating agricultural development on a vast scale: where this stimulation requires an agrarian reform this reform should be a priority;

2. by creating industrial enterprises which favour general economic development and by devising a tariff policy which encourages industry;
3. by instituting a policy of birth control.

Finally we must examine the question of international aid. It is undeniable that such aid is desirable, and if we consider the probable course of future population growth in the under-developed countries, it even seems indispensable. But it is the ways of distributing it and the amounts to be provided that raise the problem. It has to be recalled, given the gap between levels of income in the Third World and the advanced countries, that the available aid would seem relatively substantial when compared to the national product of the Third World, whereas it would not form more than a small share of the national product of the advanced world. For example, the G.N.P. of the non-communist, under-developed world at current prices, amounted to 390 billion dollars in 1970 compared to 2090 billion dollars in the western developed countries, i.e. a ratio of 5.4:1.

The target laid down by the United Nations — international financial aid amounting to 1 per cent of the national product of the advanced countries — though far from having been achieved, could be, and should be, greatly increased. A reasonable minimum level of international aid should be agreed which would allow the less-developed countries to absorb four-fifths of their own population growth and thus raise these countries to the same level, in demographic terms, as the western powers during their 'take off'. In these hypothetical conditions, and with a capital output ratio of 4.5, aid should have amounted to some 37 billion dollars in 1970, i.e. more than twice what was provided, taking the wider definition of aid. With a more realistic definition of aid, the sum would be ten times higher than what is provided. This 37 billion dollars would form 1.8 per cent of the G.D.P. at market prices of the advanced countries, or, 2.0 per cent of their national income. In future years, given the probable acceleration of population and economic growth, aid (at constant prices) should rise by an annual rate of 4 per cent to a figure of about 55 billion dollars in 1980 (at 1970 values).

Furthermore, and this is very important, the way the aid is distributed must also be modified. The aid should be multilateral and distributed by an international agency. It should comprise mainly grants and should have no strings attached. If this should not be feasible, then specific allocations of aid must be justified solely by the relative effort a beneficiary country is making towards economic development. It would, for example, be acceptable for financial aid to be used for the purchase of consumption goods if this would help to stimulate local investment. We should be aware that the multilateral character of an international agency for distributing financial or technological aid to less-developed countries might not be able to prevent the money-lending country from influencing directly or indirectly the distribution of aid. Although this state of affairs is very regrettable, it is questionable if in practice it is possible to eliminate it entirely, given the current attitudes of both eastern and western powers.

It is also essential that any aid provided by the advanced countries should not be recovered indirectly (either wholly or in part) as a result of a deterioration in the terms of trade of the Third World such as occurred after 1954. A problem of this kind could easily be solved if the advanced countries so wished, and the creation of a special section of U.N.C.T.A.D. or a re-orientation of the GATT. would be useful for this purpose.

Obviously recommendations in the field of international aid such as these have little or no chance of actually being adopted. But the western world, which forms more than two-thirds of the advanced world, ought to realize that even such an effort is a modest one — amounting as it does to barely one-third of what is spent on defence — and is justified not only on humanitarian and political grounds, but also on grounds of justice. For the colonial and trade policies of the advanced countries in former times have, even if unwittingly, upset the equilibrium of the Third World and had mostly unfavourable effects. Besides, and this is perhaps the most unfortunate feature of the situation, so far as we can draw up a balance sheet, it seems that the profit accruing to the West from its colonial and trade policies in the past was much smaller than the harm unwittingly inflicted on the less-advanced countries.

The obligation to provide aid with no strings attached is, however, incumbent not only on the western powers. Rapid economic growth in the Soviet Union and the other east European countries has resulted in their achieving a level of development high enough to allow them to contribute a substantial share of the total volume of financial aid needed by the less developed countries. The G.D.P. of the developed communist countries, expressed in western accounting terms, could be estimated in 1970 at about 600 billion current dollars, i.e. 1700 dollars per capita, compared to 2090 billion dollars and 2900 dollars per capita respectively for the western developed countries. Similarly there should be no objection to the communist under-developed countries being included amongst the beneficiaries of international financial aid. Total aid required would thereby be increased by about 70 per cent.

But if foreign aid is necessary in most cases, it is not sufficient itself to permit the under-developed countries to get their economies moving. Efforts must be made within a country to allow foreign aid to be deployed in the most efficient way. But since foreign aid can never provide more than a small part of total investment required, it is even more important to mobilize all the local resources. On the assumption of a growth rate of 6 per cent per annum and a capital-output ratio of 4.5 (which is what the U.N. experts who are drawing up targets for the next decade of development seem to expect), the total amount of investment in the under-developed countries as a whole, including the communist ones, would be about 150 billion dollars in 1970. In my opinion the target of 6 per cent, although most desirable, is probably not likely to be achieved in the next decade.

Besides this figure of 150 billion dollars, the new target (1 per cent of G.D.P. which would form 27 billion dollars of foreign aid from the entire advanced world) adopted at New Delhi in 1968 by U.N.C.T.A.D. II, but neither achieved nor even accepted to be binding, seems — to say the least — very modest. The same can be said for the target which I have proposed and which represents, for the whole of the under-developed world, foreign aid of 46 billion dollars. Quantitative juxtapositions of this sort demonstrate how important local efforts are likely to be if a growth rate of 6 per cent is to be achieved. They also show that serious consideration of the recommendations made here is more than justified.

To repeat, it goes without saying that these recommendations are no more than generalizations, necessarily imprecise and based on average conditions. Mathematically speaking, of course, an average need not apply to any of the units forming the statistical universe under consideration, especially if the statistical spread is as wide as is the case here. Thus it is obvious that restraints on population growth, which have been made a first priority, are less urgent, even though far from superfluous, for most of the countries in Latin America and Africa because they command greater reserves of land. In the case of Latin America, of course, this is also combined with a more advanced economic development than exists in Asia. On the other hand agrarian reform is more necessary and of greater urgency in the Latin-American countries than it is elsewhere. Similarly regional integration is not so imperative for most Asian countries because their domestic markets are vast enough to provide outlets, even with incomes at such a low level, for a wide spectrum of manufactures. But integration is desirable in Latin America, even more so in Central America, and in some South-East Asian countries, while in most African and Middle Eastern countries it is literally vital.

As we have just said, it is unrealistic to expect all the recommendations put forward in these pages to be considered with the same degree of priority, or to be taken as relevant to each one of the 170 different nations comprising the Third World. Each individual case deserves a detailed study (and it is interesting that many of these studies have already been made), and each needs its own remedy. But to the extent that much of what has been discussed is common to the entire Third World we have tried to show that the recommendations are mostly the indispensable preliminaries upon which national schemes for economic development should be based but which are all too often forgotten.

D. Postscript (1974)

Reading the proofs in September 1974 it is hard to resist the desire to add a brief postscript commenting on the probable effects of the sharp increase in oil prices in 1973. Should the present high price of oil be maintained for a long period the main effects would probably be as follows:

For the oil-exporting countries, representing some 3 per cent of the total population of the Third World, there would be an opportunity to use the additional financial resources for investment purposes. But the very high price of oil will in itself keep down somewhat the income from oil because the increase in the rate of consumption will be slowed down and the process of substitution will be speeded up. For the non oil-exporting, less-developed countries, representing over 95 per cent of the Third World, the new situation raises enormous difficulties. Briefly, these arise from the greatly increased cost of importing essential energy, fertilizers and food. It is also probable that the financial aid (in real terms) that they will receive from developed countries will decline and that the decline will not be wholly compensated for by aid coming from the less-developed countries which are getting rich as a result of their oil exports.

Notes

Introduction

1. P. Bairoch, *Révolution industrielle et sous-développement*, Paris, 1963 (4th ed. Mouton, The Hague and Paris, 1974).
2. These figures have already been the subject of an essay, 'L'évolution de la productivité agricole dans les pays économiquement sous-développés de 1909 à 1964', in *Développement et Civilisations*, 25 March 1966.
3. It should be noted, however, that in some aggregates calculated by the United Nations Turkey is counted as part of Europe and thus as a developed country. This point will be mentioned later.

1. Population

1. In particular *Ten Great Years* (statistical abstract, Pekin, 1960); G. Etienne, 'Quelques données recentes sur la population en Chine', *Population* (July–Sept. 1962); W. F. Wertheim, 'La Chine est-elle sous-peuplée? Production agricole et main-d'oeuvre rurale', *Population* (May–June 1965); discussion of demographic problems in *China News Analysis* (24 and 31 July 1964).
2. The analysis in this paragraph is based mainly on an excellent synthesis by R. M. Field, 'A note on the population of Communist China', *The China Quarterly*, 38, (1969) pp. 158–63; and on W. Klatt, 'A review of China's economy in 1970', *The China Quarterly*, 43 (1970) pp. 100–20.
3. J. S. Aird, 'Population growth and distribution in mainland China', in *An Economic Profile of Mainland China*, Vol. 2, Part III (Washington, Joint Economic Committee of U.S. Congress, 1967), pp. 343–400. Aird, in projections up to 1985, uses four hypotheses. For 1970 (up to Jan. 1) these hypotheses postulate — assuming that the census of 1953 is correct — a minimum of 788 and a maximum of 814 million. Aird also admits the possibility that the censuses under-estimate the total from 5 to 15 per cent (p. 363).
4. H. Gille, 'Accélération démographique en Extrême Orient', *Population* (Oct–Nov. 1961). Differences of the same order have been noted for other Far Eastern countries:

Pakistan (1951—61)   2.2% real growth instead of 1.7% forecast
Philippines (1948—60) 3.2% real growth instead of 2.5% forecast
Thailand (1947—60)   3.0% real growth instead of 2.0% forecast

5. 'Bilan et perspectives de l'économie indienne au seuil de l'année 1965' (French commercial counsellor in India), *Problèmes Economiques*, 898 (March 1965).

6. *New York Times*, 20 May 1970.

7. Figures extracted from the article by Sajal Basu and Sankar Ray, 'Impact of intra-uterine contraceptive devices', *Economic and Political Weekly* (Bombay, 8 June 1968).

8. L. Henry and R. Pressat, 'Perspectives de population dans les pays sous-développés', in *Tiers-Monde, sous-développement et développement* (Paris, 1956), pp. 189—213.

9. Thus, according to projections made by F.A.O., we can expect a surplus in the western world in 1975 of the order of 27 to 33 million tons for all cereals (depending on the hypothesis adopted); a surplus resulting mainly from that forecast for North America (between 54 and 57 million tons), *F.A.O. Agricultural Commodities Projections for 1975 and 1985*, Vol. I (Rome, Oct. 1966), We should note, however, that in the longer term (40—50 years) the margin available to cover the growing deficits of the undeveloped countries by western agriculture is problematical, as will be seen in the chapter on agriculture. (For a 1980 forecast see note 35, Chap. 2.)

10. This is the date in history when the relative share in the world total of the population of these countries was the smallest; it should not be forgotten that from the beginning of the industrial revolution up till about 1930 the population of the developed countries grew more quickly in general than did that of other regions. Thus it can be estimated that the present-day less-developed countries accounted for 75 per cent of the world population in 1750 (73 per cent in 1850 and 65.5 per cent in 1900).

11. It would, moreover, be important to know to what extent the estimates of the optimum densities of population take sufficient account of today's low costs of transport and its greater speed. This, however, touches a problem outside the scope of this study.

2. Agriculture

1. These are of course only approximate percentages: the differences between countries are considerable.

2. See the author's own studies, *Révolution industrielle et sous-développement*; and *Agriculture and the Industrial Revolution* (London: Collins, 'The Fontana Economic History of Europe', 1969).

3. The productivity index has been constructed in a very similar way to the one for my study of agricultural productivity in eleven countries during the nineteenth century. See my article, 'Niveaux de développement économique de 1910 à 1910', in *Annales (Economies, Sociétés, Civilisations)*, 6, 1965.

4. In terms of export values these commodities represent about 80 per cent of total exports of tropical commodities and about 70 per cent of total exports of agricultural commodities, fisheries and forest products of the Third World.

5. Average export price for each commodity for all the principal producing countries.

6. The index of food production is based on the following commodities: cereals, starchy roots, sugar, pulses, edible oil crops, nuts, fruit, vegetables, wine, cocoa, livestock and livestock products. To obtain an index of total agricultural production the F.A.O. adds the following commodities: fibres, rubber, tea, coffee, oil seeds (industrial oils) and tobacco.

7. It should be noted that since the end of 1967 the F.A.O. has considerably modified its ways of calculating these figures. The indices of agricultural production are henceforth calculated for the civil year and for totals of the larger regions. There was a revision in 1972 and again in 1973.

8. For these F.A.O. calculations the Middle East theoretically includes the following African countries: Libya, Sudan, Egypt, and these Asian countries: Aden, Afghanistan, Bahrein, Cyprus, Iraq, Iran, Jordan, Kuwait, Lebanon, Muscat and Oman, Katar, Saudi Arabia, Syria, Oman, Turkey and Yemen. Africa includes all the countries in the continent with the exception of South Africa and those included in the Middle Eastern group. The same applies to the Far East, except that China and Japan are also excluded. Latin America includes all America except the United States, Canada, Bermuda, Greenland and St Pierre and Miquelon.

9. Nevertheless it must be pointed out that most of the indices

could possibly be biased in the same direction, in which case the margins of error would not be reduced. A unilateral bias is quite probable and would have the effect of exaggerating growth. The exaggeration would result partly from the fact that commercial production increases more rapidly than total production (mostly, but not entirely, through a rise in the level of commercialization) and partly through the desire of the authorities not to provide excessively 'negative' figures. Lastly, it is more than probable that the levels of demographic growth are under-estimated.

10.   As we shall see in the chapter on manufacturing industry, the annual levels of growth in this sector were nearly 3 per cent.

11.   These rates have been calculated, after taking account of various factors, in my study, *Révolution industrielle et sous-développement*, p. 155.

12.   It is also possible that certain series have been revised in the interval. I have endeavoured to avoid this pitfall by using, as far as possible, figures which are not provisional.

13.   The fact that the United Arab Republic is referred to under its former name has no political significance. The choice is justified on purely statistical grounds because the material concerns solely the Egyptian part of the U.A.R., as is also the case for most of the statistics. The title U.A.R. would have risked introducing an error into the geographical range of the statistics, all the more since the union has changed in the course of time.

14.   See my article 'Niveaux de développement économique de 1810 à 1910'. English readers will find a very short resumé of this article in Section IIc of my study, *Agriculture and the Industrial Revolution.*

15.   By 'direct' or 'initial' calories is meant those which have not undergone a transformation in the course of livestock rearing. Livestock produce from the calories contained in vegetable feeding stuffs in the form of milk or meat are called 'indirect' or 'derived' calories. I shall come back later to this problem.

16.   The calorie content of meat differs greatly according to the percentage of fat which it contains, since muscle or 'pure' meat contains about 1600 calories per kilo, while 'pure' fat contains nearly 9000.

17.   F.A.O. has adopted a single coefficient of 7 for all meat in all countries (accepted also by M. Cepede and M. Lengele, *Economies alimentaires du globe*, Paris, 1953). I have preferred

to use different coefficients for each kind. For the contemporary period there is sufficient data to allow these coefficients to be determined in the form of weight gain per unit of feeding stuff. From these contemporary figures — which I worked out for the earlier study in this field — I have calculated coefficients, theoretically valid in the middle of the nineteenth century for partially-developed European countries. (The choice was based partly on the advice of specialists whom I consulted and whom I must thank for their kindness, and partly on fragmentary material about the age of slaughter. The figures thus obtained have been modified slightly on the basis of available statistics concerning the percentage of slaughtered animals.)

18. I have not made an estimate for detecting the consumption of cereals by animals for the following three reasons: a) Existing figures on the subject are fragmentary and rather unreliable. b) Animal consumption is extremely small in most of the under-developed countries, with the exception of those in Latin America. c) I have postulated a certain compensation between animal consumption of cereals and the fact that we have not taken into consideration certain agricultural commodities, namely, poultry meat, oil seeds, dairy products and cane sugar.

19. I chose the countries for which I made this correction on the basis of the production of different crops and on the relative value of exports of agricultural products (as much in relation to total exports as by the value of total agricultural production).

20. I have to thank the librarian of I.N.E.A.C. (Institut National pour l'Etude Agronomique du Congo Belge) for his kind cooperation.

21. Publication of the I.N.E.A.C., un-numbered (Brussels, 1958).

22. Out of some fifty studies and articles dealing with different commodities which I examined only the six following works contained any figures relating to labour norms: T. Eden, *Tea* (London, 1958) esp. p. 61; J. L. Collin, *The Pineapple: Botany, Cultivation and Utilization* (London, 1961) — a few facts on p. 141; Ch. Surre and R. Ziller, *Le palmier à huile* (Paris, 1963) esp. p. 111; J. Champion, *Le bananier* (Paris, 1963) esp. p. 203; L. Burle, *Le cacaoyer*, Vol. II (Paris, 1962) esp. pp. 509–17; F. Martin, *La canne à sucre* (Paris, 1935) esp. p. 183.

23. This rate is based on material relating to several tropical crops (especially in the works of Eden and Burle mentioned above).

24.   Even confined to the group of countries included here, calculating gross production alone entailed research, transcription and handling of about 20,000 statistical computations. I have to thank Monsieur H. Gelders for helping me with this part of the study.

25.   Especially for China and Cuba and for manioc and soya beans. The Chinese material was of course the most difficult to assemble. For the 'official' figures the main sources were Government statistical publications (*Dix grandes années*, Pekin, 1960) and the press communiqués of the New China Agency; the 'western' material has been drawn from the analyses in the *Far Eastern Economic Review* (Hong Kong), including the annual supplements; E. F. Jones, 'Emerging pattern of China's economic revolution' in *An Economic Profile of Mainland China*, Vol. I (Washington, 1967); R. M. Field, 'How much grain does communist China produce? in *The China Quarterly*, 33 (Jan–March 1968); S. Swamy and S. J. Burki, 'Foodgrain output in People's Republic of China, 1958–1965' *The China Quarterly*, 41 (Jan–March 1970); W. Klatt, 'A review of China's economy in 1970' *The China Quarterly*, 43 (July–Sept. 1970); and T. G. Rawski, 'Recent trends in the Chinese economy' *The China Quarterly*, 53 (Jan–March 1973).

26.   Other factors such as stature and climate help to differentiate this minimum according to region. Here, by way of example, is the amount of calories of average food available per head for some under-developed countries for which the F.A.O. has calculated these figures (general averages 1963/65– 1966/68–1969):

Latin America		Asia		Middle East/Africa	
Argentina	3,150	Burma	2,010	Algeria	1,890
Bolivia	1,760	Sri Lanka	2,160	Egypt	2,840
Brazil	2,540	India	1,940	Morocco	2,130
Chile	2,520	Indonesia	1,750	Nigeria	2,160
Equador	1,850	Pakistan	2,290	Syria	2,450
Mexico	2,610	Philippines	2,000	Tanzania	2,140
Peru	2,180	Thailand	2,020	Turkey	2,760

Year Book of Production, 1970 (F.A.O., Rome, 1971), pp. 444–7.

27.   In my study 'Niveaux de développement économique de 1810

à 1910' I have assumed 45 per cent of the population to be active during the nineteenth century in countries which are now developed. But given a very different demographic structure (especially the much greater proportion of children under 10) in the under-developed countries, I have not kept the same rate. The rate accepted here is based on figures from most of the under-developed countries for which statistics on the subject are available (see Chapter 9).

28. If a weighted average is made for the part of the employed population of under-developed countries not occupied in agriculture, this works out at about 20 per cent for Asia and Africa and more than 35 per cent for Latin America.

29. The determining of this rate is rather hazardous. It is obviously very difficult to put an exact figure on the extent of these losses.

30. It is of course a national average, and inequalities which are as much regional as assignable to social classes may lead to insufficiencies for a large part of the population. In addition it is possible and even probable that such a food availability implies qualitative nutritional scarcities due to protein or vitamin deficiencies.

31. In addition to stockraising we should also take account of the possibilities of stockpiling, but — as in the preceding case — this factor plays a negligible role in under-developed countries. Of course it is true that at the moment foreign trade allows most of the under-developed countries to keep the famine risk in check, particularly by means of surpluses of cereals from agriculture in the developed west.

32. In my study *Révolution industrielle et sous-développement* I have already expressed doubts on this subject after examining the percentage of durable goods made locally (pp. 172–3).

33. India's famine in 1966 illustrates tragically the reality of this situation. It should be pointed out that the first edition of this study was completed in the course of 1965 just when it seemed as if the food situation of that country was improving, the harvest of 1965 being better than the rather poor one of 1964.

34. Thus if cereal stocks are large in relation to the harvests of the countries with surplus production (U.S. ±50 per cent of the annual harvest; Canada ±75 per cent) the quantity is much less when compared with the volume of world production. Wheat stocks (at 31 July of each year) fluctuate around 55 million tons from 1960 to 1970, that is about 20 per cent of world

production. Stocks of all cereals averaged 130 million tons from 1960 to 1970, or ±12 per cent of world output (figures for stocks are those of the principal exporters and form the essential part of stocks). Sources: *Foreign Agriculture Circular*, U.S. Dept. of Agriculture and F.A.O. Given the yield fluctuation, it is quite conceivable that world cereal output could be 12 per cent less than the average for two successive years.

35. The level of cereals consumed by animals in the developed countries is such that it is theoretically possible to make a large quantity of cereals available in case of urgent need. To illustrate the situation here is an estimate of production and consumption of all cereals produced in the western countries (figures rounded up to millions of tons):

	Situation at 1970	Forecast for 1980
Production	380	510
Consumption	360	455
Seed	30	40
Food	80	90
Animals	250	315
Surplus	25	65

Sources: F.A.O. especially *Commodity Review 1970–71* (Rome, 1971) and *Agricultural Commodity Projection 1970–80* (Rome, 1971). Therefore, in an hypothetical situation where adverse conditions in the under-developed countries create an additional demand at a moment when supply in the west is reduced, it would always be possible, in theory, to cover the deficit by sacrificing some livestock; since in 1970 animals in western countries consumed ten times as much as the surplus exported to under-developed countries (and, in part, to the eastern countries).

36. Correlations between the two series provide the following results: for all twenty-four countries under consideration here − 0.92; for African countries − 0.91; for Latin America − 0.97; for Asian countries (including China at the 5.8 level) − 0.25.

37. Agricultural land is taken to mean arable land and land under permanent crops plus meadows and permanent pasture.

38. It should be noted that the margin of error in the productivity indices of countries where plantations are important is probably greater than for other territories because the working

population employed in plantations has to be estimated. This additional margin of error is not, however, enough to explain the gaps which are so evident.

39. Thus in France 'the final output per male agricultural worker' rises from 1,894 Frs. (Frs. 1905—14) in 1895—1904 to 4,788 Frs. in 1955—58, an increase of 151 per cent in 57 years (an annual rate of 1.7 per cent); from A. Toutain, *Le produit de l'agriculture française de 1900 à 1958*, Vol. II (I.S.E.A. pamphlet no. 115, Paris, 1961). In the U.S. the index of gross agricultural productivity per man hour rises from 45 in 1910—14 (base 100 = 1947—19) to 149 in 1953—57, an increase of 231 per cent in 42 years (an annual rate of 2.9 per cent); from *Historical Statistics of the United States* (Washington, 1960), p. 602. During the period 1948/52—1968/72 the productivity of the agriculture of all western developed countries increased by some 5.5 per cent per annum.

40. The growth of productivity in Mexico is generally attributed to agrarian reform. As I said in the Introduction, I do not seek here to provide explanations of differences, but the question may well be asked whether a part of the progress could not be attributed to the better coverage of statistics made possible by the reforms. This reflexion is not meant to cast doubt on the positive value of agrarian reform in Latin American countries, without which it is hardly likely there would have been any noticeable improvement in the economic condition of these countries.

41. Based on government figures the annual rate of growth would be 3.0—3.5 per cent.

42. It should be noted, however, that I have not been able to find a significant correlation between the rates of growth in the employed agricultural population and productivity.

43. Any degree of bias in the comparisons introduced by these differences is not large (probably less than 10 per cent) and tends to under-estimate the nineteenth-century figures in relation to the under-developed countries.

44. See my study, *Révolution industrielle et sous-développement*, pp. 75—6, 223—4 and 292—3.

45. When comparing the estimates of income per head in France, Great Britain and the U.S. at the beginning of the nineteenth century with those of the under-developed countries (allowing for changes in prices and purchasing power) I had already come to the same conclusion (see my article, 'Le mythe de la

croissance économique rapide au XIXème siècle' in *Revue de l'Institut de Sociologie*, 2, (1962), pp. 319—20).

46. Note that the small decrease in land available occurring at the start of development was only temporary and was in fact changed into an increase in cultivated land because of the decline in the practice of fallowing. As we have seen earlier, the land available today is greater due to the fall in the population employed in agriculture.

47. Estimate based on the ratio of the calorie consumption from milk, eggs and vegetables compared to total consumption in these countries; compared to the same ratio for the under-developed countries.

48. However, we should not take 'available land' for granted, for in certain countries it is certainly possible to augment it. But it pre-supposes investment on a massive scale and there is always the risk of damaging the ecological equilibrium for, as Prof. Harroy points out in 'La conservation des ressources naturelles du Tiers-Monde', in *Tiers-Monde*, 20 (Oct—Dec. 1964) the Third World countries, by reason of their geographical position, suffer from the existence of ecological conditions which are much more easily damaged than those in Europe, North America or the U.S.S.R.

49. The western countries are of course those referred to, for that is where the surpluses are. In addition the developed countries beyond the Iron Curtain seem to have entered a phase in which it is unlikely that they will have much of a surplus in the near future.

50. R. Dumont, *Développement agricole africain* (Paris, 1965), p. 211. For the problems concerning the famine menacing the Third World, another of his works should be consulted (Dumont and Rosier, *Nous allons à la famine*, Paris, 1966. English trans. *The Hungry Future*, New York, 1969).

51. Mostly based on a publication of the F.A.O. *The Green Revolution* (lecturer's guide); and *The State of Food and Agriculture* (both Rome, 1972).

52. The situation is different when it is a question of yields changing due to climatic conditions: in this case all producers are on average affected similarly and as a result there is some compensation between changes in price and the amount produced.

3. Extractive Industry

1. For the eighteenth century the figures are those collected for my study, *Révolution industrielle et sous-développement*.

Contemporary figures have been provided by the Services Techniques du Groupement des Hauts Fourneaux de Belgique and I should like to thank them for their kindness.

2. *Annuaire Statistique de la Fédération professionnelle des producteurs et distributeurs d'éléctricité de Belgique*, several years.

3. As I shall show later, it is clear that this widening gap is also partly due to the import by developed countries of products of extractive industry originating in the under-developed countries. But as a whole the gap remains due to the factors set out in this section. Thus, for all non-communist countries (developed and under-developed) and for the period 1958/60– 1968/70, the annual rate of growth of manufacturing industry was 6.0 per cent, while it was 4.7 per cent for the whole of extractive industry, and 2.4 per cent for extractive industry excluding oil and natural gas.

4. Most prices have been taken from *Metal Bulletin* and *Engineering and Mining Journal*. I have to thank here the Société Belge des Minerais and, in particular, Monsieur Lamberts for having provided me with information in this field.

5. Ivar Hogbom, *Développement de la production mondiale de matières premières*, appendix to the Report of the Commission for the study of the problem of raw materials, League of Nations, 1934; cited by *Industrialisation et commerce extérieur* (League of Nations, Geneva, 1945), p. 55.

4. Manufacturing Industry

1. It is clear that there are considerable differences between one country and another, as well as between one period and another, which arise particularly from variations in energy consumption for private use. The average used here (5 per cent) results from the calculations made for a large number of under-developed countries for which the two series (i.e. index numbers of manufacturing production and energy consumption) exist.

2. Because the index numbers are rounded off to whole numbers, the rates of annual variations for short periods contain an additional margin of error; the figure after the decimal point in my figures, is consequently no more than an indication.

3. C.f. also my article 'Le mythe de la croissance économique rapide au XIXe siècle' *Revue de l'Institut de Sociologie*, 2, 1962.

4. For the 'take off' periods of most of the countries mentioned

here, readers are referred to my study 'Niveaux de développement économique de 1810 à 1910'.

5. It might be claimed that Nazi Germany had a centralized economic régime, running parallel to a capitalist system, but this did not occur until after 1935.

6. See particularly: J. Ahmad, 'Import substitution and structural change in Indian manufacturing industry, 1950–1960', in *J. of Development Studies*, IV (April 1968); J. Ahmad, 'Measuring the influence of foreign trade and domestic demand on economic growth', *Institut International d'Économie Quantitative*, Publication 4 (Montreal, 1970); H. B. Chenery, S. Shishido and T. Watanabe, 'The pattern of Japanese growth, 1914–1954', *Econometrica*, 30, No. 1 (1962); S. Lewis and R. Soligo, 'Growth and structural change in Pakistan manufacturing industry, 1954–1964', *Pakistan Development Review*, 5, No. 1 (1965); R. Soligo and J. Stern, 'Tariff protection, import substitution and investment efficiency', *Pakistan Development Review*, 5, No. 2 (1965); United Nations, *A Study of Industrial Growth* (New York, 1963).

7. The official figures up to 1958 come from the publication *Dix grandes années* (Pekin, 1960). After 1958 figures are based on a systematic search for information about China, both in official documents and in the following reviews: *Far Eastern Economic Review; China News Analysis; The China Quarterly*, and 'Problèmes chinois' in *Notes et études documentaires (La Documentation française)*. For Western estimates, apart from miscellaneous articles and reviews in *Far Eastern Economic Review*, the following have been consulted: Cho-Ming Li's article, 'China's industrial development 1958–1963', in *Industrial Development in Communist China*, ed. Cho-Ming Li (New York, 1964), which gives the various estimates published up to 1963; and Kang Chao, *The Rate and Pattern of Industrial Growth in Communist China*, (University of Michigan Press, 1965).

8. M. Field, 'Industrial production in Communist China: 1957–1968', *The China Quarterly*, 42 (April–June 1970). For the period 1949–65 see the same author, 'Chinese Communist industrial production', in *An Economic Profile of Mainland China*, Vol. I, Part 2, pp. 269–95.

9. *Le Monde*, 2 March 1971.

10. *Le Monde*, 2–3 January 1972.

11. For the years 1950–52, according to the available western

estimate (Kang-Chao, *op. cit.* p. 88) the annual rate of growth would be 26 per cent (as against the 34 per cent given in the official index). For the period 1952—57 the four main western estimates provide very similar growth rates (as annual rates, 9.6, 14.2, 13.6 and 13.3 per cent respectively). Given that growth was faster from 1950 to 1952 than from 1952 to 1957, I have retained as the average of western estimates a rate for the period 1950—57 of 14.0 per cent. For 1958 and 1959, the rates for the four estimates are: 1958, 32.5; 19.6; 19.5 and 30.3 per cent; for 1959, 31.6; 27.0, 32.3 and 31.5 per cent. I have kept the average of these estimates (25.0 and 31.0 per cent).

12.   M. Field, 'Industrial production in Communist China: 1957—1968', *The China Quarterly*, 42 (April—June, 1970).

13.   Especially W. Klatt, 'A review of China's economy in 1970', *The China Quarterly*, 43 (July 1970), pp. 100—20 and analyses in *Far Eastern Economic Review*.

14.   Where Pakistan is concerned this is partly due to the transfer of factories, especially textile factories, following the partitition of India at independence when Mahommedan industrialists emigrated. In Taiwan the situation was similar, but was also combined with considerable financial aid and a rise in domestic demand resulting from even larger military aid. In this country, and in South Korea, the opening of western markets, particularly in the United States, re-inforced as it was by the Vietnam War, played an essential role.

15.   The cases of the United States and Morocco are an illustration of this situation. In the United States, manufacturing industry forms only 29 per cent of the Gross Domestic Product while working population so occupied forms 27 per cent of the total, that is a gap of 7 per cent between the two rates. Morocco, on the other hand, in which manufacturing industry employs only 9 per cent of the working population, this sector produces 14 per cent of the Gross Domestic Product, that is a gap of 55 per cent between the two rates.

16.   In order to have a very approximate yardstick of the productivity of manufacturing, I have calculated the value of output per worker in dollars for some of the countries examined here for which the material available enables such a computation to be made. (The figure is the value of Gross Domestic Product generated by manufacturing related to workers in the sector and expressed in U.S. dollars.) The

following are the figures for 1961—63 (annual averages):

	$ US		$ US
Morocco	550	India	190
Argentina	2030	Pakistan	210
Chile	1040	Philippines	560
Mexico	1080	Thailand	740
Peru	1100	Turkey	940

17.   Comparisons are made more difficult because of the differing changes recorded between 1930 and 1950. While India was experiencing a period of peace in which industrial expansion was not hindered, China, with the Sino-Japanese War followed by civil war, went through a troubled period which resulted in a fall in industrial production. This is why, in an attempt to reduce any statistical bias, I have chosen to compare the highest level attained in both countries before 1950. This method nonetheless favours India since the maximum levels achieved by this country in general occurred in 1949, whereas the maximum Chinese levels occurred before 1940. Here, therefore, for the four indices given in Table 25, are the maximum levels achieved before 1950 by these two countries:

	Energy	Steel	Cotton	Transport
China	±120	±3.0	±1.9	140
India	100	3.9	2.3	118

18.   As already noted, a more detailed analysis of this subject will be found in my book, *Révolution industrielle et sous-développement*, especially in Chapter 5, 'Agriculture, facteur déterminant d'amorce du développement', (pp. 73—84) and in Chapter 7, 'Le schéma explicatif du processus d'amorce du développement économique' (pp. 98—113). English-speaking readers should refer to my study *Agriculture and the Industrial Revolution*.

19.   P. Bairoch, 'Niveaux de développement économique de 1810 à 1910', except Austria which was calculated for my study *Agriculture and the Industrial Revolution*.

20.   The kind of agricultural economy is meant in which most farmers sell no more than a small part of their output. In this situation a fall in yields means that a farmer has no surplus

output for sale, and cannot therefore compensate for the fall in available income by selling produce at a higher price.

5. Foreign Trade

1. In recent literature, the reports of the two U.N.C.T.A.D. conferences — Geneva 1964 and New Delhi 1968 — are especially noteworthy: *United Nations Conference on Trade and Development, Proceedings*, 8 vols. (1964) and *Proceedings*, 5 vols. (1968). Other references are: B. A. Balassa, *Trade Prospects for Developing Countries* (Homewood, 1964); M. Z. Cutajar and A. Franks, *The Less-Developed Countries in World Trade* (London, 1967); G. de La Charrière, *Commerce extérieur et sous-développement* (Paris, 1964); H. G. Johnson, *International Trade and Economic Growth* (London, 1958); C. P. Kindleberger, *Foreign Trade and the National Economy* (New Haven, 1962); A. I. Macbean, *Export Instability and Economic Development* (London, 1966); A. Maizels, *Exports and Economic Growth of Developing Countries* (Cambridge, 1968); J. Pinkus, *Trade, Aid and Development* (New York, 1967); *Revue de l'Institut de Sociologie* special number, 'Division internationale du travail et organisation du commerce mondial' (Brussels, 1965); M. Saint-Marc, *Commerce extérieur de développement* (Paris, 1968); J. Weiller, *L'économie internationale depuis 1950* (Paris, 1965). In addition the GATT (Geneva) has published every year since 1952 a report called *International Trade . . .*, in which one section is devoted to trade in the unindustrialized regions. See also *Trends in International Trade*, published by the GATT (Geneva, 1958).

2. Readers are reminded that prices f.o.b. (free on board) mean that the prices do not include freight costs, insurance and the other charges connected with transport. On the other hand, prices c.i.f. (cost, insurance and freight) do include these costs. Exports are usually expressed in f.o.b. prices while imports are expressed c.i.f.

3. Note, however, that there is a strong possibility that the available index numbers of export prices are significantly distorted and that the increases in the volume of world exports have in fact been slightly less important.

4. In applying a correction based on the average of 1960–70, the gap between export values and world imports would be — according to my own calculations — 5.4 per cent.

5.   According to my estimates, by including the merchant fleets of Panama and Liberia amongst those of the developed countries, a figure is obtained for the merchant tonnage of the under-developed countries as at 1 January 1965 of slightly less than 6 per cent of the world total, while the trade of these countries forms about 20 per cent of the world total. We can therefore assume that approximately 70 per cent, at least, of the international maritime trade of the under-developed countries is carried in ships belonging to the developed countries. I say 'at least' since the international trade of the under-developed countries comprises a much higher proportion of sea transport than that of the international trade of the developed countries.

6.   Apart from the Asian Middle Eastern countries, the Middle East comprises Egypt, Ethiopia, Libya, Somalia and Sudan. These countries are consequently not included in Africa.

7.   See my book, *Révolution industrielle et sous-développement*, pp. 334—5.

8.   *International Trade 1968* (GATT, Geneva, 1969).

9.   Indeed the situation is not much better in Latin America. Thus in 1970 exports intended for Latin American countries formed only 11 per cent of total exports from these countries, in spite of the comparative success of two customs unions.

10.   The following, expressed in per capita terms, is the situation as far as imports coming from under-developed countries are concerned (in U.S. dollars):

	1965	*1970*
EFTA	56	69
Common Market	50	71
United States	34	49
Japan	29	84
Under-developed countries	5	6
U.S.S.R.	5	5
China	0.7	0.4

11.   In fact I have been engaged for several years on the more general study of the relationship between international trade and economic development. My research was greatly helped by a generous grant from the Canadian Council of Arts in 1970. The parts which I have been able to publish cover only the period of nineteenth-century free trade ('Commerce extérieur et développement économique: quelques enseignements de l'expérience libre-échangiste en France au XIXe siècle', in

Revue Economique XXI, no. 1 (1970); and 'Free trade and European economic development in the 19th century' in *European Economic Review*, 3, no. 3 (1972). A much larger study on trade and economic development of 19th-century Europe. will appear during 1975 in the form of a book (in French). I have not yet resumed the more specific problem of the foreign trade of the Third World, which I had begun to deal with (but not to master) during the three years I spent in the research division of the GATT. These are the reasons why the conclusions here must be considered as preliminary.

12. Including Manchuria.
13. Tea, which formed about 50 per cent of total exports in 1870 had by 1910 fallen to 9 per cent. Between the same dates the share of silk and silk articles fell from 40 to 25 per cent. A. Feuerwerker, *The Chinese Economy c. 1870—1911*, Michigan Papers in Chinese Studies, No. 5 (1969).
14. The data relating to the foreign trade of China for the period 1950 to 1965 is based almost exclusively on R. C. Price, 'International trade of Communist China 1950—1965', in *An Economic Profile of Mainland China*, Vol. 2, Part 4, pp. 579—608.

6. The Terms of Trade

1. Ever since the notion of terms of trade was first introduced by J. Stuart Mill and A. Marshall it has been widened so that we now possess three major concepts, all different, of which the most commonly employed is 'net barter terms of trade': this expression, under the name of 'terms of trade', is the only one to be used here.
2. The estimate was repeated again in another U.N. publication, *Instability in Export Markets of Under-Developed Countries* (New York, 1962).
3. W. Arthur Lewis, 'World production, prices and trade 1870—1960', in *The Manchester School of Economic and Social Studies*, XX (1952), pp. 105—34. We·may include also the index computed by Kindleberger for industrial Europe which is discussed below.
4. W. Schlote, *Entwicklung und Strukturwandlungen des englischen Aussenhandels von 1700 bis zur Gegenwart* (Jena, 1938). English translation by W. O. Henderson and W. H. Chaloner,

British Overseas Trade from 1700 to the 1930's (Oxford, 1952).

5. Annual figures are given here because in the index for industrial Europe calculated by Kindleberger data is available only for isolated years.

6. The countries included are Great Britain, Germany, France, Italy, Holland, Belgium, Sweden, Switzerland. C. Kindleberger, 'The Terms of Trade and Economic Development', in *The Review of Economics and Statistics*, special supplement, *Problems in International Economics* (Feb. 1958), pp. 72–90. For further details see also by the same author, *The Terms of Trade. A European Case Study* (Cambridge, Mass., 1956).

7. Index compiled about 1886 by A. Sauerbeck and published in 'Prices of commodities and the precious metal', in *Journal of the Statistical Society* (1886). It was continued in the review known as *The Statist.*

8. *Industrialization and Foreign Trade* (League of Nations, Geneva, 1945), p. 183.

9. Thus of the 55 articles included in Sauerbeck's index (45 products, 10 of which are included twice according to type and quality) prices for 36 are import prices, to which must be added another 10 whose prices are a direct function of import prices (e.g. price of flour = a direct function of the price of American wheat). Only 10–12 articles therefore may be considered as representing domestic prices, i.e. only 20 per cent of the total (all the articles in this index are given equal weight). Thus 80 per cent of the index is based on import prices. As will be pointed out below, this bias is not peculiar to Sauerbeck's index; it is quite general and stems from the fact that import price statistics were usually the only ones available in the nineteenth century.

10. Readers should note that although, as we have seen, the assumption of a secular deterioration in the terms of trade of raw materials is very widely accepted (especially by people dealing with the problems of the Third World), the idea that transport costs played a part in the deterioration has occasionally been formulated, but only by theorists of international trade and without any systematic effort to make an estimate of their impact (see particularly, G. Haberler, *A Survey of International Trade Theory* (Princeton, 1961) and T. Morgan, 'The long run terms of trade between agriculture and manufacturing' in *Economic Development and Cultural Change,*

VIII, 1 (Oct. 1959), and 'Les tendances des termes de l'échange et leurs répercussions' in *Les Minutes de la Conférence de Brissago* (Cahiers de l'I.S.E.A., 167 P. 11 (Nov. 1965), pp. 99—142).

11. According to the calculations of world values of trade made by the statistical office of the League of Nations (*Industrialization and Foreign Trade*) the difference between the two aggregates is as follows for the period under consideration:

1881—85	17.5%
1886—90	17.1%
1921—25	4.3%
1926—29	10.9%
1931—34	12.4%

12. A measure of the drop in insurance costs can be found in the percentage of ships totally lost or missing. For all registered ships these losses were 2.8 per cent annually between 1871 and 1880. By 1926, in spite of the much greater distances involved, the percentage fell to 0.7. (From 'Shipping wreck statistics', *Encyclopaedia Britannica*, 19th ed.)

13. Ignoring the effects of transport costs, I have concluded that the probability was an improvement of 10 to 25 per cent, which by merely adding to the 10 to 20 per cent due to freight costs gives us a figure of 21 to 50 per cent.

14. In this case all under-developed countries including the communist ones, as well as Australia, New Zealand, South Africa and Canada.

15. B. M. Bhatia, 'Terms of trade and economic development: a case study of India, 1861—1939', in the *Indian Economic Journal*, XIV (April—June, 1969), pp. 414—33.

16. The basic figures were extracted by S. Bambrick ('Australia's long-run terms of trade' in *Economic Development and Cultural Change*, 19, Oct. 1970) from R. Wilson's study, *Capital Imports and the Terms of Trade* (Melbourne, 1931).

17. Calculated by the Canadian Bureau of Statistics and repeated in M. C. Urquhart (ed.), *Historical Statistics of Canada* (Toronto, 1965), p. 184.

18. From J. Bjerke, *Langtidslinjer i norsk Økonomi, 1865—1960* (Oslo, 1966), pp. 142—4.

19. From E. Pihkala, *Suomen Ulkomaankauppa, 1860—1917: Finland's Foreign Trade* (Helsinki, 1969).

20. From A. Ølgaard, *Growth, Productivity and Relative Prices* (Amsterdam, 1968), p. 242.

21. From M. Levy-Leboyer, 'L'héritage de Simiand: prix, profits et termes des échanges au XIXe Siècle', in *Revue Historique*, 493 (Jan–March, 1970), pp. 110–11. As the domestic price series stops at 1921, I have completed it by the wholesale price index calculated by the Institut National de Statistiques (see *Annuaire Statistique de la France*).

22. From W. G. Hoffmann, *Das Wachstum der Deutschen Wirtschaft Seit der Mitte des 19. Jahrhunderts* (Berlin, 1965), pp. 562–63 and 569–70.

23. A. Montesano, 'Il movimento dei prezzi in Giappone dal 1878 al 1958' in *Giornale degli Economesti e Annali Economia* (Nov–Dec. 1967), p. 968.

24. Taken from *Etudes sur l'économie mondiale*, I, 'Les pays en voie de développement dans le commerce mondial' (U.N., 1963), p. 20.

25. As, for instance, for fuel prices, U.S. export prices have been taken. It is regrettable that the average for 1950–52 should have been chosen as a reference point for the 'fifties since it includes the boom year of 1951 which was due to the Korean War. Note that for the period after 1950 the statistical office of the U.N. have calculated an index of export prices which is more elaborate than the one used here for long-term changes.

26. 'Le commerce international en 1952' (Geneva, 1953), table on p. 130. The weighting of the index is based on output in 1929.

27. Thus, between 1929 and 1952, for example, the index of wholesale prices grew by 2,500 per cent in France, 230 per cent in Belgium, 174 per cent in Holland, about 5,000 in Italy, 165 in Sweden, and 68 even in Switzerland.

28. *Statistical Yearbook 1969* (New York, 1970), p. 54; details about the method of construction and the statistical coverage appear in a document which, so far as I know, has not yet been published.

29. Thus, between 1954 and 1962 the index of wholesale prices of primary products in the United States fell by 3.5 per cent, while that of manufactures rose by 10.2 per cent and that of capital equipment by 23.0 per cent.

30. The index of average prices of exports of capital equipment from the developed countries to the Third World is used; also the index of average prices of primary product exports from Third World countries to developed countries. The trade in both cases concerns non-communist countries.

31. For a discussion of this problem the works referred to in footnote 1 of Chapter 5 should be consulted.
32. 1951 is excluded in order to eliminate the effects of the boom caused by the Korean War.
33. World production (excluding China) of plastics and resins rose from a figure of about 2 million tons in 1953 to 10.6 million tons in 1963. In 1970 production was 30.7 million tons, i.e. a larger tonnage than that of world production of all non-ferrous metals, including aluminium.
34. The following variations in this index occurred between 1952/54 and 1964/66.

	Developed countries	Undeveloped countries
Food products	2.7%	−15.4%
Other agricultural products	−7.1%	−10.8%
Minerals	16.3%	−
Total of above	0.3%	−10.5%
Non-ferrous metals	37.9%	40.3%

35. Based on the average of the growth rate, 1934/38—1963/65 for world output (excluding U.S.S.R.) of the following products: citrus fruits (excluding U.S.) 159 per cent; ground nuts 69 per cent; bananas 175 per cent; cocoa 79 per cent; coffee 55 per cent; rubber 126 per cent; copra 36 per cent; cotton fibre (excluding U.S.) 109 per cent; palm and palm oil 157 per cent; jute 60 per cent; tea 123 per cent; cane sugar 123 per cent. The average is 105.9 per cent.
36. Thus for the United States, while between 1889 and 1937 the annual average rate of growth of production per unit of total input was 0.5 per cent in the farm sector, in non-farm sectors it was 1.7 per cent. Between 1937 and 1957 it was 3.4 and 2.1 per cent respectively. The differences for labour productivity are even more striking. (From *Historical Statistics of the United States*, pp. 599—602.)

7. The Level of Education

1. For the long-term developments in differing technological conditions, readers are referred to my study *Révolution industrielle et sous-développement*, 4th ed. especially Chapter 12, 'Les obstacles découlant des modifications du contenu de la technique', pp. 164—75.
2. Thus, to quote only a few examples, here are the rates of

growth of total population compared to that of ages 5—14:

		Total population	Population ages 5—14
India	(1951—61)	+23.0 per cent	+39.6 per cent
Philippines	(1948—63)	+57.2 per cent	+58.6 per cent
Venezuela	(1950—64)	+67.4 per cent	+69.2 per cent
Chile	(1952—60)	+24.3 per cent	+30.4 per cent
Morocco	(1952—63)	+73.0 per cent	+99.0 per cent

3. Rates prior to 1950 have been estimated on the basis of scattered data relating to the age groups in 1950. Figures for 1950—70 are based on UNESCO computations.

4. Rates are calculated from statistics on the subject in many European countries and from various sources, especially the historical sections of statistical yearbooks. Note that the rate mainly applies to the period 1830—1900 since statistics earlier than 1830 are usually lacking.

5. See especially C. M. Cipolla, *Literacy and Development in the West*, (London, 1969).

6. A rate of 95—98 per cent can be considered as the practical limit which has not up to now been exceeded in the developed countries.

7. Facts used in this chapter about education in China after 1958 have mostly been taken from: S. E. Fraser (ed.), *Education and Communism in China. An Anthology of Commentary and Documents* (Hong Kong, 1969); L. A. Orleans, 'Communist China's Education', *An Economic Profile of Mainland China* (Joint Economic Committee of U.S. Congress, Washington, 1967), pp. 499—518; Chu-Yuan Cheng, 'Scientific and engineering manpower in Communist China', *An Economic Profile of Mainland China*, pp. 519—47; *China News Analysis*, esp. 792 (20 Feb 1970), 816 (2 Oct 1970) and 868 (21 Jan 1972).

8. See *Le Monde*, 8 July 1970.

9. *Statistics of Students Abroad 1962—1968* (UNESCO, Paris, 1972).

10. Including students registered to study abroad. From *Statistical Yearbook* (UNESCO) and *Statistics of Students Abroad 1962—1968*.

11. *China News Analysis*, 792 (20 Feb 1970).

8. Urbanization

1. Small countries founded on international trade are excluded from this statement: such countries could achieve very high levels of urban concentration by reason of their role as intermediaries. Venice, the other Italian city republics, and the Low Countries spring to mind as the most obvious examples.

2. Even such factors as policies governing transport prices, especially reduced workers' fares, can have profound effects on the localization of population, and underline the ambiguity of even the most straightforward definitions of urban population.

3. These are the pairs of countries:

	Urban population percentage (1960)	Per capita (1958–63) GNP (US $)
Austria	38	805
Switzerland	28	1570
Holland	60	930
Belgium	52	1180
Hungary	38	830(*)
Czechoslovakia	25	1200(*)

*Net material product per capita. The dollar conversion has been made on the basis of the 1960 'basic rate'. On the basis of a 'non-commercial rate' the figures would be $470 for Hungary and $830 for Czechoslovakia.

4. B. Ward, 'The Poor World's Cities; the cities that came too soon', in *The Economist*, 233 (Dec 6 1969), pp. 56–62.

5. G. Jenkins, 'Africa as it urbanizes' in *Urban Affairs Quarterly*, II (March 1967), pp. 68–80.

6. P. Verhaegen, *L'urbanisation de l'Afrique noire: son cadre, ses causes et conséquences économiques, sociales et culturelles* (Bibliographical study), (Brussels, 1962).

7. P. Bairoch, *Urban Unemployment in Developing Countries. The nature of the problem and proposals for its solution* (I.L.O., Geneva, 1973).

8. *Growth of the World's Urban and Rural Population 1920–2000* (U.N., New York, 1969).

9. The definition is agglomerations of 20,000 inhabitants and more, which is clearly as arbitrary as any other definition. Selecting a single definition for all types of economy at all periods, although certainly the least objectionable solution, suffers from obvious disadvantages.

10.   United Nations projection. For reservations about this see below. According to my own estimate the figure should be 4.9 per cent.

11.   The notion of hyper- or over-urbanization came into use about twenty years ago. In particular it was at the heart of the discussions at the joint U.N. and UNESCO seminar in Bangkok in 1956 (see Ph. Hauser, ed., *Le phénomène d'urbanisation en Asie et en Extrême-Orient* (UNESCO, Calcutta, 1959). The notion had already been present in K. Davis and H. Hertz's study, 'Urbanization and the development of pre-industrial areas' in *Economic Development and Cultural Change* III (Oct 1954), pp. 6—26. The authors comment that they took the notion of over-urbanization from a communication by P. Parke Jr. at the annual meeting of the Eastern Sociological Society in 1954.

12.   I am, of course, aware of the unreliable nature of simple indicators of growth levels. But as work in progress on this problem has made no substantial progress, the indicators used here remain the least objectionable of those available. I have used here figures from my study 'Les écarts des niveaux de développement économique entre pays développés et sous-développés de 1770—2000' in *Tiers-Monde*, XII (July—Sept. 1971).

13.   Making fairly crude corrections to account for differences in purchasing power produced a lower difference — about 65 per cent.

14.   There is a vast literature on this problem. The following recent studies can be selected from it: E. J. Berg, 'Wages and unemployment in less-developed countries' in *The Challenge of Unemployment to Development and the role of Training and Research Institutes in Development* (O.E.C.D. Development Centre, Paris, 1970), pp. 111—41; J. C. Caldwell, *African Rural-Urban Migration: The Movement to Ghana's Towns* (London, 1969); M. P. Todaro, 'A model of labor migration and urban unemployment in less-developed countries', in *American Economic Review*, 59 (March, 1969), pp. 138—48; C. R. Frank Jr., 'Urban unemployment and economic growth in Africa' in *Oxford Economic Papers*, 20 (July, 1968), pp. 250—74.

15.   One method of testing the increase in the gap which is sometimes used is to compare agricultural and industrial prices.

But this is only valid in certain circumstances and when the rates of growth in productivity are similar.

16. R. Dumont, *False Start in Africa* (London, 1966), p. 88 (translated from the French, *L'Afrique Noire est mal partie*, Paris, 1966, new ed.).

17. L. Roussel, 'Measuring rural-urban drift in developing countries: a suggested method' in *International Labour Review*, 101 (March, 1970), pp. 229–46.

18. It goes without saying that the relationship 'level of education = propensity to emigrate' is not only applicable to less-developed countries and that it also exists in industrialized societies.

19. If they were not actually urban centres created *de novo*, then they were centres whose rapid growth arose from the choice of the site as a focus of trade penetration and therefore, because of this, they were almost always ports. Such were, in Asia: Bombay, Calcutta, Madras, Manila, Djakarta, Singapore, etc; in Africa: Niamey, Brazzaville, Dakar, Yaoundé, Pointe Noire, etc. Because of European settlement Latin-American, and some North African, cities do not come into this category. Articles and reviews on these problems will be found in the special number of *Annales, E.S.C.* on 'Histoire et Urbanization' (No. 4, July–Aug. 1970). See also G. Hamdam, 'Capitals of New Africa', in *Economic Geography* (July, 1964), reprinted in G. Breeze (ed.), *The City in Newly Developing Countries*, (Englewood, N.J., 1969), pp. 146–61.

20. See in this connexion A. Landry (under the direction of), *Traité de démographie* (Paris, 1945), p. 194; M. G. Mulhall, *Dictionary of Statistics* (London, 1899), pp. 181–9. The industrial character of the town is not by itself the cause of the higher mortality, because, as E. A. Wrigley notes in *Population and the Industrial Revolution*, mortality was higher than in rural areas even when cities were administrative centres.

21. W. Petersen, *Population* (London, 1969), p. 551.

22. B. Benjamin, *Social and Economic Factors affecting Mortality* (The Hague and Paris, 1965), p. 35.

23. The figures presented here are mostly based on the following sources; E. Ni, *Distribution of the Urban and Rural Population of Mainland China*, International Population Reports, U.S. Dept. of Commerce, No. 56 (Washington, Oct. 1960, in roneotype); J. P. Emerson, 'Manpower training' in J. W. Lewis

(ed.), *The City in Communist China* (Stanford, 1971); J. S. Aird, 'Population growth and distribution in mainland China', in *An Economic Profile of Mainland China*, Vol. 2, Part III (Washington, 1967).

24. It should be noted, however, that according to forecasts by the population department at the U.N. (see *Monthly Bulletin of Statistics* for November, 1971), the percentage of urban population measured according to national definition (which in China begins at 1000 persons insofar as 75 per cent of these have no agricultural employment) moved from 18.3 per cent in 1960 to 24.8 per cent in 1970.

9. The Labour Force and Employment

1. *Labour Force Projections 1965–1985*, Part V (World Summary), I.L.O., Geneva, 1971).

2. For the methods used to make the estimates and the importance of the margins of error, see P. Bairoch and J-M. Limbor, 'Changes in the industrial distribution of the world labour force by regions, 1880–1960' in *International Labour Review*, 98, (Oct. 1968), pp. 311–36.

3. For further details, see P. Bairoch, 'La structure de la population active du Tiers-Monde, 1900–1970' in *Tiers-Monde*, X (April–June, 1969), pp. 393–403. Part I of this chapter is largely based on this article.

4. For further details and regional changes, see P. Bairoch and J-M. Limbor, *op cit.* Also S. Baum, 'The world's labour force and its industrial distribution, 1950 and 1960', in *International Labour Review*, 95, (Jan–Feb. 1967), pp. 96–112.

5. It should be noted, however, that as the process of economic development tends towards specialization, rural 'industrial' labour (especially textiles and construction) gradually disappears, which leads to an increase in the statistical importance of the secondary sector of employment.

6. Austria, Belgium, Czechoslovakia, Denmark, France, Germany, Holland, Italy, Luxemburg, Norway, Sweden, Switzerland.

7. It should be noted that, according to projections made by W. Schulte, L. Naiken and A. Bruni in 'Projections of world agricultural population' in *Monthly Bulletin of Agricultural Economics and Statistics*, 21, (F.A.O., Rome, Jan. 1972) the fall in the relative importance of the agricultural labour force will be greater than the one I have projected. According to

these authors, the percentage of the agricultural labour force compared to total labour force would fall from 71.3 per cent in 1960 to 65.2 per cent in 1970 and from 57.7 per cent in 1980 to 53.7 per cent in 1985. These rates appear to me to assume much too great a fall in the relative size of the agricultural sector. In fact from 1950 to 1960 the latter fell by an average rate of 0.6 per cent per annum; from 1960–70 by 0.8 per cent; and the rate expected between 1970 and 1985 would be 1.1 per cent.

8. J. Berque, *Le village* (mimeographed), (Paris, 1959), p. 16.
9. *Shorter Oxford English Dictionary.*
10. O. Bloch and W. U. Wartburg, *Dictionnaire étymologique de la langue française* 5th ed. (Paris, 1968).
11. This was due to the combined effects of a rise in the daily hours of work and a fall in the number of days' employment on saints' and holy days. The number of hours worked daily on 'industrial' activities in the seventeenth and early eighteenth centuries seems to have been on average nine to ten. J. E. Van Dierendonck, 'Historisch Overzicht' in P. J. Verdoorn, *Arbeidsduur en Wewaartspeil* (Leiden, 1947). In addition to Sundays the number of holy days was from 60 to 100 or even more, to which were added periods of enforced seasonal inactivity which reduced still more the total number of days worked. One of the most detailed surveys of the average number of days worked during the year in pre-industrial societies is Vauban's, in which he estimated that at the end of the seventeenth century day-labourers and craftsmen worked no more than 180 days during the course of the year.
12. D. Turnham assisted by I. Jaeger, *The Employment Problem in Less Developed Countries. A Review of Evidence*, (O.E.C.D., Paris, 1971).
13. According to D. Turnham, *op cit.,* p. 57, and *Yearbook of Labour Statistics* 1971 (I.L.O., Geneva, 1972).
14. See D. Turnham, *op. cit.* and *The World Employment Programme,* (I.L.O. Geneva, 1969), pp. 42–5.
15. G. Ardant, *Le plan de lutte contre la faim* (Paris, 1964).
16. This section is mainly based on my study (especially Chapter 3) entitled *Urban Unemployment in Developing Countries: The nature of the problem and proposals for its solution.* This study may be consulted for further details.
17. The definition used here is the same as was used in the last chapter, i.e. agglomerations of 20,000 inhabitants and more.

18.   Without detailed studies to explore this aspect of the problem it is obviously difficult to offer any reasons. But it is at least probable that the concentration of government offices with lower accidental and cyclical unemployment at least partly explains why the difference should exist. General considerations of public order or simply prestige may also help to put a brake on the immigration of workless people.

19.   Instead of a figure for urban population of 19.7 per cent of the total which is the one forecast by the United Nations projections, I have adopted a figure of 21 per cent which assumes a pace of urbanization slightly below what was achieved between 1950 and 1960.

20.   D. Turnham, *op. cit.,* pp. 48—50.

21.   G. W. Jones, 'Under-utilization of manpower and demographic trends in Latin America' in *International Labour Review,* 98 (Nov. 1968), pp. 451—69.

22.   I do not make any distinction here between *overt under-employment* — defined as the percentage of workers with a job in which the working time is less than normal or who are seeking or would accept a supplementary job, and *disguised under-employment* — defined as a situation characterized by a poor distribution of manpower resulting in especially low returns and under-utilization of skills or a low level of productivity (see in this connexion *Eleventh International Conference on Labour Statistics* (I.L.O., Geneva, 1966).

23.   See especially, *The World Employment Programme.*

10. Macro-Economic Data

1.   A. Eckstein, *The National Income of Communist China* (New York, 1961), p. 84. Also the same author, 'The strategy of economic development in Communist China', in *The American Economic Review* (May 1961), p. 509.

2.   W. W. Hollister, 'Capital formation in Communist China' in *Industrial Development in Communist China,* ed. Choh-Ming Li (New York, 1964), p. 40.

3.   P. Bairoch, *Révolution industrielle et sous-développement,* pp. 132—4.

4.   Readers should consult my book quoted in note 3; for the mechanisms thus set in motion see especially Chapters 6 and 7; for the causes of the difference between the western and the under-developed countries see Chapters 12 and 13.

5. T. Mende, *From Aid to Recolonisation. Lessons of a Failure* (London, 1973). The book is, as the author says, 'an ambitious attempt to reconsider an immense subject, namely, the relations of the industrial powers of the northern hemisphere with the ex-colonial countries in the southern hemisphere'. The attempt is not only most successful but the book itself reads like a novel.

6. Development Assistance Committee of the O.E.C.D. which in 1972 included sixteen of the developed countries of the West (Australia, Austria, Belgium, Canada, Denmark, France, Germany, Italy, Japan, Netherlands, Norway, Portugal, Sweden, Switzerland, United Kingdom and United States). The national product of these countries forms 98 per cent of the total of all western developed countries.

7. *Resources for the Developing World. The Flow of Financial Resources to Less-Developed Countries 1962—1968* (O.E.C.D., Paris, 1970). *Development Assistance* (O.E.C.D., Paris, 1971).

8. The following is the relative importance of the aid for the principal developing countries in 1960/62 and 1969/71 (as a percentage of Gross National Product at market prices).

	1960/62	1969/71		1960/62	1969/71
Belgium	1.3	1.1	Netherlands	1.5	1.5
Canada	0.3	0.7	Sweden	0.3	0.7
France	2.0	1.2	Switzerland	1.8	0.7
Germany	0.9	1.0	United Kingdom	1.1	1.1
Italy	0.8	0.9	United States	0.8	0.6
Japan	0.6	0.9			

(According to *Development Assistance 1972*, O.E.C.D., Paris, 1972.) The relative size of aid from the developed countries of eastern Europe is even lower — about 0.2 to 0.3 per cent of G.N.P. including a rough estimate for aid to the communist under-developed countries.

9. See below section B; also General Conclusions.

10. These figures and the following ones come from the annual reports of B.I.R.D. and A.I.D.

11. Figures assembled for the non-communist under-developed countries as defined for this study (U.N. definition; see above Introduction). Changes in the public debt (end of December) and servicing the debt (in billions of dollars) for the eighty or so under-developed countries for which precise information is available were as follows:

	Debt	Service
1965	33.4	3.0
1966	38.4	3.4
1967	43.4	3.6
1968	48.7	4.0
1969	53.1	4.5
1970	59.7	5.2

(According to *World Bank and I.D.A. Annual Report 1972*, Washington, 1972.)

12. This certainly does not exclude, as we shall shortly see, the possibility or even the probability of an over-estimation of recent rates of growth.

13. L. J. Zimmerman, 'The distribution of World Income, 1860–1960', in *Essays on Unbalanced Growth*, (Institute of Social Studies, 's Gravenhage, 1962).

14. Frequent revisions are made in this series, as in others, which often result in considerable modifications to the figures. Thus, the figures available to the end of 1966 were used for growth rates for the period 1957–63, but the figures published after 1968 modified these rates. To quote only one example, the growth rate of G.D.P. for the non-communist developing countries was changed from 4.2 to 4.7 per cent.

15. S. Kuznets, 'Problems in comparing recent growth rates for developed and less-developed countries' in *Economic Development and Cultural Change*, 20, No. 2 (Jan. 1972), pp. 185–209.

16. For a recent study on international differences of income structure see *Income Distribution in Latin America* (E.C.L.A., U.N., New York, 1971).

17. Calculated in my article 'Le mythe de la croissance rapide au XIXe siècle'.

18. It should be pointed out here that rates for the developed communist countries are higher still; thus, for the period 1950–70 growth of Gross Product at constant prices for the U.S.S.R. and other eastern countries was 8 per cent per annum. It should be remembered of course that the methods of calculating the Gross Product are different in the communist countries (e.g. services are excluded); however the differences do not result in much variation in growth rates.

19. W. W. Hollister (*China's Gross National Product and Social Accounts 1950–1957*, M.I.T., 1958) gives an estimate of

G.N.P. at constant prices (pp. 132—3) which gives us for the period 1950—57 an annual growth rate of 9.3 per cent. The author thinks that this perhaps is an over-estimate of 1.5 points, which would leave us with the figure of 7.8 per cent (p. xviii). Later the same author revised his estimates ('Estimates of the Gross National Product of China' in *The Realities of Communist China*, Yuan-Li Wu (ed.), 1960) and advanced the rate to about 8.5 per cent. Ta-Chung Liu and Kung-Chia Yen ('Preliminary estimates of the national income of the Chinese mainland 1952—1959' in *American Economic Review*, May 1961) give five estimates of national income which indicate an annual growth rate of 5.9 per cent from 1952 to 1957. But growth was faster between 1950 and 1952 than between 1952 and 1957 (according to official figures 20 per cent and 9 per cent respectively); on the other hand growth in 1957 was slower. Choh-Ming Li (*Economic Development of Communist China*, Los Angeles, 1959), by converting the figures of Chinese accounting according to western methods, obtains a growth rate of 8.9 per cent between 1952 and 1957 (the same trend as quoted above: a peak in 1952 and a trough in 1957). But Choh-Ming Li thinks these rates are too high due to an over-estimate of industrial prices. But he does not give revised estimates to allow for this. See also Ta-Chung Liu's synoptic study 'The Tempo of Economic Development of the Chinese Mainland, 1949—1965' in *An Economic Profile of Mainland China*, pp. 47—75.

20. Ta-Chung Liu and Kung-Chia Yen, *op. cit.* (13 per cent for 1958 and 16 per cent for 1959); W. W. Hollister, 'Estimates of the Gross National Product of China' (20 per cent in 1958 and 8 per cent in 1959). Y. L. Wu, F. P. Hoeber and M. M. Rockwell (*The Economic Potential of Communist China*, Stanford, 1963, quoted by Cho-Ming Li in *Industrial Development in Communist China*, New York, 1964) show an increase of 16 per cent in G.N.P. between 1957 and 1959 and a fall of 25 per cent between 1959 and 1962, which would place the 1962 level below the 1957 level. This seems to me extremely unlikely and smacks more of wishful thinking than of scientific computation. Ta-Chung Liu (*op. cit.*) places the total product for 1965 at the same level as 1958.

21. Thus long-term credits (excluding repayments) rose to a total of 1720 million roubles from 1950 to 1957 (Choh-Ming Li, *op. cit.*, p. 174), i.e. 430 million dollars at the then rate of exchange

which is $0.1 per capita per annum. This is a very low figure, because net public aid per capita in all non-communist countries taken together alone rose to $4.4 per annum in 1968–70. It should be remembered, moreover, that after 1960 aid from Russia and the other countries of the communist block was reduced to practically nothing and that since then China herself has supplied aid to other under-developed countries.

22. L. J. Zimmerman, 'The Distribution of World Income, 1860–1960', *op. cit.*

23. A. Eckstein, *op. cit.* p. 69.

24. W. W. Hollister, *China's Gross National Product and Social Accounts 1950–1957,* p. 3.

25. For further discussion of this problem see p. 192.

26. A brief but complete historical survey of the various attempts made in this field will be found in the study of W. Beckerman, *Comparaison internationale du revenu réel* (O.E.C.D., Paris, 1966); he also gives an account of his own method of evaluating real levels of per capita consumption based on seven non-monetary indicators (per capita volume: steel and meat consumption; cement output; letters; radio receivers; telephones; and motor vehicles).

27. J. P. Delahaut and E. S. Kirschen, 'Les revenus nationaux du monde non communiste' in *Cahiers Economiques de Bruxelles,* **10** (April, 1961). For 1957 the coefficients used to correct income expressed in dollars on the basis of exchange rates into income based on the real structure of prices are: 2.11 for per capita incomes lower than $50: 1.98 for incomes from $50–99; 1.82 for incomes from $100–144; 1.71 for incomes from $150–199; and 1.61 for incomes from $200–299. I have not used the most interesting figures given by W. Beckerman (*op. cit.*) since it is impossible to calculate from them a valid estimate for the under-developed world taken as a whole. This is because the countries for which he provides both private consumption calculated with the help of official rates of exchange and 'real' private consumption calculated by means of his own method form (population-wise) only 19 per cent of all non-communist under-developed countries.

28. For a discussion of factors bearing on this question my article 'Les écarts des niveaux de développement économique entre pays developpés et pays sous-developpés de 1770 à 2000' in *Tiers Monde,* XII (July–Sept. 1971), pp. 497–514, should be

consulted. The other articles in this number, which is entirely devoted to the Third World in the year 2000, are of great interest.

29. For a recent survey of the Chinese economy see T. G. Rawski, 'Recent trends in the Chinese Economy' in *The China Quarterly,* 53 (Jan—March, 1973), pp. 1—33.

General Conclusions

1. The problem, however, is far from straightforward, since, insofar as the use of synthetic materials is rapidly spreading, it is more than likely that many natural raw materials will lose much of their commercial value in the future.

Appendix: Synoptic Table

Synoptic table summarizing the recent state of economic and social development in selected Third World countries

The table set out on the four following pages shows by means of nineteen indices the recent state of the economic and social development in ninety developing countries, each of which has a population of over 500,000 people. Taken together, these countries account for over 99 per cent of total population in the Third World.

It would have been possible to give more up-to-date statistics in some cases, but in the interests of homogeneity I have decided to give either figures for 1970 or else figures for the yearly growth rate between 1960 and 1970. The advantage of this is that the reader can, if he wishes, use the data in the table as the basis for deducing further information (e.g. by multiplying 'per capita G.D.P.' by 'Total population' it is possible to obtain 'Total G.D.P.').

Sources: F.A.O. documents (mainly *Production Yearbook*)

I.M.F. documents (mainly *International Financial Statistics* and *Direction of Trade*)

I.L.O. documents (mainly *Yearbook of Labour Statistics*)

U.N.C.T.A.D. documents (mainly *Handbook of International Trade and Development Statistics*)

U.N. documents (mainly *Statistical Yearbook, Monthly Bulletin of Statistics, Population and Vital Statistics Report*, and *Demographic Yearbook*)

WORLD BANK documents (mainly *World Bank Atlas, Trends in Developing Countries*, and *Annual Report*)

And statistical yearbooks of individual countries.

EXPLANATION OF HEADINGS IN THE TABLE

The sign —	Means that no recent valid data is available.
Population	The total figures represent estimates of population at mid-year.
Urban population	The ratio of urban population (according to local definition) to total population.
Infant mortality	The number of deaths of infants under one year per 1000 corresponding live births.
Active populations	The percentage of each sector has been calculated in relation to total economically

active population, excluding (whenever such categories are reported) activities not adequately described, persons seeking work for the first time, and unemployed persons who are not counted in the sector in which they were previously employed. Agriculture includes mining, manufacturing, construction and electricity. Services include commerce, transport and services.

Gross Domestic Product	For a large number of countries the data contains a wide margin of error. The figures have not been corrected for differences in the purchasing power of currencies (see Chapter 10, section C).
Calories supply per capita	This represents the daily net per capita food supply (average for a number of years around 1970).
Total agricultural production	Gives the yearly growth rate (in this case for the period 1961–65 to 1968–72) of the F.A.O. index number of total agricultural production.
Consumption of energy per capita	This is the estimated apparent inland consumption of modern forms of energy (excluding wood) expressed in kgs of coal equivalent.
Consumer prices	In cases where there are two indices of consumer prices (for 'European' and 'non-European') the figures reported are based on the index for 'non-European'.
Foreign trade	Relates generally to special trade in which imports are expressed in c.i.f. values and exports in f.o.b. values.
International liquidity	The reason why there is not data for a large number of non-communist countries is that some of them are part of a monetary union. The figures include gold, foreign exchange, reserve position in the I.M.F., and special drawing rights. The figures relate to the situation at the end of 1970.
External public debt	Represents the situation of the external public debt outstanding (including undisbursed) at the end of 1970.

1970 situation or 196·

	DEMOGRAPHY				ACTIVE POPULATION %			
	Total population		Urban popula- tion %	Infant mo·tality %o	Year	Agriculture	Industry	Service
	1,000	*						
LATIN AMERICA								
Argentina	23,210	1.5	80	58	60	20	36	44
Bolivia	4,930	2.6	34	77	—	—	—	—
Brazil	93,390	2.9	56	—	70	47	17	37
Chile	8,860	2.3	76	79	71	20	34	47
Colombia	21,120	3.2	60	70	64	49	20	31
Costa Rica	1,740	3.3	36	56	63	50	19	31
Cuba	8,470	2.1	60	35	—	—	—	—
Dominican Rep.	4,060	3.0	40	50	70	52	14	33
Ecuador	6,090	3.4	38	77	62	59	18	23
El Salvador	3,530	3.7	38	52	71	58	13	29
Guatemala	5,280	3.1	31	83	70	66	14	20
Guyana	720	2.4	29	40	65	33	28	39
Haiti	4,870	2.0	18	—	—	—	—	—
Honduras	2,580	3.3	32	39	61	70	11	19
Jamaica	1,870	1.2	37	26	60	40	25	36
Mexico	49,090	3.5	59	61	70	42	24	34
Nicaragua	1,980	3.5	46	45	71	47	16	37
Panama	1,430	3.3	48	38	70	43	16	41
Paraguay	2,390	3.1	36	36	62	56	19	25
Peru	13,590	3.1	52	72	67	49	21	30
Puerto Rico	2,720	1.4	58	27	73	7	34	59
Trinidad and Tobago	1,030	2.1	12	35	71	21	37	42
Uruguay	2,890	1.3	78	40	63	20	31	49
Venezuela	10,400	3.5	76	49	71	20	27	53
ASIA								
Afghanistan	17,090	2.0	7	—	—	—	—	—
Burma	27,580	2.1	19	66	—	—	—	—
China (official fig.)	—	—	—	—	—	—	—	—
China (western est.)	773,660	1.8	25	—	—	—	—	—
Hong Kong	3,960	2.6	92	18	71	4	54	41
India	539,860	2.3	20	—	71	72	12	16
Indonesia	115,460	2.0	17	75	71	66	10	24
Khmer Rep.	6,840	3.2	12	—	62	82	4	15
Korea Dem. Pop. Rep.	13,890	2.7	38	—	—	—	—	—
Korea Rep. of	31,020	2.6	41	—	71	48	18	34
Laos	2,960	2.4	15	—	—	—	—	—
Malaysia	1,040	3.1	28	39	—	—	—	—
Mongolia	1,250	3.0	45	—	—	—	—	—
Pakistan	114,190	2.7	13	140	68	70	12	18
Philippines	36,850	3.0	32	62	70	55	17	29
Singapore	2,070	2.3	81	20	70	3	30	66
Sri Lanka	12,510	2.4	20	50	63	56	14	30
Taiwan	14,040	2.9	64	—	—	—	—	—
Thailand	34,380	3.1	15	25	70	83	5	12
Viet-Nam Dem. Rep.	21,150	2.8	18	—	—	—	—	—
Viet-Nam Rep..of	18,330	2.6	24	37	—	—	—	—

*Yearly growth rate (percentage) for the period 1960 to 1970, except in the case of total agricultural production

70 yearly increase

| GROSS DOMESTIC PRODUCT | | | | | | FOREIGN TRADE | | | | |
Volume total*	Per capita in $U.S.	Calories supply per capita	Total agricultural production*	Consumption of energy per capita	Retail prices*	Imports $ millions	Exports $ millions	*	International liquidity $ millions	External public debt $ millions
4.2	1055	3200	1.2	1687	21.4	1685	1773	5.1	673	2457
5.7	195	1800	3.9	193	5.6	159	227	16.1	46	529
6.0	365	2800	3.7	478	44.0	2849	2739	13.6	1187	3809
4.4	795	2600	1.9	1275	26.5	931	1247	9.8	388	2503
5.2	315	2100	4.2	653	11.2	843	736	4.7	206	1720
6.1	530	2400	6.7	423	2.4	317	231	10.4	16	217
–	530	2500	1.5	1076	–	1300	1043	5.3	–	–
4.5	345	2100	3.3	253	2.0	278	221	2.4	32	282
5.3	265	2000	2.7	293	4.3	248	218	4.1	83	337
5.6	295	1900	2.1	205	0.7	214	228	6.9	63	120
5.5	350	2000	4.0	239	0.9	284	299	9.8	78	176
4.4	330	2100	0.9	1071	2.3	134	134	6.0	20	113
0.8	90	1900	1.2	27	2.7	55	40	2.0	4	–
5.0	250	2200	5.5	222	2.3	221	171	10.4	20	139
5.1	590	2300	1.8	1271	4.1	522	343	7.5	139	180
7.0	660	2700	3.1	1236	2.7	2461	1402	6.2	744	3791
7.3	435	2300	4.1	380	–	198	175	12.1	49	224
8.0	710	2400	5.6	700	1.2	353	111	14.7	304	234
4.7	245	2600	2.7	149	1.7	64	64	9.0	18	142
5.2	435	2200	2.0	629	9.6	619	1044	9.2	329	1184
8.1	1650	2500	-3.4	3242	2.7	–	–	–	–	–
4.5	800	2400	3.9	4604	3.0	542	480	5.3	43	90
1.4	820	2700	-0.2	909	41.0	233	233	6.0	175	318
5.6	920	2400	4.8	2598	1.4	1713	2691	1.0	1021	806
2.5	90	2100	1.7	26	–	75	86	5.6	46	689
3.7	75	2000	1.1	58	–	169	108	-7.1	94	–
3.5	350	–	–	–	–	–	–	–	–	–
1.7	160	2200	2.7	530	–	2800	2200	1.5	–	–
2.9	885	2400	2.5	1010	2.9	2905	2514	13.8	–	–
3.7	95	2000	2.3	182	6.3	2124	2026	4.3	1006	9235
3.5	105	1900	2.8	109	237.0	893	1009	1.8	–	3463
3.3	110	2200	1.7	48	4.4	54	39	-5.6	–	–
5.1	330	2300	–	2185	–	–	–	–	–	–
8.7	260	2500	3.7	785	13.9	1983	835	38.0	610	2637
4.3	75	2200	5.6	93	20.7	114	7	22.6	–	–
6.3	355	2500	5.4	468	0.9	1490	1762	4.0	733	549
–	460	2500	-0.3	885	–	–	–	–	–	–
4.6	125	2400	5.1	94	3.6	1151	723	6.2	182	4302
5.0	265	2000	3.0	292	4.1	1210	1119	7.1	251	822
9.4	960	2500	8.7	808	1.0	2461	1554	3.1	294	283
4.9	170	2300	2.1	149	3.0	389	339	-1.3	43	516
7.1	390	2600	–	925	3.4	1524	1428	24.0	624	985
7.9	175	2300	3.8	256	2.0	1293	710	5.7	906	456
7.9	100	2100	–	172	–	–	–	–	–	–
3.6	200	2200	1.1	302	21.4	325	7	-21.6	242	–

where the period under consideration is 1961/65 to 1968/72 (see also the notes of explanation given on p. 244).

	Total population		Urban population %	Infant mortality ‰				
	DEMOGRAPHY				ACTIVE POPULATION %			
	1,000	*			Year	Agriculture	Industry	Servi⬛
AFRICA								
Algeria	14,330	3.1	40	86	66	59	14	27
Angola	5,570	1.3	14	21	60	69	12	19
Burundi	3,540	2.0	3	150	—	—	—	—
Cameroon	5,840	2.1	20	137	—	—	—	—
Central African Rep.	1,610	2.6	27	—	—	—	—	—
Chad	3,640	1.8	7	—	—	—	—	—
Congo People's Rep.	936	1.9	30	—	—	—	—	—
Dahomey	2,690	2.9	13	—	—	—	—	—
Ethiopia	24,630	2.2	9	—	—	—	—	—
Gabon	500	1.1	32	—	63	85	7	8
Ghana	8,640	2.6	31	—	60	61	15	23
Guinea	3,920	2.6	11	—	—	—	—	—
Ivory Coast	4,310	3.0	21	—	—	—	—	—
Kenya	11,230	3.1	10	55	—	—	—	—
Liberia	1,520	3.0	26	159	62	81	9	10
Madagascar	6,750	2.6	14	55	—	—	—	—
Malawi	4,440	2.6	6	148	—	—	—	—
Mali	5,050	2.1	12	—	—	—	—	—
Mauritania	1,170	1.9	7	187	—	—	—	—
Mauritius	810	2.3	44	65	62	38	27	35
Morocco	15,520	2.9	34	—	71	56	18	25
Mozambique	8,150	1.9	6	92	—	—	—	—
Niger	4,020	2.9	8	—	60	94	1	5
Nigeria	55,070	2.9	23	—	—	—	—	—
Rwanda	3,680	3.0	3	16	—	—	—	—
Senegal	3,930	2.1	26	—	—	—	—	—
Sierra Leone	2,550	1.4	14	136	63	77	12	11
Somalia	2,790	2.4	20	—	—	—	—	—
Southern Rhodesia	5,310	3.3	18	—	61	11	27	62
Sudan	15,700	2.9	12	18	—	—	—	—
Togo	1,970	2.9	13	—	—	—	—	—
Tunisia	5,140	3.0	43	78	66	46	19	35
Uganda	9,810	2.7	10	—	—	—	—	—
Un. Rep. of Tanzania	13,270	2.5	7	160	—	—	—	—
Upper Volta	5,380	2.1	4	182	—	—	—	—
Zaire	21,570	2.8	15	—	—	—	—	—
Zambia	4,180	2.5	31	—	69	32	24	43
MIDDLE EAST								
Cyprus	633	1.0	39	25	72	38	28	34
Egypt	33,330	2.5	42	116	66	56	16	28
Iran	28,660	2.9	41	—	66	47	27	26
Iraq	9,440	3.5	58	20	—	—	—	—
Israel	2,910	3.2	82	20	71	9	33	59
Jordon	2,310	3.5	47	36	61	43	26	30
Lebanon	2,790	2.8	41	14	70	19	25	56
Libyan Arab Rep.	1,940	3.7	27	—	—	—	—	—
Saudi Arabia	7,740	1.7	24	—	—	—	—	—
Syrian Arab Rep.	6,250	2.9	43	23	70	51	20	28
Turkey	35,230	2.5	39	153	65	74	11	15
Yemen	5,770	2.3	6	—	—	—	—	—

*Yearly growth rate (percentage) for the period 1960 to 1970, except in the case of total agricultural producti⬛

GROSS DOMESTIC PRODUCT						FOREIGN TRADE				
Volume total*	Per capita in $U.S.	Calories supply per capita	Total agricultural production*	Consumption of energy per capita	Retail prices*	Imports $ millions	Exports $ millions	*	International liquidity $ millions	External public debt $ millions
.0	305	1900	0.9	460	—	1257	1009	6.0	339	—
.3	300	1900	2.7	156	—	369	423	13.0	—	—
.8	65	2300	4.7	8	—	22	24	18.0	15	10
.7	170	2300	4.0	91	2.4	242	232	9.1	—	218
.3	135	2200	1.7	62	5.0	34	31	7.1	—	29
.2	70	2200	0.1	23	4.9	61	30	8.4	—	51
.0	250	2100	-1.4	222	4.1	57	31	5.6	—	173
.7	95	2200	4.0	36	—	64	33	6.0	—	55
.6	70	2000	3.1	33	5.2	172	122	5.3	71	270
.4	630	2200	3.2	887	3.5	80	121	9.9	—	115
.7	270	2100	2.9	170	7.7	411	433	3.9	58	572
.9	80	2100	2.3	97	—	78	56	0.7	—	378
.9	340	2500	4.6	231	3.8	388	469	12.0	—	413
.6	140	2200	3.4	148	1.8	397	217	6.8	220	394
.7	230	2300	2.7	296	—	150	213	9.9	—	177
.6	120	2300	2.3	67	2.6	170	145	6.8	—	138
.8	80	2400	4.4	46	—	86	60	8.9	29	156
.5	100	2100	1.6	20	—	47	33	9.9	1	288
.7	155	2000	1.7	133	—	56	89	51.0	—	39
.1	225	2400	1.4	168	1.8	76	69	5.8	46	43
.9	210	2200	4.9	198	2.3	684	488	3.2	140	855
.8	240	2200	2.5	151	2.9	324	156	7.8	—	—
.7	80	2300	2.1	19	3.5	58	32	9.7	—	63
.7	105	2300	0.4	46	4.4	1059	1240	10.0	224	683
.4	55	2000	5.0	10	—	29	25	32.0	8	12
.3	180	2200	-0.8	133	2.5	193	152	2.8	—	114
.1	160	2200	3.0	114	4.1	116	101	1.9	35	85
.5	65	1800	2.6	38	4.3	45	31	3.2	21	105
.7	270	2600	0.9	578	2.1	329	355	7.4	—	248
2.9	120	2200	5.6	119	3.3	311	293	4.8	22	339
3.3	145	2300	3.8	60	1.7	65	55	13.9	—	40
5.1	235	2200	2.0	258	2.9	305	183	4.3	60	787
4.7	135	2300	3.0	72	4.5	121	246	7.4	57	184
6.7	100	1700	5.5	42	2.1	272	238	5.6	65	576
3.0	60	2100	2.8	13	—	47	18	15.6	—	31
4.9	110	2100	4.5	83	21.0	533	781	4.5	186	579
6.1	405	2300	2.9	494	4.2	477	1001	10.7	514	616
6.3	845	2500	7.1	1320	1.1	238	108	7.2	209	49
4.6	200	2800	3.1	263	3.7	787	762	3.0	167	1768
9.0	355	2100	4.0	895	1.7	1658	2355	11.2	208	3022
5.8	300	2100	5.2	617	2.1	509	1093	5.3	462	276
8.9	1485	3000	6.4	2524	5.6	1422	734	13.2	449	2022
6.4	285	2400	-5.7	295	—	184	34	11.9	256	170
4.4	530	2500	4.2	719	—	568	198	17.3	386	—
2.6	1670	2600	4.8	578	—	554	2366	71.0	1590	—
0.0	585	2200	3.2	827	—	692	2423	10.4	662	—
6.6	260	2500	0.3	457	2.5	357	203	6.3	55	244
5.6	340	2800	3.3	481	6.4	894	589	6.2	431	2626
4.2	80	1900	0.8	13	—	143	15	-2.6	59	—

here the period under consideration is 1961/65 to 1968/72 (see also the notes of explanation given on p. 244).

Bibliography

This list is not intended to be a complete bibliography on the problems of the less-developed countries, but merely to give some indications for further research. For this reason it is divided into four sections: the first gives a short list of some general works; the second collects together the principal international statistics; the third is devoted to bibliographical works (or parts of works) dealing with the subject; and the fourth is a select list of the specialized journals devoted to the problems of the Third World.

A. General works

AUSTRUY, J. *Le Scandale du développement*. Paris, Marcel Rivière, 1965.

BAIROCH, P. *Révolution industrielle et sous-développement*. Paris, 1963; 4th edition, Paris and The Hague, Mouton, 1974.

BALDWIN, R. E. *Economic Development and Growth*. New York, J. Wiley, 1966.

BALOGH, T. *The Economics of Poverty*. New York, Macmillan, 1966.

BARAN, P. A. *The Political Economy of Growth*. New York, Monthly Review Press, 1957.

BAUR, P. T. (ed.) *Dissent on Development. Studies and Debates in Development Economics*. Cambridge (Mass.), Harvard University Press, 1972.

BROOKINGS INSTITUTE, *Development of the Emerging Countries*. Washington, D.C., 1962.

BROWN, L. R. *Seeds of Change. The Green Revolution and the Development in the 1970s*. New York, Praeger, 1970.

CAIRNCROSS, A. K. *Factors in Economic Development*. London, Allen and Unwin, 1962.

CLARK, C. *The Conditions of Economic Progress*. 3rd ed., London, Macmillan, 1957.

COTTA, A. *Analyse quantitative de la croissance des pays sous-développés*, Paris, Presses Universitaires de France, 1967.

DOMAR, E. D. *Essays in the Theory of Economic Growth*. New York, Oxford University Press, 1957.

DUMONT, R. and ROSIER, B. *The Hungry Future*. New York, Praeger, 1969.

FALKOWSKI, M. *Les problèmes de la croissance du tiers-monde vus par des économistes des pays socialistes*, Paris, Payot, 1968.

FRANK, G. *Capitalism and Under-Development in Latin America*, revised ed., New York, Modern Reader Paperback, 1969.

FURTADO, C. *Development and Underdevelopment*. University of California Press, 1964.

GALBRAITH, J. K. *Economic Development*. Cambridge (Mass.), Harvard University Press, 1964.

GARZOUZI, E. *Economic Growth and Development. The Less Developed Countries*. New York, Vintage Press, 1972.

GENDARME, R. *La pauvreté des Nations*. Paris, Cujas, 1963.

HAGEN, E. E. *The Economics of Development*. Homewood, Ill., Irwin, 1968.

HIGGINS, B. H. *Economic Development; Principles, Problems, Policies*. revised ed., New York, W. W. Norton, 1968.

HIRSCHMAN, A. O. *The Strategy of Economic Development*. New Haven, Conn., Yale University Press, 1958.

HOROWITZ, D. *The Abolition of Poverty*. London, Pall Mall Press, 1970.

JALEE, P. *Le tiers-monde dans l'économie mondiale*. Paris, Maspero, 1968.

JOHNSON, H. G. *Economic Policies Towards Less-Developed Countries*. Washington, The Brookings Institute, 1967.

KINDLEBERGER, C. P. *Economic Development*. Cambridge (Mass.), M.I.T. Press, 1965.

KUZNETS, S. *Economic Growth and Structure*. London, Heinemann, 1966.

LACOSTE, Y. *Géographie du sous-développement*. Paris, Presses Universitaires de France, 1965.

LEBRET, L. J. *The Last Revolution: the Destiny of Over- and Under-developed Nations*. Dublin, LOGDS, 1965.

LEWIS, W. A. *The Theory of Economic Growth*. London, Allen and Unwin, 1955.

MEIER, G. M. and BALDWIN, R. E. *Economic Development: Theory, History, Policy*. New York, J. Wiley, 1957.

MENDE, T. *From Aid to Recolonisation, Lessons of a Failure*. London, Harrap, 1973.

MYINT, H. *The Economics of the Developing Countries*. 3rd ed., London, Hutchinson, 1965.

MYRDAL, G. *Economic Theory and Under-Developed Regions*. London, Duckworth, 1957.

MYRDAL, G. *The Asian Drama: An Inquiry into the Poverty of Nations*. New York, Panthon, 1968.

NURKSE, R. *Problems of Capital Formation in Under-Developed Countries.* New York, Oxford University Press, 1960.

PEARSON, L. B. (ed.) *Partners in Development, Report of the Commission on International Development.* New York, Praeger, 1969.

PERROUX, F. *L'économie des jeunes nations.* Paris, Presses Universitaires de France, 1963.

PIATIER, A. *Equilibre entre développement économique et développement social.* Paris, Génin, 1962.

SACHS, I. *La découverte du Tiers-Monde.* Paris, Flammarion, 1971.

SAUVY, A. *Malthus et les deux Marx. Le problème de la faim et de la guerre dans le monde.* Paris, Denoël, 1963.

SEERS, O. (ed.) *Development in a Divided World.* Harmondsworth, Penguin, 1971.

SINGER, H. W. *International Development: Growth and Challenge.* New York, McGraw-Hill, 1964.

TINBERGEN, J. *The Design of Development* (International Bank for Reconstruction and Development), Baltimore, Johns Hopkins Press, 1958.

U.N.C.T.A.D. *Towards a Global Strategy for Development.* Report by the Secretary-General of the United Nations. Conference on Trade and Development Document TD/3/Rev. 1., United Nations, New York, 1968.

B. Principal international statistical sources

Important sources of information will of course be found in statistical yearbooks and periodicals of the different countries. Only works including statistics for a great number of less-developed countries or for a group of those countries are given here.

F.A.O. — Food and Agricultural Organization of the United Nations — (Rome)
Production Yearbook
Trade Yearbook
Monthly Bulletin of Agricultural Economics and Statistics
The State of Food and Agriculture
F.A.O. Commodity Review
GATT. — General Agreement on Tariffs and Trade — (Geneva)
International Trade . . .

I.L.O. — International Labour Office — (Geneva)
  Yearbook of Labour Statistics
  Bulletin of Labour Statistics
I.M.F. — International Monetary Fund — (Washington)
  Annual Report
  Direction of Trade
  International Financial Statistics
  The Balance of Payments Yearbook
League of Nations (Geneva, until 1940)
  Statistical Yearbook
  Monthly Bulletin of Statistics
  World Production and Prices
  International Trade Statistics
O.E.C.D. — Organization for Economic Co-operation and Development — (Paris)
  Development Assistance Review
U.N.C.T.A.D. — United Nations Conference on Trade and Development — (Geneva)
  Handbook of International Trade and Development Statistics
  Review of International Trade and Development . . .
UNESCO — United Nations Educational Scientific and Cultural Organization — (Paris)
  Statistical Yearbook
UNITED NATIONS (New York)
  Publications issued several times per year:
    Commodity Trade Statistics
    Economic Bulletin for Asia and the Far East
    Economic Bulletin for Latin America
    Monthly Bulletin of Statistics
    Population and Vital Statistics, Reports
  Annual Publications:
    Demographic Yearbook
    Statistical Yearbook
    Statistical Yearbook for Asia and the Far East
    Studies on the Economic Situation of Asia and the Far East
    World Economic Survey
    Yearbook of International Trade Statistics
    Yearbook of National Accounts Statistics
WORLD BANK (Washington)
  Annual Report
  Trends in Developing Countries
  World Bank Atlas

C. Bibliographical studies

CAIRE, G. 'Esquisse d'un état des travaux en matière de développement', in AUSTRUY, J. *Le scandale du développement*, op. cit. pp. 327—512.

CANADIAN COUNCIL FOR INTERNATIONAL COOPERATION, *Bibliography of International Development*, Ottawa, 1969.

DE GREEF, G. 'Eléments de bibliographie critique du sous-développement économique', in *La Belgique et l'aide économique aux pays sous-développés*, Institut Royal des Relations Internationales, The Hague, 1959, pp. 453—512.

ECONOMIC DEVELOPMENT INSTITUTE, *Selection Readings and Source Materials on Economic Development.* A list of books, articles and reports recommended as reading material for general development course of the Economic Development Institute, 1965—66. International Bank for Reconstruction and Development, Washington, 1966.

F.A.O. *Selected Bibliography on Cooperation*, 1957.

GEIGER, H. *National Development 1776—1966.* A selected and annotated guide to the most important articles in English; Scarecrow, 1969.

HAZLEWOOD, A. *The Economic Development.* An annotated list of books and articles, 1959—1962; Oxford, 1964.

KABIR, A. K. M. *Social Change and National Building in the Developing Areas.* A selected annotated bibliography. National Institute of Public Administration, Dacca, 1965.

KATZ, S. M. and McGOWAN, F. Selected list of U.S. Readings on Development, prepared for the United Nations conference on the application of science and technology for the benefit of the less developed areas. U.S. Government Printing Office, Washington, 1963.

LAMBERG, V. *Literatur über Entwicklungsländer*, Hanover, 1966.

LAWRENCE, M. M. *Decade of Development.* Compendium of U.S. sponsored Center of Economic Publications, 1959—1969. Washington (?), 1970.

O.E.C.D. *Economic Growth.* Special annotated bibliography no. 17—18. Paris, 1968.

O.N.U. *Bibliographie des ouvrages relatifs aux méthodes et aux problèmes de l'industrialisation dans les pays sous-développés*, 1956.

PIATIER, A. Bibliography in A. Piatier, *Equilibre entre développement économique et développement social*, pp. 105—81.

REQUA, E. S. and STATHAM, J. *The Developing Nations, A Guide to Information Sources*, Detroit, 1965.

STRACK, H. B. *Bibliographie uber Entiwcklungsländer nach Sach-gebieten*, Hanover, 1965.

TARR, R. 'Bibliographie commentée sur les problèmes du sous-développement' in *Problèmes de l'Europe*, No. 8 and 9, pp. 228–42, 258–74.

TRAGER, F. N. 'A Selected and Annotated Bibliography on Economic Development 1953–1957', in *Economic Development and Cultural Change*, July 1958, pp. 257–329.

D. Specialized journals in the problems of development

In addition to the journals mentioned here, studies dealing with the problems of less-developed countries will often be found in journals devoted to economics, sociology and geography as well as to countries or regions of the Third World.

Community Development Journal (Manchester)
Croissance des Jeunes Nations (Paris)
Cultures et Développement (Louvain)
Desarrollo Economico (Buenos Aires)
Development Digest (Washington)
Développement et Civilisations (Paris)
Economic Development and Cultural Change (Chicago)
Finance and Development (Washington)
France d'Outre-Mer (Paris)
International Development Review (Washington)
Journal of Development Economics (Amsterdam)
Journal of Development Studies (London)
Journal of Developing Areas (Macomb, Ill.)
Journal of Developing Economies (Berkeley)
Monde en développement (Paris)
Présence Africaine (Paris)
Terzo Mondo (Milano)
The Developing Economies (Tokyo)
The Journal of Development Studies (London)
The Pakistan Development Review (Karachi)
Tiers-Monde (Paris)
World Development (Oxford)

Index

aggregate wage outlay, 60-1

agricultural revolution, 196-8

agriculture: export crops, 14-16
 generation of purchasing power, 90
 levels of development, 89
 output: growth rates, 17-20, 196,
   201; index, 16-17, 19-21; per
   capita, 17-18; totals, by country,
   247, 249
 productivity: average levels, 29-31,
   35-6; changes since 1900, 35-9;
   China, 37; comparison with
   advanced countries during
   take-off, 39-45; effect on terms
   of trade, 134; European influence,
   34; future estimates and
   requirements, 195, 203; index,
   13-14, 21-6, 35-6, 38; and land
   availability, 32-4; and plantation
   agriculture, 34; thresholds, 26-9,
   31-2
 relationship with manufacturing,
   88-91
 research, 45-8
 share of labour force, 13, 160-2,
   246, 248
 subsistence, 16, 34
 yields, 28-9

aid: financial flow, 177-181
 future distribution and requirements,
   207-8
 geographical distribution, 182
 internal distribution, 209
 private, 177, 179-80
 proportion of G.D.P., 180
 public, 177, 179
 sources, 208

Aird, J. S., 6

balance of trade, 93, 95-7

birth control, campaigns and policies,
   9-10, 203-4

Borlaug, N. E., 45

capital formation: as an indicator of
   economic development, 172
 China, 173-5
 European experience, 176-7
 rates, 173-4
 share of imports, 175-7

capital-output ratio as an indicator of
   economic development, 172

centralized economies:
 Chinese experience, 202
 manufacturing growth, 69
 see also state intervention

China: agriculture, 37, 201
 birth rate, 9
 capital formation, 173-5
 education, 139, 143
 exports, 109-10
 foreign trade, 109-10
 Gross Domestic Product, 188-90,
   193
 growth rates, 188-90
 manufacturing industry, growth of
   72-6
 per capita income, 191-3, 201-2
 population, 5-7
 productivity, 37
 urbanization, 156-7

Clark, C., 78

colonialism; effect on development in
   India, 202
 effect on urbanization, 153-4
 provision of infrastructure, 201

construction, employment, 160

cotton, consumption as an indicator
   of development, 84, 86

Delahaut, J. P., 192

demand, domestic, 70
 elasticity of, in manufactures, 129

demographic inflation, 7-8

Dumont, R., 45, 203

Eckstein, A., 191

Rockefeller Foundation, 45
rural-urban migration, 150-5, 200

Sauerbeck, A., 115
Schlote, W., 114
services, employment, 160-1, 246
Snow, E., 73
social structure: and agricultural
    improvements, 47
    restraints, effect on urban growth,
    153
state intervention, and economic
    development, 205-7
steel production, as an indicator of
    development, 83-4, 86
synthetics: effect on raw material
    prices, 129-31
    share of market, 131

'take off': and agricultural
    productivity, 13, 18, 39, 41,
    196
    agricultural and industrial
    development, 88, 91
    availability of land, 34
    China, 200-4
    foreign trade, 177, 198-9
    G.D.P., 187, 206
    level of literacy, 135
    population growth, 8, 195
    unemployment, 170
technological progress, and extractive
    industry, 49-50
    and primary product prices, 129
Teheran Agreement, 60

terms of trade: causes of deterioration,
    128-34
    definition, 111
    effect of changes on world trade,
    94, 199
    effect of production increases, 131
    historical comparisons, 112,
    120-34
    post-war changes, 125-8
transport, as an indicator of
    development, 84, 86
    costs, and primary product prices,
    115-19; and manufactured
    goods, 118; employment, 160

underemployment: definition, 166-7
    rural, 167-8
    urban, 168, 170-1, 200
unemployment: definition, 165-6
    rural, 167
    urban, 168-70, 200
United Nations Conference on Trade
    and Development, 127, 132, 180,
    209
United Nations Organization: aid, 178
    index of export prices, 124
    index of per capita income, 190
    indices of GDP, 183-6
urban inflation, causes, 150-6
urbanization: China, 156-7
    growth rates, developing
    countries, 145-7, 149;
    Europe, 147-9; relationship
    with industrialization, 151
    India, 156-7

Zimmerman, L. J., 183-4